THREE RIVERS COOKBOOK

"The Good Taste of Pittsburgh"

Cover Design and Illustrations by Susan Gaca.

CHILD HEALTH ASSOCIATION OF SEWICKLEY, INC.

Sewickley, Pennsylvania

1973

Our thanks to The H. J. Heinz Company for making possible the inclusion of color in our first edition.

First Printing	12,500	October 1973
Second Printing	10,000	December 1973
Third Printing	10,000	March 1974
Fourth Printing	20,000	August 1974
Fifth Printing	20,000	May 1975
Sixth Printing	20,000	January 1976

For additional copies, use the order blanks
in the back of the book or write directly to:
THREE RIVERS COOKBOOK
Child Health Association of Sewickley, Inc.
Post Office Box 48
Sewickley, Pennsylvania 15143
Checks should be made payable to Child Health Association of Sewickley, Inc. for the amount of $5.00 plus 50¢ postage and handling. Pennsylvania residents please add 30¢ tax.

Printed in the United States of America

by

William G. Johnston Co.
Pittsburgh, Pennsylvania

CHILD HEALTH ASSOCIATION
OF SEWICKLEY

In 1923, the Child Health Association began a series of unique programs, many well ahead of their time in the area of child welfare. Their first important projects were supplying milk to schools in the area, employing a public health nurse to provide medical care for families of limited means, and establishing a dental hygiene program which exists to this day. A pioneer study of the effects of water fluoridation proved so effective that the program was adopted locally, with financial aid from Child Health.

Since its modest beginnings, Child Health has raised $400,000 with which it has supported community agencies and projects especially related to child welfare in Allegheny County. Members are also required to serve a certain number of volunteer and project hours annually.

The money-raising events were as imaginative as the projects themselves. In 1936, a Golden Gloves boxing championship was sponsored; later, the group was paid $1,000 to sit around a tea table smoking cigarettes for an advertising campaign in a magazine. More conventional methods of fund-raising, an annual ball and seventeen house tours, have been increasingly successful projects. The Arnold Palmer Golf Exhibition of 1972 was the greatest financial success in Child Health's history.

Current activities range from an innovative adventure playground for the Pittsburgh Home for Crippled Children to sponsoring an "Art in Motion" booth at the Three Rivers Arts Festival.

In 1973, fifty years later, the Child Health Association looks back with pride on a half century of community service. It is this heritage that will serve as our inspiration in the years ahead.

Jacqueline P. Cavalier
President

3

In the years Pittsburgh has been my home, ever since I left New York city in the Fall of 1962, I have been regularly accosted by the same question (usually asked with a solemn air): "Are you now adjusted to Pittsburgh?"

It is a question for which I have yet to find a reasonable answer.

Nobody of sound mind and body has to "adjust" to Pittsburgh, unless you've just checked in from Utopia, U.S.A. The good things about this city were evident to me from the very beginning. How nice to take a Pittsburgh taxi and see the driver actually get out of his seat to open the door for me! How nice to have a saleswoman come to me and pleasantly ask if she could be of help!

Voila! My love affair with Pittsburgh was off to a rousing start. In the years since, give or take a few unhappinesses with politicians whose horizons are smaller than the potential of this city, I have been charmed, amused, gratified and exhilarated as a Pittsburgh resident. We don't have to arm ourselves to take a walk at night. Some of the world's art treasures are in our museums and our performing arts enjoy international repute. All this in a city that is a scenic gem; rivers, hills and dales, lush greens and winding streets.

So what if there's a pothole up ahead. That's part of the Pittsburgh character, and if there weren't potholes around, how else could we in Pittsburgh satisfy the human need to complain!

I did not have to adjust to Pittsburgh. It was love at first sight!

Marie Torre

MARIE TORRE
KDKA

4

Pittsburgh and its surrounding communities reflect a rare combination of sophisticated appreciation of the arts and the refreshing charm and warmth of our people.

As a unique industrial, cultural and academic center, Pittsburgh has been heavily influenced by the traditions and customs of its many ethnic backgrounds. Through them, the fine art of culinary expression has taken shape in the impressive array of foods featured by the area's eating establishments and prepared in the homes of Pittsburgh residents.

Because of the popularity of these international favorites, recipes for many of them are included in the pages that follow. It is our sincere hope that you will enjoy reading this book and preparing the recipes.

Ferdinand E. Metz
President, Chefs' Association of Pittsburgh
and Manager, New Product Development
Heinz U.S.A. Division of H. J. Heinz Company

THE COMMITTEE

How do you thank a city? Nearly 1,400 recipes were submitted by friends — and strangers who became friends. After months of testing, we have discovered that there are enough top-notch recipes to fill another book. Our thanks to everyone who sent them in, and our apologies to those whose favorites, for reasons of space, were omitted.

We are especially grateful to John Besanceney of the Pittsburgh Convention and Visitors Bureau and other members of the business community who encouraged us to believe that there would be a market for a regional cookbook. The Pittsburgh History and Landmarks Foundation, the Carnegie Library of Pittsburgh and the Carnegie Institute Museum of Art deserve special credit for providing materials for our artist's use. The area's professional chefs were extraordinarily generous with their recipes, time and advice.

Finally, without the Child Health members, associates, and the husbands who have been so patient, there would have been no THREE RIVERS COOKBOOK.

Mrs. Edward I. Sproull, Jr. — Chairman
Mrs. Thomas M. Garrett — Co-Chairman
Mrs. Frank F. Brooks III — Associate Chairman
Mrs. Giles J. Gaca — Graphics Chairman
Mrs. William H. Riley — Testing Chairman
Mrs. John G. Zimmerman, Jr. — Testing Co-Chairman

CONTENTS

FOREWORD/1

BREADS/33

ENTREES/45

VEGETABLES/111

SALADS/131

SWEETS/149

CHEFS' SPECIALTIES/193

NATIONALITY FAVORITES/217

INDEX OF ILLUSTRATIONS

FOREWORD/1

OPENERS/9

BREADS/33

ENTREES/45

VEGETABLES/111

SALADS/131

SWEETS/149

CHEFS' SPECIALTIES/193

NATIONALITY FAVORITES/217

OPENERS

9

ROLLING ROCK

The Rolling Rock Club in Ligonier, located on a magnificent forested site which was personally chosen by the late Richard King Mellon, is famous for beautiful scenery, trout fishing, golf, shooting and riding. It is the site of the annual Rolling Rock Races, a famous steeplechase which benefits the Home for Crippled Children.

Additional illustrations in this section:

GEORGE I BRITANNIA SILVER OCTAGONAL TEAPOT — Maker: Edward Barnet — London 1718 — Ailsa Mellon Bruce Collection.

CHARLES II TANKARD — Maker's Mark: */EC in cartouche — London 1683 — Ailsa Mellon Bruce Collection.

Mexican War Streets Doorway — Pittsburgh's North Side.

Classical music flows from the American Wind Symphony barge, "Point Counterpoint", during mid-summer months.

Bas-relief gargoyles at Heinz Hall.

Mexican War Streets — Window.

ʙEVERAGES

BLOODY MARY

⅔ cup V-8 juice
⅓ cup Snap-E-Tom
1 shot vodka
black pepper
salt
celery salt
Worcestershire sauce
dash Tabasco
wedge of lime

Add freshly ground black pepper, salt, celery salt, Worcestershire, and Tabasco to V-8, Snap-E-Tom, and vodka. Pour over ice and serve garnished with a wedge of lime. To prepare ahead combine all ingredients except vodka. Add vodka just before serving.

Preparation: 5 min.

Easy
Can do ahead

Serves: 1
Can increase

W. Lukens Ward

PLUM BRANDY
"A recipe for patient people."

2 lbs. Damson plums
1½ lbs. cubed sugar (1 box)
1 fifth gin

Wash plums and punch each plum 5 times with fork. Place in crock. Spread sugar cubes over plums. Cover with gin. Cover with foil or Saran wrap. Place in cool spot in basement. Let sit at least 3 months. DO NOT MOVE. When ready to top crock — use a dipper gently and strain through a linen handkerchief.

Preparation: 30 min. Easy
Standing: At least 3 months

Mrs. Richard P. Simmons

CAFÉ BRULOT

"Delightful at the end of a special dinner."

8 cups strong coffee
3 or 4 sticks cinnamon
peel of 1 lemon
peel of 1 orange
3 tsp. brown sugar
1 cup cognac, bourbon or
  brandy

Add cinnamon, lemon and orange peel to coffee and simmer for 10 minutes. Dissolve sugar in liquor and pour into simmered coffee immediately before serving.

| Preparation: | 10 min. | Easy | Serves: 8 |
| Cooking: | 15-20 min. | Can do ahead | |

Mrs. Leon G. Krasinski

A CUP A CUP A CUP

"This is an ancient Child Health recipe."

1 cup black coffee
1 cup vanilla ice cream (other
  flavors can be used, not
  strawberry)
1 cup bourbon or blended
  whiskey

Put all in blender. Serve immediately after dinner or morning after.

| Preparation: | 5 min. | Easy | Serves: 4 |

Mrs. Charles W. Dithrich

BANANA DAIQUIRI

"Refreshing fruit drink!"

1 oz. banana liqueur
1½ oz. white rum
½ banana
crushed ice (4-5 cubes)
lemon or sugar to taste

Combine all ingredients in blender. Blend at high speed until very well mixed. Multiply as needed.

| Preparation: | 3 min. | Easy | Yield: 1 cocktail |
| | | Serve immediately | |

William H. Riley

EASY EGG NOG

"Make sure you're having a short cocktail hour or you will have a short party. This is very smooth and people should be warned!"

2 qts. egg nog
1 fifth blended whiskey
1 fifth rum
1 pt. brandy
nutmeg to grate at time of serving

Mix and refrigerate. This should be made well ahead and allowed to sit in the refrigerator for a day or two. Keeps for weeks in refrigerator.

| Preparation: | 5 min. | Easy | Yield: 1 gal. |
| | | Must do ahead | |

The Committee

CHRISTMAS EGG NOG

"An adaptation of a family recipe — it is very potent!"

1 doz. large eggs
1 qt. half and half
1 pt. heavy cream
1 pt. light cream
½ gal. milk (whole or 2%)
1 fifth rum
1 fifth brandy
12 oz. bourbon or whiskey
2½ cups granulated sugar
nutmeg (optional)

Separate eggs and beat whites until stiff. Beat yolks. Fold whites into yolks. Add cream and milk and stir well — do *not* beat. Add rum, brandy, whiskey, sugar, and stir well. Ladle into glass jars for storage. Keeps a week to 10 days in refrigerator. Shake well before serving and sprinkle nutmeg on top for those who like it.

Preparation: 30 min.   Easy   Yield: 7½ - 8 qts.
                              Must do ahead

Mrs. Edward A. Montgomery, Jr.

PARTY PUNCH

"Terrific luncheon punch!"

1 large can frozen orange juice
1 box frozen mandarin oranges
1 box frozen strawberries
2 cups real lemon or lime juice
1-2 cups grenadine
1 pt. vodka
2 qts. ginger ale
sliced oranges, if preferred

Slightly defrost orange juice, oranges and strawberries. Mix all ingredients together, adding well-chilled ginger ale just before serving. Add sliced oranges, if desired.

Preparation: 10 min.   Easy   Yield: about 2 gal.
                              Can do ahead

Mrs. James R. Smith

PARTY PUNCH FOR CHILDREN

"A favorite of the younger set."

1 large can frozen
  lemonade
1 large box frozen sliced
  strawberries
1 large can well-chilled
  Hawaiian Punch
2 qts. well-chilled ginger ale

Partially defrost the lemonade and strawberries. Pour ingredients into a punch bowl, adding the ginger ale last. Strawberries, mint leaves, and pineapple chunks can be frozen in a ring of Hawaiian Punch and floated in the center of the bowl for a special touch.

Preparation: 5 min.   Easy   Yield: 30 "punch cups"

Mrs. Donald H. Bryan

WINE PEACH BOWL (PUNCH)

"Great for a summer luncheon."

3 lbs. ripe peaches, peeled &
  sliced
¼ cup sugar
¼ cup brandy
1 fifth red wine well chilled
1 fifth white wine well chilled
1 bottle champagne well chilled

Add sugar and brandy to peaches and let stand 3 to 4 hours. Place in punch bowl and add the red wine and white wine. Chill well. Just before serving, add a block of ice and the champagne.

Preparation: 20 min.   Easy   Serves: 10
Standing: 3 - 4 hours   Must do ahead

Mrs. Jon E. McCarthy

CHAMPAGNE PUNCH

½ cup lemon juice
½ cup water
1 cup sugar
3 oz. brandy
3 oz. Curacao
3 oz. maraschino juice
1 bottle sparkling water
  (well chilled)
3 bottles champagne
  (well chilled)

In punch bowl, dissolve sugar in water and lemon juice. Add brandy, curacao, and maraschino. Mix well. Just before serving, pour in chilled sparkling water and champagne. Stir gently. Garnish with fresh strawberries or pineapple.

Preparation: 10 min.   Easy

Mrs. William A. Gordon, Jr.

RED SANGRIA

1 gal. good domestic red
  burgundy
juice of 1 lemon, & its rind
  in slices after juicing
juice of 1 lime, & its rind
  in slices after juicing
slices of 1 peach or apple
  (in season)
4 oz. brandy
4 oz. light rum

Combine all ingredients and steep in the refrigerator all day before serving. Do not dilute with soda water unless serving to a guest who desires a very diluted drink. You may strain off all fruit rinds and slices if desired before serving.

Preparation: 15 min.   Easy   Yield: 1 gal.
                            Must do ahead

Edward A. Montgomery, Jr.

14

WHITE SANGRIA

1 gal. good domestic chablis
juice of one lemon (and slices of
  rind after juicing)
juice of one orange (and slices of
  rind after juicing)
juice of one lime (and slices of
  rind after juicing)
sugar to taste
8-10 sprigs fresh mint
8-10 strawberries

Combine all of these ingredients and steep all day before serving. Do not dilute with soda water unless serving to a guest who desires a very diluted drink. You may strain off all fruit rinds, mint and strawberries before serving if you wish.

Preparation: 20 min.   Easy   Yield: 1 gal.
    Must do ahead

Edward A. Montgomery, Jr.

SCOTCH SOURS

"These are not too sweet."

1 can lemonade
1 can water
1 can scotch
1 can club soda

Place all in blender and serve over ice or straight up! Use lemonade can as measure.

Preparation: 5 min.   Easy   Serves: 4 - 6
    Can do ahead

Mrs. Jon E. McCarthy

SLUSH

"Something to try when you've read too many recipes."

2 cups sugar
9 cups water
1 12-oz. can frozen orange
  juice
1 12-oz. can frozen lemon
  juice
2 cups gin
7-Up or Squirt

Bring sugar and water to a boil, simmer 15 minutes, then cool. Add juices and gin, then freeze. When ready to serve, fill glass half full with slush, then fill remaining part with 7-Up or Squirt.

Preparation: 5 min.   Easy   Yield: 2½ qts.
Cooking: 15 min.   Must do ahead

Mrs. Edward J. Klein

𝒜PPETIZERS

CHEESE IN A BREAD BOWL

*"This is a conversation piece that men like.
Be sure you call ahead to the bakery for the big bread."*

1½ lbs. sharp cheese,
  grated
¼ lb. Roquefort or
  blue cheese
1 tsp. dry mustard
2 tbsp. soft butter
1 tsp. Worcestershire
  sauce
2 tsp. grated onions
  or chives
1 12-oz. bottle of beer
1 3 to 5 lb. loaf of rye,
  round or oval, *not* long &
  thin if possible
an extra loaf of party rye
paprika
parsley

Hollow out the big bread, reserving as much as possible to slice thinly for the dip. "Sawtooth" the crust as you would a watermelon. While you are doing this, put all ingredients except beer in a bowl to soften; 30 minutes or longer. Add beer slowly and beat until smooth and fluffy. Fill bread bowl with this mix, garnish with paprika and parsley, and refrigerate. Serve on a big bread board with reserved, sliced rye. You will need the extra party rye.

Preparation: 10 min.   Must do ahead   Serves: 20-30

Mrs. Edward I. Sproull, Jr.

BEEF CHEESE LOGS

1 8-oz. pkg. cream cheese,
   softened
1 tbsp. mayonnaise
½ tsp. Worcestershire sauce
2 tbsp. chopped ripe olives
1 tbsp. minced parsley
1 tsp. finely chopped onion
½ cup finely snipped dried beef

Blend softened cream cheese
with mayonnaise and Worcestershire sauce. Add olives, parsley,
onion. On waxed paper, shape
into 1½" diameter 8-10" roll.
Chill until firm. Roll in dried
beef.

Preparation: 15 min.   Easy   Serves: 6-8
                             Can do ahead

Mrs. R. Allen Moulton, Jr.

CHEESE PASTRY HORS D'OEUVRES
"Rich and good looking."

2½ cups flour
1 cup butter
1 cup sour cream
seasoned salt
pepper
3 cups shredded
  Cheddar cheese
paprika

Combine flour, butter and
sour cream in bowl and mix.
Divide into 4 portions. Wrap
and chill. Roll out 1 at a time
on floured surface to 12 x 6"
rectangle. Sprinkle each with
seasoned salt and pepper, then
with ¾ cup cheese. Starting
with 12" side, roll up jelly-

roll style. Seal edge and ends. Place seam side down on ungreased
cookie sheet. Cut rolls halfway through at 1" intervals. Sprinkle
with paprika. Bake at 350° for 30 to 35 minutes.

Preparation: 30 min.   Easy   Yield: 48
Cooking: 35 min.   Must do ahead   Can freeze

Mrs. Philip Beard

CHEESE PUFFS

5 oz. extra sharp Cheddar
  cheese, grated
4-6 slices crisp bacon,
  crumbled
1 tsp. grated onion
  (more if desired)
1 small egg
bread rounds

Toast small bread rounds
lightly on one side under
broiler. Mix ingredients
and spread, mounding slightly
on untoasted side. If mixture
is not thick enough, add more
grated cheese. Broil at medium
heat, until puffed and slightly
browned.

Preparation: 15 min.   Can do ahead   Freezes well

Mrs. Charles Lang

PARMESAN CHEESE SQUARES

Italian or French Bread,
  a day old
1 stick margarine
paprika
Parmesan cheese

Remove crusts from day old bread. Cut into 1½" cubes. Melt margarine and add paprika for color. Put grated parmesan cheese in small bowl. Dip cubes in margarine, then roll in cheese. Place on cookie sheet so cubes don't touch and freeze. Once frozen, put into plastic bags and return to freezer until ready to use. Bake at 400° for 12-15 minutes.

Preparation: 10 min.   Easy   Freeze
Cooking: 12-15 min.   Must do ahead

Beth Adams

CRAB ALMOND SPREAD

1 7-oz. can crabmeat
1 8-oz. pkg. cream cheese
8 drops Tabasco sauce
1 tbsp. Worcestershire sauce
1 tbsp. lemon juice
¼ tsp. Lawry's Seasoned Salt
½ cup blanched slivered
  almonds browned in 1
  tbsp. butter

Mix together all ingredients reserving about $1/3$ of the almonds for top. Form into loaf and heat 15 minutes at 450°. Serve hot.

Preparation: 30 min.   Can do ahead   Serves: 12-15
Baking: 15 min.   Can freeze

Mrs. Frank L. Seamans

CRAB, CREAM CHEESE & CHILI SAUCE

8 oz. pkg. cream cheese
1 can well picked over
  crabmeat

Sauce:

½ cup chili sauce
1 tsp. horseradish
1 tsp. Worcestershire sauce
¼ tsp. Tabasco Sauce
2 tbsps. lemon juice
1 tsp. chopped chives
¼ tsp. parsley
1 tsp. salt

Slice cream cheese in half and cover with crabmeat. Just before serving, top with chili sauce mixture. Serve with crackers.

Preparation: 15 min.   Easy

Mrs. Lowell W. Monroe

HOT CRABMEAT

1 can Alaskan Crab,
  picked over
8 oz. pkg. cream cheese
2 tbsp. mayonnaise
lemon juice
curry powder
Worcestershire sauce
small amount of chopped
  onion
grated Parmesan cheese

Combine crab, cheese and mayonnaise. Add lemon juice, curry powder, Worcestershire and onion to taste. Put into a shallow baking dish, top with grated Parmesan cheese and bake at 400° for 30 minutes. Serve with Triscuits.

Preparation: 15 min.   Easy

Mrs. Lowell W. Monroe

CRABMEAT CANAPÉS

½ cup salad dressing
½ tsp. prepared mustard
1 tsp. Worcestershire sauce
2 tsps. horseradish
1½ cups flaked crabmeat
½ cup grated Parmesan cheese

Mix first 4 ingredients with crabmeat. Spread on bread rounds or crackers. Sprinkle cheese on top, and heat until brown at 350°.

Preparation: 10 min.   Easy   Yield: 16-18
Baking: 5 min.   Can do ahead

Mrs. Harry Baumgartel

HAM AND CHICKEN ROLL-UPS
"Gets rave reviews from everyone."

Ham
8 slices ham
¼ lb. braunschweiger
4 tsp. soft butter
2 tsp. chopped chives
2 tsp. chopped parsley
1½ tbsp. sherry

Chicken
8 slices chicken loaf
½ lb. Roquefort cheese
½ lb. cream cheese
1 tbsp. Worcestershire sauce
4 tbsp. sour cream
1 small garlic clove, minced

Ham: Mix all ingredients and spread on ham slices. Roll up. *Chicken:* Mix all ingredients and spread on chicken loaf slices. Roll up.

Preparation: 20 min.   Easy   Serves: 8
                           Can do ahead

Mrs. William F. Duncan

DILLWEED DIP

¾ cup mayonnaise
¾ cup sour cream
2 tbsp. minced onion flakes
2 tsp. Beaumonde
  (Spice Island)
2 tsp. dillweed

Mix and serve with chips or
fresh vegetables.

Preparation: 5 min.

Easy
Can do ahead

Yield: 1½ cups

Mrs. Calvert G. deColigny

HERBLETS

"Keep these on hand for unexpected guests."

thinly sliced Pepperidge
  Farm bread
shallot buds
butter
dill
basil
thyme
marjoram

Slice each piece of bread into
4 sections. Do not remove the
crusts. Cut shallot buds in slices
and gently sauté. Dip each section
in melted butter sautéed with
shallots. Remove from dip and
place on cookie sheet. Sprinkle
with finely chopped herbs.
Use any one, or make a
variety of toasts. Toast in 350° oven for approximately 10 minutes
or until browned. Cool and store. Will keep indefinitely in air tight
containers. Use for soups, salads or cocktails.

Preparation: 15 min.
Cooking: 10 min.

Easy
Can do ahead

Mrs. Howard G. Wilbert

HOT APPETIZER PIE

"Make ahead — bake later. A crowd pleaser."

1 8-oz. pkg. cream cheese
2 tbsp. milk
1 2½-oz. jar dried beef,
  cut fine
2 tbsp. finely chopped
  green pepper
2 tbsp. finely chopped
  onion
½ tsp. pepper
½ cup sour cream
¼ cup chopped walnuts

Soften cream cheese and blend
with milk. Mix other ingredients with this, except nuts.
Pat into 8" pyrex pie plate.
Spread ¼ cup chopped walnuts
over top. Bake at 350° for 15
minutes. Serve hot with
crackers or sturdy potato chips.

Preparation: 30 min.
Baking: 15 min.

Easy
Can do ahead

Mrs. J. Norman McDowell, Jr.

PICKLED SHRIMP

"Mother always served this."

2½ lbs. cooked
  shelled shrimp
3 sliced onions
cracked bay leaves
  (about 3 tbsp.)
3 tbsp. whole cloves
1½ cups salad oil
1 cup white vinegar
1 tsp. salt
3 tbsp. capers
3 tbsp. celery seed
1 tbsp. garlic salt

Arrange shrimp and onion, bay leaves and cloves in layers in flat glass dish. Mix other ingredients. Pour over shrimp and chill for 2 days. Drain and serve.

Preparation: 15 min.   Easy
                           Must do ahead

Mrs. William P. Snyder, IV

SHRIMP SPREAD

1 8-oz. pkg. cream cheese
2 tbsp. butter or
  margarine
2 tbsp. lemon juice
salt & pepper to taste
1 chopped onion
1 can shrimp

Mix together the cream cheese, butter, lemon juice, salt and pepper. Let shrimp stand in cold water for ½ hour. Drain and separate with fork. Mix shrimp, cheese mixture and chopped onion. Refrigerate until firm.

Note: An equal amount of fresh or frozen shrimp may be substituted for the can of shrimp.

Preparation: 15-20 min.   Easy   Yield: 1½ cups
                             Must do ahead

The Committee

SHRIMP AND PINEAPPLE APPETIZER

fresh pineapple
cooked, cooled medium-
  sized shrimp
Dressing:
1 cup mayonnaise
½ cup sour cream
a little red maraschino
  cherry or beet juice

Cut fresh pineapple in half lengthwise. Cut out the meat of the pineapple in as large chunks as possible, then cut into 1" pieces. Scoop out the rest of the pineapple leaving a medium thick wall. Place the 2 halves in the center of a large serving dish. Fill with special dressing which should be served very cold. Surround the pineapple halves with shrimp, pineapple chunks and toothpicks for dipping.

Preparation: 30 min.   Easy   Serves: 10
                           Can do ahead

Mrs. Raymond D. Ryan

SHRIMP MOLD

"This is most attractive in a fish mold."

1 can tomato soup
1 8-oz. pkg. cream cheese
1½ envelopes gelatin
½ cup cold water
1 cup mayonnaise
1½ cups diced celery
½ cup diced onion
1 lb. cooked, cut-up shrimp
mayonnaise

Bring undiluted soup to boil. Add cream cheese. Heat until melted. Dissolve gelatin in water. Add to hot mixture. Add all other ingredients and cool. Pour into mold, lightly coated with mayonnaise. Refrigerate 3 hours or longer.

Preparation: 30 min.   Easy
Cooling: 3 hours   Must do ahead

Mrs. Joseph Wilcox Jenkins

SHRIMP SAUCE

"The ultimate in shrimp sauce."

½ cup mayonnaise
½ cup sour cream
¼ tsp. Tabasco sauce
2 tbsps. chili sauce
1 tbsp. lemon juice
½ tsp. curry powder
  (optional)
¼ tsp. salt
1 tbsp. capers (optional)

Blend mayonnaise and sour cream. Stir in Tabasco sauce. Add remaining ingredients and mix thoroughly. Refrigerate until ready to serve with well-chilled shrimp.

Preparation: 5 min.   Easy   Yield: 1 cup
Can do ahead

Mrs. James Harris

SMOKED SALMON PATÉ

1 lb. can salmon
1 8-oz. pkg. cream cheese
2 tbsp. grated or finely
  chopped onion
¼ tsp. salt
1 tbsp. lemon juice
¼ tsp. pepper or
  dash of Tabasco
1 tbsp. liquid smoke
1 tsp. prepared horseradish
  (optional)
chopped nuts
parsley
paprika

Drain salmon and remove skin and bones. Flake and combine with next 7 ingredients. Chill several hours. Decorate with chopped nuts and parsley or paprika. Serve with crackers.

Preparation: 10 min.   Must do ahead   Serves: 16-20

Mrs. Stephen W. Menzel, Jr.

MUSHROOM ROLLS

1 lb. mushrooms,
  chopped fine
½ cup butter
6 tbsp. flour
1½ tsp. salt
½ tsp. monosodium
  glutamate
2 cups light cream or
  coffee cream
2 tsp. lemon juice
1 tsp. onion salt
1½ loaves bread

Sauté mushrooms in butter for 5 minutes. Cool. Add flour and blend well. Add salt and MSG. Stir in cream and cook until thick, stirring constantly. Add lemon juice and onion salt. Cool. Remove crust from bread and roll slices flat. Spread the mixture and roll. Freeze slightly and cut into thirds. Dip in melted butter. Bake at 375° for 15 to 20 minutes.

Preparation:	1-1½ hour	Easy	Yield: 7 or 8 doz.
Baking:	20 min.	Can do ahead	Can freeze

Mrs. Robert L. Brush

PICKLED MUSHROOMS
"A sure thing."

1 lb. mushrooms
½ cup water
½ cup white vinegar
Marinade:
¼ cup olive oil
2 tsp. salt
2 tsp. peppercorns
2-4 garlic cloves, minced
1 tsp. mace
white vinegar

Clean and trim mushrooms. Boil mushrooms in ½ cup water and ½ cup white vinegar for 3 minutes. Drain and cool. Place mushrooms in jar or covered Tupperware type bowl. Add marinade and cover with the white vinegar. Place in refrigerator for at least 2 days. Shake once or twice.

Preparation: 20 min.   Easy
                              Must do ahead

Mrs. J. Robert Van Kirk

CURRY — OLIVE DIP
"A constant winner."

1 can cream of shrimp soup
1 8-oz. pkg. cream cheese
1 4-oz. can black olives,
  drained & chopped
2 tsp. lemon juice
½-1 tsp. curry powder,
  to taste
garlic salt
salt & pepper
Fritos

Combine ingredients in top of double boiler. Blend well and heat. Serve hot as a dip with Fritos.

Preparation:	5 min.	Easy	
Cooking:	10 min.	Can do ahead	*Mrs. John M. Webb*

SAUERKRAUT BALLS

"They are worth every bit of the trouble to make them."

8 oz. sausage meat, crumbled
¼ cup finely chopped onion
1   14-oz. can sauerkraut,
  well drained & snipped
2 tbsps. dry bread crumbs
1   3-oz. pkg. cream cheese,
  softened
2 tbsps. parsley
1 tsp. prepared mustard
garlic salt
¼ tsp. pepper
¼ cup all-purpose flour
2 well-beaten eggs
¼ cup milk
1 cup more bread crumbs

In skillet, cook sausage and onion until meat is brown. Drain. Add sauerkraut and 2 tablespoons bread crumbs. Combine cream cheese, parsley, mustard, touch of garlic salt, and pepper, stir into sauerkraut mixture. Chill. Shape into small balls, coat with flour. Add milk to beaten eggs. Dip balls into egg-milk mixture and roll into bread crumbs. Fry in deep fat to brown. Bake in 375° oven for approximately 15 to 20 minutes.

Preparation: 1 hour
Baking: 15 min.

Can do ahead
Can freeze

Mrs. James Smith

STEAK TARTARE

2½ lbs. ground round or
  sirloin (have butcher
  trim & grind twice)
4 tbsp. dry red wine
3 cloves minced garlic
¾ tsp. Tabasco sauce
2 tsp. dry mustard
1 tsp. salt
2 tbsp. Worcestershire
  sauce
1 tsp. hickory smoked salt
1 tsp. curry powder
1 tsp. Escoffier Sauce
  Diable

After mixing all ingredients, refrigerate for 2 hours. Mound on a pretty plate and decorate the top with well-drained capers. Serve with thinly sliced dark rye or party rye. Chop fine hard-boiled eggs and red onions. Put in bowls alongside.

Preparation: 10 min.

Easy
Must do ahead

Mrs. William C. Campbell

SOUPS

CREAM OF ARTICHOKE-MUSHROOM SOUP

1 can drained artichokes
3 tbsp. butter
2 tbsp. finely chopped
  onion
½ cup thinly sliced fresh
  mushrooms
2 tbsp. flour
1 can chicken broth
  (College Inn)
2½ cups half & half cream
½ tsp. salt
cayenne to taste
parsley as garnish

Drain artichokes and dice. Heat butter and sauté onions and mushrooms 5 minutes. Stir in flour. Cook slowly for 2 minutes. Slowly add broth then cream. Heat very slowly to thicken. Stir in artichokes and seasonings.

Preparation: 30 min.   Easy   Serves: 6
                               Can do ahead

Mrs. William S. Pampel, Jr.

25

CORN CHOWDER

"Good for family dinner — great with cole slaw, bread and 'Voila'."

5 slices of bacon, cooked
— save 3 tbsp. grease
1 onion sliced
3 med. potatoes, diced
(about 2½ cups)
2 cups water
1   17-oz. can cream style
corn
2 cups milk
salt
pepper
butter

Add onion to grease and sauté.
Add potatoes and water. Cook
until tender. Add remaining
ingredients and warm. Serve
with bacon and butter on top.

Preparation: 40 min.   Easy   Serves: 4-6
                                Make ahead

Mrs. James R. Smith

CHICKEN CURRY SOUP

2 lbs. chicken necks and backs
1 tbsp. salt
1 onion, quartered
water
3 tbsp. margarine
1 tsp. curry powder
1 medium onion, chopped
½ cup heavy cream
chopped parsley
flour, (optional) to thicken

Cover chicken with water. Add
quartered onion and salt when
water begins to boil. Simmer 2-3
hours, skimming foam if
necessary. Cool, strain stock,
and refrigerate overnight. The
next day, remove fat from
congealed stock. Melt margarine
in a deep, heavy pot. Add curry
powder and onion and sauté
until onion is limp but not brown. Remove from heat. Add hot stock,
return to heat, and stir while bringing to boiling point. Simmer for one
minute, add cream, garnish with parsley, and serve immediately.

Preparation: 10 min.   Easy   Serves: 4
Cooking: 2-3 hours   Must do ahead

Mrs. William I. Jack

UNCLE ED'S FAVORITE CHEESE SOUP

"Ed and I always quadruple this recipe and freeze containers of this soup for later treats."

5 slices bacon
½ cup grated carrot
½ cup chopped celery - chop fine
½ cup chopped onion - chop fine
½ cup green pepper - chop fine
¼ cup flour
4 cups chicken or beef broth (or combination)
3 cups shredded Old English cheese
2 cups milk
2 tbsp. dry sherry
5 oz. pimento stuffed olives, sliced
pepper - coarsely ground
parsley to garnish

In a large saucepan, cook bacon until crisp. Drain in paper towel and crumble. Sauté carrot, celery and green pepper in bacon drippings on low heat until tender, but still crisp - do not brown. Blend in flour, then gradually add broth. Cook over low heat until mixture thickens and boils. Cook for 5 minutes. Add cheese and stir until cheese is melted. Stir in milk, sherry and olives. Simmer 10 minutes. Season to taste with pepper. Serve garnished with crumbled bacon and parsley.

Preparation: 1 hour   Freezes well   Yield: 2 qts.

Mrs. Ed Schaughency

CUCUMBER SOUP

1½ lbs. cucumbers
½ cup minced shallots or combination of shallots, scallions and/or onions
3 tbsp. butter
6 cups chicken stock
1½ tsp. wine vinegar
¾ tsp. dill or tarragon
4 tbsp. Cream of Wheat or Farina
salt, pepper and more liquid if necessary
1 cup sour cream
fresh dill, tarragon or parsley

Peel cucumbers. Cut 18-24 slices paper thin to serve later. Cut rest in ½ " chunks; should have about 4½ cups. Cook shallots, scallions or onions in butter until tender but not brown. Add cucumbers, chicken broth, vinegar and herbs. Bring to a boil, then stir in Farina. Simmer, partially covered for 20-25 minutes. Purée and return the soup to pan. Thin with more liquid if necessary, season. Bring to a simmer before serving, beat in ½ cup sour cream. Ladle soup into bowls, place a dollop of sour cream in each bowl. Float cucumbers and sprinkle with herbs.

Preparation: 25 min.   Make ahead   Serves: 4-6
Cooking: 20-25 min.

Mrs. Richard B. Lord

WHITE GAZPACHO

3 med. cucumbers (peeled)
1 clove garlic
3 cups chicken broth
(cooled) or 3 bouillon
cubes
3 cups sour cream (3 small
containers)
3 tbsp. white vinegar
2 tsp. salt
Topping: (chop in small
pieces and sprinkle on top)
½ cup sliced green onions
¾ cup toasted almonds
(chopped)
½ cup chopped parsley
2 chopped tomatoes

Cut cucumbers in chunks and whirl in blender a very short while with a little chicken broth. Combine with remaining ingredients and whirl just enough to mix. Chill. Serve in soup bowls.

Preparation: 30-45 min.

Easy
Must do ahead

Serves: 6-8

Mrs. Jack Diederich

COLD GREEN SUMMER SOUP

"Great for the diet-conscious."

5 cups white chicken stock
(homemade if possible)
2 cups chopped green beans,
raw
2 cups chopped romaine,
raw
2 cups chopped zucchini,
raw
2 cups raw peas or 1 box
frozen (unthawed)
1 cup chopped celery
½ cup chopped scallions
¼ cup chopped parsley
salt
pepper
chopped parsley

In saucepan, combine all ingredients except salt and pepper. Simmer the vegetables, partially covered for 15-20 minutes or until tender. Put through the blender about 1 cup at a time until all is smooth. Season with salt and pepper. Chill thoroughly and garnish each serving with chopped parsley.

Preparation: 30 min.
Cooking: 25 min.

Easy
Must do ahead

Serves: 6-8
Can freeze

Mrs. John Gould

NONIE'S LEMON SOUP

2 qts. chicken broth
5 celery stalks, chopped
1 carrot, chopped
1 large onion, chopped
salt & pepper
3 egg yolks
juice of 1 lemon
lemon slices

Simmer broth, celery, carrot and onion for 1 hour. Salt and pepper to taste. In a double boiler, beat the egg yolks and slowly add the lemon juice. Beat. Strain broth and add to egg mixture, stirring quickly. To serve, float a slice of lemon on top. Serve hot or cold.

Preparation: 20 min.   Easy   Yield: 16 cups
Cooking: 1 hour

Mrs. F. Gordon Kraft

SPINACH SOUP

"Good served hot or cold."

2 pkg. frozen spinach
1 tbsp. grated lemon peel
½ cup water
2 env. concentrated
  chicken stock or cubes
¼ tsp. seasoned pepper
about 1½ cups half & half
dill weed

Cook spinach in water with all seasonings. When barely cooked, put all in blender. Add equal amount half & half. Either reheat to boiling (do not boil) or refrigerate. Sprinkle dill weed on top when ready to serve. Zucchini with ends cut off, skins left on, and

chunked for cooking, may be substituted and is at least as good. Add a bit more water. May also be made with broccoli.

Preparation: 10 min.   Easy   Serves: 4-6
                          Can do ahead

Mrs. Edward I. Sproull, Jr.

SAUERKRAUT SOUP

1 lb. short ribs of beef
½ cup chopped onion
2 tbsp. cooking oil
1 can (1 lb. 11 oz.) sauerkraut
6 cups fat-skimmed stock or
  6 cups bouillon made with
  cubes
1 can (1 lb.) tomatoes
10 peppercorns
2 bay leaves

Remove fat from bones, but leave meat. Brown onion and meat in oil, then add sauerkraut. Add remaining ingredients; bring to boil and simmer for 40 minutes. Lift out bones, pepper and bay leaves. Scrape off all meat from the bones, cut into chunks and add to soup. Check salt seasoning and serve.

Preparation: 25 min.   Can do ahead   Serves: 12
Cooking: 40 min.   Can freeze

Mrs. James Harris

EASY BOOKBINDER'S SOUP

1 can tomato soup
1 can pea soup
1 cup sherry
1 can lobster

Heat in double boiler. If too thick, add milk.

Preparation:	10 min.	Easy	Serves: 4-6
Cooking:	10 min.	Make ahead	

Mrs. James O. Borden

CLAM BISQUE

"A delicious bisque that goes from shelf to table in 15 minutes."

1½ tbsp. minced onion
6 tbsp. butter or margarine
6 tbsp. flour
3 7½-oz. cans minced clams
 & liquor
3 cups clam juice
paprika, salt, pepper to taste
1½ cups light cream
butter
dry vermouth (optional)

Sauté onions in butter until golden. Stir in flour. Add liquor from clams (you will get about a cup from 3 cans). Add clam juice and seasonings and heat until slightly thickened. Add cream and clams. At this point chill if serving it cold. Before serving, sprinkle with chopped parsley. If serving hot, put in top of double boiler and add

a lump of butter while it heats. Sprinkle with paprika and croutons. A little dry vermouth is a nice addition.

Preparation:	3 min.	Easy	Serves: 6
Cooking:	10 min.		

Mrs. Mary Cooper Robb

EVANCHO POTATO SOUP

8 med. potatoes
3 med. onions
6 celery sticks
¼ lb. fresh mushrooms
2 or 3 sprigs parsley
½ lb. butter or margarine
½ gallon milk
1 pint table cream
3 tbsp. flour
salt
pepper

Dice celery, onions and mushrooms; combine in a deep fry pan and sauté in butter. Peel and dice potatoes. Add to sautéed mixture a layer of raw, diced potatoes and chopped parsley. Cover with water and boil until potatoes are cooked. (Excess potatoes can be boiled in a separate saucepan, then drained.) Do not drain water from potatoes

in sautéed mixture. Combine into large soup kettle entire sautéed mixture, additional potatoes, milk and cream. Simmer slowly for approximately 5 minutes. Brown 3 tablespoons flour in small frying pan, then add slowly to soup. Salt and pepper to taste.

Preparation:	1 hour	Can do ahead	Serves: 6-7

Nicholas Evancho

MUSHROOM BISQUE

"A treat for mushroom fans."

1 lb. fresh mushrooms
1 qt. chicken broth
1 med. onion, chopped
6 tbsp. butter
6 tbsp. flour
3 cups milk
1 cup heavy cream
1 tsp. or more salt
white pepper
Tabasco sauce
2 tbsp. sherry, if desired

Grate, grind or chop the mushrooms and stems very fine. Simmer, covered in broth, with chopped onion, 30 minutes. Melt butter in saucepan, add flour and stir with whisk until blended. Meanwhile, bring milk to a boil and add all at once to flour mixture, stirring vigorously until sauce is thick and smooth. Add cream. Combine mushroom broth mixture with sauce and season to taste.

Preparation: 45 min.

Easy
Can do ahead

Yield: 2 qts.
Can freeze

Mrs. Foster A. Stewart

VICHYSSOISE SOUP

"This will keep several days in the refrigerator."

4 med. potatoes, peeled and
  cubed
3 cups boiling water
5 chicken bouillon cubes
3 tbsp. butter
5 leeks, minced finely,
  including 3" of green top
  (or 1½ cups minced onion)
1 cup heavy cream
1 cup milk
1 tsp. salt
¼ tsp. pepper
minced chives
paprika

Place potatoes in large saucepan. Add water, bouillon cubes, butter and leeks or onions. Cover and cook until potatoes are very tender (about 30 minutes). Press mixture, without putting through sieve. Or put through blender to achieve complete smoothness. Pour into saucepan. Add cream, milk, salt and pepper. Mix well. Serve very cold with garnish of chives and paprika or reheat and serve very hot.

Preparation: 20 min.   Easy   Serves: 6-8
Cooking: 30 min.   Must do ahead

Mrs. George P. O'Neil

VEGETABLE SOUP

"Very tasty and very easy."

½ cabbage, shredded
  (green)
several carrots
bay leaf
1 soup bone or 4 tbsp. beef
  flavored instant bouillon
1 can tomato soup or ¾ cup
  tomato catsup
margarine
1 can mixed vegetables or
  pkg. frozen vegetables or
  leftover vegetables like
  cauliflower, broccoli, etc.
½ cup barley
2 tbsp. parsley
3 tbsp. sugar
salt & pepper to taste

Shred cabbage and slice carrots. Sauté both in margarine until cabbage just begins to brown. Add sugar, salt and pepper. Mix well. Add remaining ingredients. Add enough water to make 1½ quarts liquid. Bring to a boil then simmer 1½ to 2 hours.

Preparation: 30 min.   Easy   Yield: 1½ qts.
Cooking: 1½-2 hours   Freezes well

Mrs. Giles J. Gaca

BREADS

THE AILSA MELLON BRUCE COLLECTION

The decorative art on the preceding page is from the extensive collection of the late Mrs. Ailsa Mellon Bruce, daughter of Andrew W. Mellon. In the Fall of 1974, these pieces will be exhibited in the new Nationality Rooms at the Museum of Art, Carnegie Institute.

Illustrated are:

TILT-TOP MAHOGANY TEA TABLE
English, c. 1760

PAIR OF MAHOGANY STOOLS
English, c. 1760

CHIPPENDALE FALL-FRONT MAHOGANY SECRETARY
WITH PIERCED TOP IN THE CHINESE TASTE
English, c. 1770-75

CHINOISERIE WALLPAPER IN THE MID-18TH CENTURY
EUROPEAN TASTE

Additional illustrations in this section:

Local artists, sculptors and photographers exhibit their work in early June during the Three Rivers Arts Festival in Gateway Center.

Frieze of Pittsburgh's Carnegie Institute Music Hall.

Gateway Center tulips.

ᴄBREADS

BREAD

"So good, you may never buy store-bought bread again."

2 pkg. yeast
½ cup warm water
2 cups water & milk
  mixed to taste
2 eggs
½ cup melted butter
1 tbsp. salt
½ cup honey
1½ cups wheat germ
7-8 cups unbleached flour⁻

Sprinkle yeast over ½ cup warm water, let sit 5 minutes. Mix in milk and water, eggs, butter, salt, honey and wheat germ. Beat in flour until kneadable. Knead at least 5 minutes. Let rise, covered, in warm place. After 1½ hours, punch down dough, flatten to rectangle, divide in two, and roll tightly. Tuck ends under, put seam on bottom. Place in well-greased loaf pans. Place in cold oven. Turn heat to 400° for 15 minutes, lower to 350° and bake 20-30 minutes. Brush with butter and set loaves on side.

Preparation:	2 hours	Easy	Yield: 2 loaves
Baking:	35-45 min.	Can do ahead	Can freeze

True light Beavers

DATE AND NUT LOAF

1 lb. chopped walnut meats
1 lb. chopped dates
1 cup sugar
1 tsp. salt
4 eggs, beaten separately
1 cup flour
2 tsp. baking powder
1 tsp. vanilla

Mix nuts and dates, sugar and salt. Stir in egg yolks with flour and baking powder. Add vanilla. Fold in beaten egg whites. Form into 2 loaves in wax papered greased bread pans. Bake 1 hour at 325°.

Preparation: 30 min.
Baking: 1 hour

Can do ahead

Yield: 2 loaves
Can freeze

Mrs. Scott Sawhill

IRISH SODA BREAD

"Food for Leprechauns!"

¼ cup shortening
3 cups flour
¼ cup sugar
3 tsp. baking powder
1 tsp. baking soda
pinch salt
1 well beaten egg
1½ cups buttermilk
1½ cups raisins or currants
1 tbsp. caraway seed

Rub shortening into flour with sugar, baking powder, baking soda and a pinch of salt. Add well beaten egg, buttermilk, raisins and caraway seeds. Knead on a floured board and bake in skillet with cross cut in top of dough. Bake for 1 hour at 375°.

Preparation: 30 min.
Cooking: 1 hour

Easy

Yield: 1 loaf
Freezes well

Mrs. Bridget Flaherty

PUMPKIN BREAD

4 eggs
⅔ cup water
1 cup Crisco Oil
1 can pumpkin pie filling
  (or 1 lb. can of pumpkin
  & increase spices to taste
  — generously)
3½ cups flour
3 cups sugar
2 tsp. soda
1½ tsp. salt
1 tsp. cinnamon
1 tsp. nutmeg
cloves to liking
nuts (optional)
also use pumpkin seasoning
  & allspice

Beat eggs; add oil, water and pie mix. Add dry ingredients. Mix well. Bake in greased and floured tins at 350° for 1 hour. Makes 2 large and 1 small or 6 small loaves.

Preparation: 20 min.
Baking: 1 hour

Easy
Can do ahead

Yield: 2 large and
  1 small loaves
Can freeze

Mrs. Richard Webster

OATMEAL MOLASSES BREAD

"Makes three big loaves!"

1½ cup quick oats
1 qt. milk
¾ cup molasses
2 tsp. salt
¼ cup shortening
1 yeast cake dissolved
  in ¼ cup warm water
7¾ to 8 cups flour

Cook oats in milk 10 minutes, stirring constantly. Add molasses, salt and shortening. Cool to lukewarm. Add yeast. Work in flour. Turn on lightly floured board and knead until smooth and elastic. Place in greased bowl. Cover, let rise to double bulk. Punch down and shape into 3 loaves. Let rise to almost double again. Bake 400°, 10 minutes. Reduce oven to 375°. Bake 40 minutes more. Remove from pans. Brush with shortening. Cool.

Preparation: 3 hours
Baking: 50 min.

Yield: 3 loaves
Can freeze

Mrs. Robert H. Bartlett

ORANGE BREAD

1 cup sugar
½ cup butter
2 eggs
1 cup sour cream
rind of 1 orange, grated
2 cups sifted cake flour
1 tsp. baking soda
½ cup sugar
juice of 1 orange

Cream sugar and butter. Add eggs, sour cream and rind of 1 orange. Sift flour and soda. Mix into other ingredients. Bake at 350° for 50 minutes in 2 medium bread pans. Mix together sugar and orange juice and pour over bread while still hot in bread pans. Cool 10 minutes and invert.

Preparation: 20 min.
Baking: 50 min.

Easy
Can do ahead

Yield: 2 loaves
Can freeze

Mrs. Robert H. Smith

LEMON LOAF

"Rich, delicious bread."

8 oz. butter or
  margarine
2 cups sugar
4 eggs
grated rind of 2 lemons
3 cups flour
2 tsp. baking powder
1 tsp. salt
1 cup milk
½ cup sugar dissolved
  in juice of 2 lemons

Cream together butter and sugar. Add eggs one at a time, beat well. Add lemon rind. Sift together dry ingredients, add alternately with milk. Pour into 3 medium loaf pans. Bake at 350° about 45 to 60 minutes. Turn from pans to cake rack, covered with wax paper. Drizzle over the loaves the sugar and juice mixture. Cool. Double wrap to freeze. For tea party, slice thin, spread with soft cream cheese and toast sandwiches lightly.

Preparation: 15-20 min.
Baking: 45-60 min.

Yield: 3 med. loaves
Can freeze

Mrs. Joseph Blackhurst

PHOTOGRAPHER'S NUT BREAD

1 cup sugar
1 egg
1½ cups milk
3½ cups sifted flour
4 tsp. baking powder
1 tsp. salt
2 cups cut-up nuts

Combine sugar and egg, beating until well-mixed and fluffy. Stir in milk gradually. Sift together flour, baking powder and salt and add gradually to sugar-egg-milk mixture. Finally stir in nuts. Use either one pan 2½ x 4½ x 13" or in 2 pans sized 2½ x 4¾ x 8¾". Grease and lightly flour the pans. Pour in mixture and let stand to rise about 20 minutes. Bake in a 350° oven. Bake larger size about 1 hour or until done. The smaller pans about 45 to 50 minutes or until they test done.

Preparation:	10-15 min.	Easy	Yield: 1 large or
Baking:	45-60 min.	Can do ahead	2 small loaves
			Can freeze

Mrs. Charles Stuebgen

APPLE SPICE MUFFINS

¾ cup milk
1 beaten egg
¼ cup melted shortening
2 cups sifted flour
½ cup sugar
1 tbsp. baking powder
½ tsp. salt
1 tsp. cinnamon
1 cup finely chopped apples
¼ cup raisins

Add milk to egg, stir in shortening. Mix dry ingredients together, and add apples and raisins. Add liquid to dry ingredients and stir *just* until moistened. Will be lumpy. Fill well-greased muffin tins ⅔ full. Bake at 400° for 20 to 25 minutes.

| Preparation: | 15 min. | Easy | Yield: 1 doz. |
| Baking: | 20-25 min. | Can do ahead | Can freeze |

The Committee

HERB ROLLS

"Try this in a ring mold or bundt pan — great for a buffet dinner."

¼ cup butter or margarine
1½ tsp. parsley flakes
½ tsp. dill seed
¼ tsp. onion flakes
1 pkg. refrigerated buttermilk
 biscuits

Put first 4 ingredients in a 9" pie pan. Let melt. Blend well. Cut biscuits in quarters. Swish each one in melted mixture. Arrange pieces touching in the pie pan. Bake in a 425° oven for 12 minutes or until golden brown. Let stand a short time to absorb the butter and herbs.

| Preparation: | 5-6 min. | Easy | Serves: 6 |
| Baking: | 12 min. | | |

Mrs. Robert A. McKean, III

ICEBOX BRAN ROLLS

1 cup shortening
¾ cup granulated sugar
1½ tsp. salt
1 cup boiling water
1 cup All-Bran
½ large cake yeast
1 cup lukewarm water
2 eggs, well beaten
6 cups all-purpose flour,
  measured after sifting
Crisco

Combine shortening, sugar and salt. Add the water and All-Bran and stir until melted. In a separate bowl, dissolve the yeast in lukewarm water. When first mixture is lukewarm, add the eggs and dissolved yeast. Add flour. Beat batter and put in a bowl in refrigerator for 24 hours. Take out and roll in rounds and cut like pie. Brush each with Crisco and roll from wide end. Pinch end down so it will not rise up when baked. Let rise in a warm place about 2 hours or until light. Grease cookie sheet and bake for 25 minutes at 375-400°.

Preparation: 30 min.   **Must do ahead**   Yield: 5 doz.
Baking: 25 min.

Mrs. Robert Trunick

STICKY BUNS

"Perfect for a morning Coffee."

Dough:*

1 pkg. dry yeast
1 cup scalded milk,
  lukewarm
½ cup sugar
1 tsp. salt
2 eggs or 4 yolks, beaten
½ cup melted shortening
4½ cups all-purpose flour

Spread:

soft butter
1 cup sugar
2 tbsp. cinnamon

Topping:

1 cup butter
1⅓ cups brown sugar
4 tsp. light corn syrup

Place yeast in bowl. Add lukewarm milk and stir until dissolved. Stir in sugar, salt and eggs. Add half the shortening and half the flour. Beat until smooth. Add remaining flour, mix well. Add remaining shortening and mix. Knead until smooth. Place in greased bowl, cover, and let rise until double. Roll out the dough into two rectangles 9 x 18". Spread each rectangle with soft or melted butter and sprinkle with sugar and cinnamon mixture. Roll up tightly from the long side. Pinch edges together. Cut in 1" slices.

Topping: Melt butter, add sugar and corn syrup. Bring to a rolling boil and take off heat immediately. Do *not* overcook. Pour into two 9 x 13" pans. Place rolls cut side down in pans. Cover and let rise until *double* in size. Bake at 375° for 20-30 minutes. Turn immediately over onto aluminum foil. *One package Pillsbury Hot Roll mix can be substituted for the dough and will make one 9 x 13" pan. Halve spread and topping accordingly.

Preparation: 25 min.   **Can do ahead**   Yield: two 9 x 13" pans
Rising: 2½-3 hours   of rolls
Baking: 20-30 min.

Mrs. James E. Cavalier

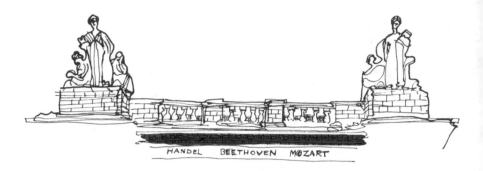

HANDEL   BEETHOVEN   MOZART

BUTTERSCOTCH RAISIN PECAN ROLLS

"They are scrumptious."

1 pkg. compressed or
  dry yeast
¼ cup lukewarm water
1 cup milk, scalded
¼ cup sugar
¼ cup butter or margarine
1 tsp. salt
3-3½ cups sifted flour
1 egg, beaten
soft butter or shortening
½ cup chopped pecans
¼ cup raisins
2 tsp. ground cinnamon
½ cup brown sugar, packed
1 tsp. water
3 tbsp. light corn syrup

Topping:

¼ cup light corn syrup
1 tbsp. water
2 tbsp. butter or
  margarine
1 cup butterscotch bits
  (6 oz. pkg.)
1 cup pecans
¼ cup raisins

Soften yeast in lukewarm water (use warm water for dry yeast). Combine scalded milk, sugar, butter or margarine and salt in large bowl. Cool to lukewarm. Add 1 cup flour. Beat well. Beat in softened yeast and egg. Add remaining flour gradually to form a soft dough. Mix well. Brush top lightly with softened butter. Cover and let rise in warm place until double, 1½ to 2 hours. Meanwhile, prepare topping.

Topping: Combine corn syrup, water, butter or margarine and butterscotch bits in 10" skillet or baking pan. Cook until bits are melted and mixture heated. Place pecans in bottom of skillet. Sprinkle with raisins. Punch down dough. Turn out on lightly floured surface. Roll out into rectangle 14 x 28". Brush with softened butter or shortening. Sprinkle pecans and raisins over surface. Blend cinnamon and brown sugar. Sprinkle over pecans and raisins. Blend water and corn syrup. Drizzle over surface. Roll as for jelly roll, beginning with long side. Seal edge. Cut roll into 1½ to 2" pieces. Place cut side down in topping in skillet. Cover and let rise in warm place until doubled, 35 to 45 minutes. Bake in 350° oven, 30 to 35 minutes. Let cool in pan for 5 minutes. Loosen edges with point of knife. Turn upside down on rack to cool slightly. Serve warm or as desired.

| Preparation: | 1 hour + | Can do ahead | Yield: 14 |
| Baking: | 30-35 min. | | Will freeze |

Mrs. Carl O. Hughes

SO-EASY NUT STRUDEL

1 cup sour cream
3 tbsp. butter
5 tbsp. sugar
1/8 tsp. baking soda
1½ tsp. salt
2 eggs, beaten
1 small cake yeast, crumbled
3 cups flour

Carefully bring sour cream to a boil in a large saucepan. Remove sour cream from heat, and add butter, sugar, baking soda and salt. Stir until well blended. Cool until mixture is lukewarm. Stir in eggs, add yeast and stir until dissolved. With wooden spoon stir in flour. Turn dough on lightly floured board and knead gently to form a smooth ball. Cover ball with clean tea towel and let stand 5 minutes. Roll dough about ¼" thick, spread with nut filling,* and roll as if for jelly roll. For easier handling, you may want to roll out dough on a lightly floured tablecloth. Also you may divide dough in 2 parts, to make 2 rolls, or twist the single roll in pan to fit. Greased roasting pan will do or a baking sheet. Let rise in pan for about 1½ hours. Brush top with beaten egg. Bake in 350° oven about 35 minutes or until done. *See nut filling on page 42.

Preparation: 30 min.   Make ahead   Yield: 1 large strudel
Rising & baking: 2 hours

Miss Zora Unkovich

AUNT TOT'S CIMMACUCA

"Be sure to try this breakfast cake. It's wonderful."

1 cup milk, heated
¼ cup sugar
½ tsp. salt
butter or margarine
  the size of a walnut
1 cake yeast, dissolved
  in ¼ cup warm water
4 cups flour
2 eggs
5⅓ oz. can of evaporated
  milk
2-3 tbsp. butter

Brown sugar mixture:

1 cup brown sugar
½ tsp. salt
¼ cup white sugar
1 tbsp. flour
1 tbsp. cinnamon

Dissolve sugar, salt and butter in heated milk in large bowl. Mix in 2 cups of flour. Beat in yeast mixture. Beat in eggs, then mix in 2 more cups of flour. Cover and let rise, will double in bulk. For a large breakfast cake, grease a 9 x 13" pan or grease two 8 x 8" pans. Punch the dough down and pat in pan. (It does not need to rise again.) Pour ½ can of condensed milk over dough, then cover with brown sugar mixture. Cut 2-3 tablespoons butter in small pieces and place on top of brown sugar. Dribble the rest of the condensed milk over this. Bake at 365° for about ½ hour or until it looks just right. Very versatile. You can substitute other fillings for the brown sugar, such as apples, jelly or poppyseed.

Preparation: 1½ hours   Yield: 1 9 x 13" cake or
Baking: 30 min.   2 8 x 8" cakes

Mrs. Willard O. Mitchell

41

MAMA'S NUT ROLLS

8 cups flour
¾ cup sugar
1 tsp. salt
1 lb. shortening —
  sometimes Mama used
  ½ lb. Crisco and ½ lb.
  butter
1 cake Fleischman's yeast
1 cup milk
4 eggs, beaten
1 tsp. vanilla (optional)

Sift flour, sugar and salt. Cut in shortening to the size of peas. Dissolve yeast in warm milk and add beaten eggs to mixture. Add to flour mixture and knead until it comes away clean from the fingers. Place in large bowl or pan, cover with tea towel and place in cold spot overnight. The refrigerator will do. When ready to bake, let dough stand at room temperature until dough softens. Mama used to place a white tablecloth on the kitchen table and roll thin the entire chunk of dough over the whole of the floured surface. However, it's easier to cut the dough into 4 sections, rolling one at a time on a large floured board or cloth. (Roll thin, remember.) Spread nut filling (see below) over all the dough surface. Roll as for jelly roll. Brush top with beaten egg and bake for 45 minutes at 375°. Mama used a roasting pan for her giant Nut Roll, arranging the whole along the length and breadth of the pan. You can use regular baking sheets.

Nut Filling The Way We Like It

6 cups ground walnuts
2 cups milk
2 cups sugar, or honey
1½ tsp. vanilla

Mix together in saucepan. Bring to a slow boil. Take off heat and let cool before spreading on dough. (Leave some nut mixture on sides of pan for children to lick. It's a rare holiday treat.) For a smaller family cut ingredients in half. If you want a less rich filling, use 4 cups of walnuts, ground, 1⅓ cups sugar or honey, and 1 tsp. vanilla.

Preparation: 1 hour +   Yield: 1 large or 4 small
Cooking: 45 minutes

Miss Zora Unkovich

MAGLINE LAKE COFFEECAKE
"Quick, easy, and inexpensive."

1 loaf bakery bread, unsliced
¼ cup soft butter
½ cup brown sugar
1 tbsp. cream

Cut off all crusts from bread (top, bottom, and sides). Slice loaf in half lengthwise and make 6 or 7 cuts crosswise in each piece and 1 lengthwise cut. *Do not cut through bottom.* Mix rest of ingredients and spread over each lengthwise section of loaves and into each cut. Place in tin loaf pans and bake at 450° for 20 minutes. Can be frozen before baking and can also be baked in foil.

Preparation: 15 min.   Easy   Serves: 6
Baking: 20 min.   Can do ahead   Can freeze

Mrs. Albert L. Brahm

CY'S WALNUT COFFEE CAKE

1½ cups flour, sifted
½ tsp. salt
2 tsp. baking powder
¾ cup sugar
4 tbsp. butter or margarine
½ cup milk
2 eggs
1 tbsp. flour
½ cup brown sugar,
  well packed
1 tsp. cinnamon
1 cup walnuts
2 tbsp. butter (optional)

Combine sifted flour, salt, baking powder, sugar, shortening and milk. Add eggs, beating an additional 2 minutes. For the topping, combine 1 tablespoon flour, the brown sugar, cinnamon and walnuts. Add the butter here if you want it. Mix well. Pour half the batter in greased pie pan. Spread with half the topping mixture, then pour on rest of batter and the rest of the topping. Bake in 350° oven for about 30 minutes. Cut in wedges and serve warm. The result is crumbly, but that is the way it is supposed to be.

Preparation: 20 min.   Easy
Baking: 30 min.

Cy Hungerford

MERK'S COFFEE CAKE

"Everyone who tastes it — loves it."

½ cup shortening
¾ cup sugar
1 tsp. vanilla
3 eggs
2 cups sifted flour
1 tsp. baking powder
1 tsp. baking soda
½ pt. sour cream
Brown sugar mixture (Mix well)
6 tbsp. soft margarine
1 cup brown sugar
2 tsp. cinnamon
1 cup chopped nuts

Cream shortening, sugar and vanilla. Add eggs beating well. Add flour, baking powder and soda alternately with sour cream. Spread ½ batter in a greased 10" tube pan, or bundt pan. Cover with one half of brown sugar mixture. Add remaining batter, then sugar mixture. Bake at 350° for 50 minutes.

Preparation: 30 min.   Easy   Serves: 10-12
Baking: 50 min.   Can do ahead   Can freeze

Mrs. R. Allen Moulton, Jr.

BLENDER APPLE PANCAKES

1 egg
1 tbsp. sugar
1 tbsp. soft butter
1 med. apple, peeled & sliced
1 cup evaporated milk
1 cup pancake mix

Place egg, sugar, butter, apple and milk in blender. Blend. Add pancake mix and blend. Fry as for ordinary pancakes.

Preparation: 3-4 min.   Easy   Can freeze
Cooking: 3-4 min.   Can do ahead

Mrs. Foster A. Stewart

DR. CYERT'S PANCAKES

"Serve with strawberries or any favorite sauce."

1 cup presifted flour
2 tsp. sugar
¾ tsp. baking powder
¼ tsp. salt
1¼ cups buttermilk
½ tsp. baking soda
2 egg yolks, lightly beaten
2 tbsp. peanut oil
2 egg whites, stiffly beaten

Mix together flour, sugar, baking powder, and salt. Combine buttermilk, baking soda and egg yolks. Mix dry ingredients and buttermilk mixture. Stir in oil. Fold in egg whites. Cook on hot, greased skillet.

Preparation: 15-20 min.

Yield: 8 large

Dr. Richard M. Cyert

FEATHERWEIGHT PANCAKES

½ cup flour
½ tsp. salt
¾ cup small curd
  cottage cheese
3 eggs, separated

Mix flour, salt and cheese together. Beat egg yolks lemon colored. Add to flour mixture. Beat egg whites stiff, but not dry. Fold in egg whites. Drop in small spoonsful on a griddle and brown on both sides. A lid helps cook these through.

Preparation: 10 min.   Yield: 12 3" pancakes
Cooking: 5-8 min.

Mrs. Roger S. Brown, Jr.

ENTRÉES

U. S. STEEL — THE HOMESTEAD WORKS

Steel, red hot from the furnace of Pennsylvania's largest steel mill, the U. S. Steel Homestead Works, projects strength and energy. Here steelmaking open hearth furnaces and rolling mills squeeze bulky ingots into primary steel shapes, giant structural beams or wide flat plates one hundred feet in length. Pittsburgh — the center of iron and steel production — the hearth of the nation.

Additional illustrations in this section:

Phipps Conservatory in Schenley Park, Oakland, is the second largest of its type in the country with 2½ acres under glass and year-round displays.

Bas-relief gargoyles at Heinz Hall.

The stern-wheeler W. P. Snyder, Jr. was once the workhorse of our great inland water system. Now in a river museum at Marietta, Ohio, she retains many 19th century characteristics reminiscent of Mark Twain's day.

South Side Market Street Relief.

Kaufmann's Clock at the corner of Smithfield Street and Fifth Avenue is a favorite meeting spot for Pittsburghers.

Gateway Center Tulips.

The "Horn" trademark of the Joseph Horne Co.

The Steel Puddler on the building at 300 Wood Street. "Pure Pittsburgh and apothesis of Art-Deco on local stores."

The Block House Sun Dial.

Pittsburgh Steeler and Penguin Emblems.

Pittsburgh Pirates' Emblem.

WHITE PORCELAIN COCK ON TREE STUMP — Chinese, Yung Cheng Period (1723-35) — Ailsa Mellon Bruce Collection.

The Gateway Party Liner — a pleasure-sightseeing boat.

The Pittsburgh Civic Arena's retractable dome is the only one of its kind in the country.

In 1869 H. J. Heinz used a horse-drawn wagon to deliver his main product, freshly grated horseradish.

CHEESE & EGGS

SWISS CHEESE SCRAMBLE
"Great Brunch"

8 pieces bacon, fried crisp,
  drained & crumbled
2 cups soft bread cubes,
  no crusts
1¾ cups milk
8 slightly beaten eggs
¾ tsp. salt
⅛ tsp. pepper
2 tbsp. butter or margarine
¼ tsp. seasoned salt
½ lb. sliced Swiss cheese
2 tbsp. melted butter
½ cup fine dry bread crumbs

Combine bread cubes and milk. Drain after 5 minutes. Combine milk drained with eggs, salt and pepper. Melt in skillet the butter. Add egg mixture and scramble until soft, not quite fully cooked. Add soaked bread cubes and turn into a 9" square or round shallow baking dish. Sprinkle with seasoned salt. Arrange the Swiss cheese over the top. Combine the melted butter and dry bread crumbs and sprinkle over cheese. Top with crumbled bacon. Bake in a hot oven, 400°, 10 to 15 minutes until the cheese bubbles around the edge of the dish and cheese at center is melted. Serve immediately.

Preparation: 15 min.   Easy   Serves: 8
Baking: 10-15 min.   Serve immediately

C. F. Spengler, Jr.

ENTREE CREPES & SPINACH FILLING

"Everyone adores this. Use your blender for the batter."

1 cup cold water
1 cup cold milk
4 large eggs
½ tsp. salt
2 cups all-purpose flour
4 tbsp. melted butter

Place all ingredients, except flour, in your blender jar and combine well. Add flour gradually with blender still running. Refrigerate for at least 2 hours.

Use approximately ¼ cup batter for each crepe, pour into pan after butter is starting to smoke, but not burned. Put wax paper in between crepes after they are cooked so they won't stick together.

Preparation:	5 - 10 min.	Easy	Yield: 24
Cooking:	45 min.	Must do ahead	Can freeze

Spinach Filling

This filling may be made in the morning and the crepes assembled then or just before baking.

4 tbsp. butter
5 tbsp. flour
2¾ cups milk
½ tsp. salt
pepper (white if you have it)
  to taste
¼ cup heavy cream
1 cup coarsely grated
  Swiss cheese
2 pkg. frozen chopped
  spinach, cooked according
  to directions and very well
  drained
1 cup cottage or Ricotta cheese
1 egg
1 cup diced fresh mushrooms
  (or 1 4-oz. can mushroom bits
  and pieces) sautéed in butter
  with 2 tbsp. minced shallots,
  green onions or onion

Melt butter, stir in flour and cook slowly for 2-3 minutes without browning. Add milk after taking saucepan off the heat, add salt and pepper. Cook, stirring, until it thickens and bubbles around edge of pan. Beat in cream and all but 2 tbsp. cheese. Correct seasoning after simmering until cheese is melted.

Add cottage cheese, slightly beaten egg, mushrooms, and 4-6 tbsp. of the sauce to the spinach.

Fill crepes with approximately 2 tbsp. each of this mixture, folding sides over, and place, seam side down, in a greased flat baking dish, side by side.

When all filling and crepes are used, pour rest of sauce over and sprinkle rest of cheese over and dot top with butter. Bake in 350° oven until very hot and bubbling, approximately 45 minutes.

This freezes well assembled, except for the grated Swiss cheese topping and butter dots which should be added just before baking. Defrost casserole all day before baking and serving.

Preparation:	1 hour	Easy	Yield: 12 crepes
Cooking:	45 min.	Can do ahead	Serves: 4 - 6
			Freezes well

Mrs. Edward A. Montgomery, Jr.

DELECTABLE CHEESE CROQUETTES

Can be appetizer or luncheon dish.

4 tbsp. butter or margarine
1/3 cup sifted all-purpose flour
1½ cups milk
1/8 tsp. white pepper
1/8 tsp. nutmeg
3 egg yolks
3¾ cups (approx. 16 oz.)
  shredded natural Swiss cheese
2 eggs
½ cup milk
½ cup all-purpose flour
1 cup fine dry bread crumbs
cooking oil

Tomato Sauce

1/3 cup diced onion
1 slice bacon, diced
1½ tbsp. butter
1 can condensed beef broth
½ cup tomato puree
¼ cup catsup
2 tbsp. diced carrots
1½ slices white bread

In skillet, melt butter; blend in 1/3 cup flour. Add the 1½ cup milk all at once; cook and stir until thickened. Add pepper and nutmeg. Mix a small amount of hot mixture into egg yolks. Add to rest of mixture in saucepan. Cook 10 minutes, stirring continually. Add cheese — stir until smooth — spread into oiled 11 x 7 x 1½" pan. Chill until firm. Cut into 12 portions. Beat 2 eggs; add ½ cup milk. Roll croquettes in flour, dip in egg mixture, roll gently in crumbs. Fry in deep fat (375°) til golden brown, 2-3 minutes.

Put 2 tbsp. hot tomato sauce on plate — 2 croquettes on plate with a garnish of parsley.

Tomato Sauce:
In saucepan, cook onion and bacon in butter til tender. Stir in remaining ingredients. Cover. Cook over low heat for 30 minutes. Press through sieve, reheat to serve. Makes 1¼ cups sauce. Sauce and croquettes can be made and kept in refrigerator at least 2 days ahead. Last minute only requires frying croquettes — goes very quickly.

Preparation:	1 hour	Must do ahead	Serves: 6
Cooking:	30 min.-sauce		Can freeze
	20 min.-croquettes		*Mrs. J. Robert Van Kirk*

BRUNCH DISH

12 slices Canadian bacon
12 slices Swiss cheese
1 dozen eggs
½ pt. cream
Parmesan cheese, grated

Line a shallow pan; e.g., 9 x 13" baking dish, with the Canadian bacon. Add the layer of Swiss cheese. Break eggs over all, being careful not to break the yolks. Drizzle the cream over the whites until the yolks peek through. Bake at 450° for 10 minutes. Remove and sprinkle well with grated Parmesan cheese. Return to oven and bake 8 to 10 minutes longer. Cut in squares and serve.

Preparation:	10 min.	Easy	Serves: 8
Baking:	20 min.	Serve immediately	

Mrs. James E. Cavalier

NIPPY CHEESE FONDUE

2 rolls Kraft Nippy Cheese
2 rolls Kraft Garlic Cheese
1 can mushroom soup
½ cup milk
2-3 drops Tabasco
1 tsp. Worcestershire sauce
2-4 tbsp. cooking sherry
bread or ham cubes

Cut cheese into chunks. Combine all ingredients except sherry in saucepan over medium low heat. Stir until melted. Just before serving, add sherry. More milk can be added if mixture appears too thick. Use bread or ham cubes for dunking.

Preparation: 15 min.   Easy   Serves: 4

Mrs. Timothy W. Merrill, Jr.

CHEESE SOUFFLÉ

1 tbsp. butter
1 tbsp. grated Parmesan or
 Cheddar cheese
2 qt. pyrex dish
Roux: 3 tbsp. butter
       3 tbsp. flour
       1 cup milk
       salt, pepper
4 egg yolks
6 egg whites
1 cup grated cheese
 (Cheddar or Swiss or
 ½ Swiss and ½ Parmesan)

Butter sides and bottom of dish. Line with cheese.
In saucepan, melt butter, add flour and mix. Add milk and mix, cook well and keep mixing.
Add grated cheese and melt over hot water. Remove from heat, add egg yolks gradually, beating well. Can be set aside at this point. When ready to bake, add beaten whites. (Add a generous spoonful of whites first, then fold in remaining whites.) Pour

in prepared dish (cut a circle in the middle for the hat to rise up). Bake at 350° for 30 minutes or until nicely browned.

You can substitute ham, mushrooms or broccoli for the cheese.

Preparation: 30 min.   Serves: 4
Baking: 30 min.
                               Mrs. Richard B. Lord

JANE'S SOUFFLÉ

6 slices bread (buttered)
6 eggs
2½ cups liquid:
 ½ cup white wine
 ½ cup chicken broth
 1½ cups milk
8 oz. grated Gruyere
 cheese
1 can sliced mushrooms
parsley, onion salt &
 pepper to season

Place bread buttered side down in bottom of large flat casserole. Mix eggs and liquids together in blender. Combine with cheese, mushrooms, parsley, etc. Refrigerate at least two hours. Bake at 350° for 30 minutes.

Mrs. W. Kendall Jones

Preparation: 10 min.   Easy   Serves: 4 - 6
Baking: 30 min.   Must do ahead

CHEESE GRITS

"Try this instead of potatoes at your next party."

4 cups boiling water
1 tsp. salt
1 cup grits (Quaker Quick Grits)
½ stick butter or margarine
2 cups or more grated sharp cheese
3 eggs, well beaten

Slowly pour the grits into the boiling, salted water, stirring constantly until mixed. Cook 2½ to 5 minutes, stirring occasionally. When grits are cooked, add butter, cheese and eggs and mix well. Pour into greased 1½-quart baking dish and bake 30 to 40 minutes at 350°.

Preparation:	10 min.	Easy	Serves: 8-10
Baking:	40 min.	Can do ahead	

Mrs. Monro B. Lanier, II

NEVER FAIL CHEESE FONDUE

½ lb. Gruyere or Swiss cheese
1½ tbsp. flour
1 clove garlic, split
1 cup dry Swiss white wine or vermouth
salt & pepper to taste
3 tbsp. kirsch, or to taste
1 loaf French bread, cut into bite-sized pieces

Shred the cheese and toss in the flour. Set aside.

Rub the inside of a heatproof, glazed earthenware casserole with garlic and add wine. Place on stove or burner with an adjustable flame. When heated to a point below boiling where air bubbles rise to the surface, stir with a fork and add cheese, a handful at a time. Let each handful melt before adding another. Add salt and pepper and finally stir in the kirsch.

If fondue becomes too thick, it may be thinned with a little preheated dry white wine.

Preparation:	10 min.	Easy	Serves: 2 - 6

Mrs. Thomas M. Garrett

BEEF

STEAK AND KIDNEY PUDDING
"Old English recipe — must like kidneys."

Crust:
2 cups flour
2 cups grated hard suet
½ tsp. baking powder
½ tsp. salt

Filling:
small peeled onion
2 lbs. lean beef (stewing beef, round steak or chuck roast, no fat or gristle)
6 or 7 lamb kidneys or 1 beef kidney (beef kidney should be boiled 10 min. before using)
flour
salt and pepper
1 tbsp. Worcestershire sauce
boiling water

Crust: mix all ingredients in bowl with barely enough cold water to make dough. Knead thoroughly. Roll out to about ¼ inch thick. Filling: cut beef and kidneys into cubes. Dredge with flour, salt and pepper, keeping beef and kidneys separate. Use bowl with rim — either metal or crockery. Grease bowl. Line bowl with pastry — do not trim. Place small peeled onion at bottom. Fill bowl with alternate layers of beef and kidney. Make holes to bottom of bowl. Pour in 1 tbsp. Worcestershire sauce and fill holes with boiling water. Fold pastry over top. Cover top with ½ yard unbleached muslin, sterilized in boiling water. Tie cloth with string about 2 inches below rim of bowl. Pull up 4 corners of cloth and knot at top of pudding. Put into boiling water to cover. Simmer 4-6 hours. Save a few pieces of beef and cook down with a little water to make a natural gravy to be added to pudding when served. Serve with brussel sprouts.

Preparation: 1 hour
Cooking: 4 - 6 hours

Serves: 6

Mrs. Dorothy Ryan Cochrane

BAKED STEAK EDWARD

"Makes a sirloin sensational."

1 2" thick sirloin steak
  (2nd or 3rd cut)
1½ tbsp. butter
1½ tbsp. oil
salt & pepper
Sauce:
2 tbsp. butter
2 tbsp. oil
1 chopped onion
4 minced garlic cloves
½ bottle red wine
1 tsp. Wilsons BV gravy mix
2 bouillon cubes
1½ tbsp. tomato paste or
  ketchup
1 stick butter, frozen &
  sliced
parsley

Preheat oven to 350°. Pat steak dry and have at room temperature. Melt butter and oil in pan. Salt and pepper steak each side and sear each side 5 minutes. Put in casserole and bake for 35 minutes.

Sauce: Melt 2 tablespoons butter and 2 tablespoons oil. When hot, add onion and garlic cloves. Cook 10 minutes. Do not brown. Add wine, BV mix, bouillon cubes, tomato paste and let boil until thick. At last minute add 1 stick frozen, sliced butter and melt in sauce. When meat is done keep warm, and when blood runs add blood to sauce. Then pour sauce on steak and sprinkle with parsley.

Preparation: 20 min.	Easy	Serves: 6-8
Baking: 35 min.		

Mrs. Douglas E. Cox

SAUCY SHORT RIBS

3½ to 4 lbs. beef short ribs
  cut into 2" pieces
salt & pepper
1 bottle Heinz Barbecue
  Sauce with onions
¼ cup honey
¼ cup orange or pineapple
  juice
2 slices pineapple, drained
  & cut into small pieces, or
  1 tbsp. orange rind

Brown ribs in preheated 500° oven, uncovered, for 30 minutes. Pour off fat.

Sprinkle with salt and pepper. Combine barbecue sauce with remaining ingredients and pour over ribs. Cover and return to 350° oven for 45 minutes. Baste well. Continue to bake an additional 15 minutes or until very fork tender.

Uncover, place under broiler for 5-10 minutes, turning frequently until well glazed and crusty. Serve with hot rice. If making ahead, remove the ribs from the sauce after baking and chill separately. Then remove layer of fat that forms on top of sauce. Reheat meat in sauce for 15 minutes before serving.

Preparation: 15 min.	Easy	Serves: 4-6
Baking: 1 hour 40 min.	Can do ahead	

Beth Adams

SYMPHONY BEEF

"A nice brunch dish. Everything in it comes right off the shelf."

2 tbsp. butter
½ lb. chipped beef, or
  dried beef, torn into
  bite-size pieces
1 tbsp. flour
1 pt. sour cream
½ cup dry white wine or
  dry vermouth
1 heaping tbsp. grated
  Parmesan cheese
1 10-oz. can artichoke
  hearts, thinly sliced
split, toasted and buttered
  English muffins, buttered
  toast or noodles
Paprika

Melt butter in a skillet over low heat (an electric skillet set at 180° is safest). In it, frizzle the beef until crimpy and crisp on the edges. Sprinkle the flour on, mix and add the sour cream and wine. Stir thoroughly until smooth. Add the cheese, and finally the artichoke hearts. Stir gently — don't disintegrate the artichoke hearts. Keep warm at 180° until serving time. Spoon over muffins, toast or noodles and sprinkle paprika on top.

Preparation: 10 min.   Easy   Serves: 4

Mrs. Thomas M. Garrett

HARMONIST STEW

"Made by members of Harmony Society
at Economy Village circa 1830."

flour
5 lbs. beef, cut in 1" squares
fat for browning
2 med. onions, chopped fine
12 cups hot water
3 tbsp. lemon juice
4 tsp. Worcestershire sauce
2 bay leaves
2 tbsp. salt
2 tsp. sugar
1 tsp. pepper
1 tsp. paprika
12 carrots, cubed
12 potatoes, cubed

Spaetzels:

2 eggs
pinch of salt
½ cup flour
water to thin

Flour and brown meat in a little fat in an iron skillet. Add onions to meat and cook briefly. Add meat and onions to a large pot containing hot water and seasonings. Add carrots to mixture. Cook for approximately 2 hours; then add potatoes. Cook for 45 minutes longer. Add spaetzels and cook (covered) for 15 minutes.

Spaetzels: Beat eggs with salt. Add flour (enough to make a thick paste). Stir well. Add water to thin (until it is the consistency of thin pancake batter). Pour mixture through a slotted spoon into bubbling stew. Put lid on pot and cook

15 minutes. Stew goes well with cole slaw and homemade bread.

Preparation: 20 min.   Can do ahead   Serves: 20
Cooking: 3 hours

Old Economy

5-HOUR BEEF STEW

3 lbs. cubed stewing beef
1 large can tomatoes (#2½)
1 box frozen peas or green beans
6 whole carrots
3 medium potatoes, cubed
3 medium onions, coarsely chopped
1 cup chopped celery
3 tbsp. Minute tapioca
1 tbsp. sugar
1 tbsp. salt
generous grinding of black pepper
pinch of thyme, marjoram, and
  rosemary
2 oz. red wine

Put all ingredients in deep casserole, cover tightly and bake 5 hours at 225°. It is not necessary to brown the meat. Serve with parsley dumplings. Drop dumpling batter into hot stew ½ hour before serving. Cover.

Preparation:	15 min.	Easy	Serves: 8
Baking:	5 hours	Can do ahead	

PARSLEY DUMPLINGS

2 cups flour
1 tsp. salt
¼ tsp. pepper
4 tsp. baking powder
1 cup fresh, chopped parsley
1 egg, well beaten
milk — enough for fairly moist,
  stiff batter (slightly more than
  1 cup)
3 tbsp. melted butter

Sift together: flour, salt, pepper, baking powder. Add parsley. Stir in beaten egg, milk and shortening. Drop batter — ¼ cup at a time into hot stew. Cover and bake for ½ hour.

Preparation:	20 min.	Easy	
Baking:	30 min.		*Mrs. Francis J. Sullivan*

JOE'S ZOO STEW

2½ cups sliced onions
4 tbsp. butter
4 lbs. cubed beef
2 tbsp. flour
2 cups beer
1 tbsp. vinegar
2 tsp. salt
½ tsp. pepper
1 tsp. sugar
2 bay leaves
½ tsp. thyme
3 tbsp. parsley

Brown onions in butter; remove and brown meat in remaining butter. Sprinkle with flour. Add other ingredients and stir well. Cover and cook in 350° oven for 3 hours or until meat is very tender.

Suggested menu: Stew served with noodles, red cabbage wedges, apple pie with cheese.

Preparation:	30 min.	Easy	Serves: 12-16
Baking:	3 hours	Can do ahead	Can freeze

Joseph F. Bissonnette

COUNTRY BEEF STEW

"Best cooked the day before — good for winter suppers."

½ lb. salt pork cut in small pieces
2 lbs. beef stew meat
seasoned flour
1½ cloves chopped garlic (some
  prefer only one)
1 large chopped onion
1 bouillon cube dissolved in
  1 cup of hot water
8 oz. can tomato sauce
10 peppercorns
3 whole cloves
¼ cup chopped parsley
½ bay leaf
½ cup sherry or dry white wine
6 pared quartered carrots
6 medium quartered potatoes
1 stalk of chopped celery
a few fresh mushrooms

Sauté pork in a large skillet over a slow fire and brown the meat in the drippings over a quick fire. Sprinkle with seasoned flour.

Combine next 8 ingredients and heat until boiling. Place meat in heavy saucepan and pour these ingredients over it. Cover tightly and simmer for 4 hours.

After cooking meat 3 hours, add wine.

Cook vegetables separately until tender. Add to stew and cook 15 minutes.

Preparation: 30 min.
Cooking: 4 hours

Serves: 6

W. H. Krome George

SUKIYAKI

*"If you have never tried cooking Japanese food,
this is the recipe to start with!"*

1 lb. sliced sirloin
6 green onions, sliced
6 pieces celery, sliced diagonally
¼ lb. mushrooms, sliced
1 can beef broth
soy sauce
1 can water chestnuts
1 can bean sprouts
1 can bamboo shoots
½ lb. spinach

Brown meat, green onions. Add celery, mushrooms, 1/3 of the broth, soy sauce to taste. Steam 10 minutes. Add Chinese vegetables and 1/3 more broth. Steam 10 minutes more. Add spinach, rest of broth (more soy sauce if desired). Steam again. Vegetables should be crunchy, spinach not mushy. If a thicker sauce is desired, add ¼ cup of cornstarch to some soy sauce, and bring to a boil. Boil until thick. Serve on hot rice or noodles.

Preparation: 45 min.

Can do ahead
Serve immediately

Serves: 4 (amply)

Mrs. Robert Y. Kopf

BOEUF BOURGIGNONNE
(BEEF BURGUNDY)
"Do this today and serve tomorrow."

2 lbs. lean beef (sirloin tip or top round cut in ½" pieces)

Marinate beef 1 day in:
  2 tbsp. lemon juice
  2 tbsp. oil
  1 small onion, chopped
  2 or 3 cloves of garlic
  salt and pepper
2 tbsps. butter
24 small white onions
12 large mushrooms, quartered
1 tbsp. tomato paste
1 tsp. beef glaze (Bovril)
3 tbsp. flour
1 cup beef consomme (or 1 bouillon cube dissolved in cup of water)
1 cup red burgundy

Heat butter in skillet. Brown meat quickly. (When making larger quantities, brown a little meat at a time to avoid the formation of juices.) Transfer meat to casserole and salt lightly.

In butter remaining in skillet (add a little, if needed) sauté whole white onions and mushrooms, lightly — until nicely coated. Add to meat in casserole.

To remaining liquid in skillet, stir in tomato paste, Bovril and flour. Add slowly the consomme and ¼ cup of wine. Stir until mixture comes to a boil. Season to taste and pour over contents in casserole.

Bake in slow oven at 300° for 2 to 3 hours depending on whether using 2, 4, or 6 pounds of meat, until fork tender, stirring and adding rest of wine, at intervals. Cover casserole for first 2/3 of cooking time, then leave uncovered. Mix to avoid too much browning on top. Serve from casserole.

Serve with rice and tossed salad.

Preparation: 30 min.   Serves: 4 - 5
Baking: 2 - 3 hours   Must do ahead

Mrs. Robert H. Bartlett

BURGER BUNDLES
"Easy and different ground beef dish the whole family will enjoy."

1 lb. ground beef
⅓ cup evaporated milk
1 cup Pepperidge Farm stuffing (prepared as directed)
1 can golden mushroom soup

Mix milk and ground beef and divide into 4 or 5 flat patties 6" in diameter. In the center of each patty, put ¼ cup stuffing. Mold the meat around the stuffing to form a ball. Place in an 8 x 8" pan and add the soup. Bake at 350° for 1 hour. Baste several times.

Preparation: 20 min.   Easy   Serves: 4
Baking: 1 hour   Can do ahead   Will freeze

Mrs. Thomas R. Wright

FAYE'S FLANK STEAK

¼ cup soy sauce
3 tbsp. honey
2 tbsp. vinegar
½ tsp. minced garlic
½ tsp. ground ginger
¾ cup salad oil
1 chopped onion
1 flank steak

Combine all ingredients, except steak. Marinate the steak a minimum of 8-12 hours. Cook 3 to 5 minutes on each side, depending on whether you want meat rare or medium-well.

Mrs. James D. Darby, Jr.

Preparation: 10 min. Easy
Cooking: 6-10 min. Must do ahead

COMPANY FLANK STEAK

"Tastes like fillet."

1½ lb. flank steak
meat tenderizer
seasoning salt, garlic powder,
  basil, thyme, oregano, etc.
3 tbsp. oil
½ cup red wine
1 tbsp. beef extract or
  Kitchen Bouquet

Tenderize each side of flank steak 1 hour. Sprinkle with seasonings. Add oil, wine and extract. Marinate overnight in shallow roasting pan. Turn next day. Broil or charcoal in sauce or with sauce 5 minutes one side and 3 minutes other. Slice on diagonal. Serve with tomatoes and toasted croutons.

Preparation: 20 min. Easy Serves: 4
Cooking: 8 min. Must do ahead

Mrs. John M. Webb

CHUCK WAGON STEAK

"Second time around . . . cut meat into bite-sized pieces, serve over noodles."

2-3 lbs. round or chuck steak
⅓ cup flour
½ tsp. salt
½ tsp. pepper
3 tbsp. Crisco oil
1 can beef broth
½ cup water
½ cup bottled barbecue
  sauce
1 tsp. chili powder
1 green pepper, diced
6-8 carrots, peeled & cut
  into pieces

Mix flour, salt and pepper, and rub or pound mixture into both sides of meat. Heat oil in heavy skillet and brown meat well on all sides. Mix together beef broth, water, barbecue sauce and chili powder and pour over meat. Cover and simmer 1 hour. Add green pepper. Cover and simmer 1 hour. Add carrots and simmer ½ hour. Skim any fat and thicken gravy if desired. Good served with mashed potatoes.

Preparation: 15 min. Easy Serves: 5-6
Cooking: 2½ hours Can do ahead

Mrs. Donald H. Bryan

POT ROAST
"A nice spicy type of pot roast."

4 lb. pot roast
2 tbsp. cooking oil
2 cups water
2 med. cans whole tomatoes
3 tsp. salt
1½ tsp. pepper
2 tsp. chili powder
2 bay leaves
1 tsp. thyme
1 large onion, quartered
¼ cup sherry
parsley

Dredge roast in flour and brown in cooking oil.

Add all ingredients and simmer for 2½ hours, covered.

Serve in sauce surrounded by parsley.

| Preparation: | 10 min. | Easy | Serves: 4 - 6 |
| Cooking: | 2½ hours | Serve immediately | |

Mrs. William Penn Snyder IV

MOTHER'S MEATLOAF
"This proves Mother was a good cook."

2 lbs. lean ground beef
1 lb. bulk pork sausage
2 eggs
¾ cup milk
1 cup corn flake crumbs
½ cup ketchup
1 medium onion, chopped
1 can tomato soup

Combine all ingredients except tomato soup in large bowl. Mix well with hands, shape mixture into loaf and place in 9 x 13" pan. Bake at 325° for 1½ hours. During last 10 minutes, spread soup over top and sides of meatloaf.

| Preparation: | 15 min. | Easy | Serves: 8 |
| Baking: | 1½ hours | Can do ahead | |

Mrs. Jon E. McCarthy

SALISBURY STEAK

"Try this old favorite with a tangy sauce."

2 lbs. ground sirloin
2 tbsp. grated onion
2 tbsp. finely chopped
 green onion
dash of garlic powder
2 tbsp. minced parsley
2 tsp. salt
½ tsp. pepper
¼ tsp. paprika
⅛ tsp. marjoram
flour

Sauce:

½ cup chili sauce
3 tbsp. butter or margarine
⅛ tsp. Tabasco
1 tsp. Worcestershire sauce
½ tsp. dry mustard
3 tbsp. sherry

Mix first 9 ingredients and form into steak shaped patties, ¾" thick. Dip lightly in flour and broil about 10 minutes.

Sauce: Combine first 5 ingredients. Simmer gently 5 minutes. Add sherry. Arrange meat on hot platter. Pour sauce over.

Mrs. Gilbert L. Dailey, Jr.

Preparation:	15 min.	Easy	Serves: 6-8
Broiling:	10 min.	Can do ahead	

STUFFED CABBAGE

"Best we've ever tasted."

½ cup white raisins
1 head cabbage
1 cup beef stock broth
½ cup lemon juice
½ cup brown sugar
5 ginger snaps
3 10-oz. cans tomato sauce
 or 2 10-oz. cans tomato
 paste
1 cup applesauce
2 large onions, chopped &
 sauteed
2 lbs. ground beef
1 egg
2 cups cooked rice
garlic salt
salt & pepper

Pour enough boiling water over raisins to cover. Set aside.

Core cabbage and put into enough boiling salted water to cover. With a fork in one hand and knife in the other, cut off leaves as they become slightly wilted. Set aside to drain. Shred leaves that are too small to use. Drain raisins and add to beef stock along with lemon juice, brown sugar, ginger snaps, tomato sauce, applesauce and onion. Add shredded leaves. Cook until shredded cabbage is soft.

Combine ground beef, egg, rice and garlic salt with salt and pepper to taste. Place about 2 tablespoons meat mixture on each cabbage leaf. Roll once from stem end — fold in sides, then continue to roll. Place in a greased 3-quart casserole, open edge down. Pour sauce over cabbage rolls. Bake at 350° for 1 hour.

Preparation:	50 min.	Can do ahead	Serves: 4-6
Cooking:	1 hour		

Judith Dunn Fisher

FLANK STEAK ORIENTAL STYLE

1 flank steak (1½ lbs.)
meat tenderizer
1 tbsp. cornstarch
3 tbsp. soy sauce
3 tbsp. cooking oil
1 sliced onion
1 sliced green pepper
1 can bean sprouts drained —
   reserve liquid
chow mein noodles

Slice flank steak thinly across the grain. Sprinkle with meat tenderizer and let sit for 10 minutes.

Mix cornstarch and soy sauce in large bowl. Add meat and stir until well coated. Let sit 10 minutes.

In large frying pan put cooking oil and fry the onion and green pepper rapidly. (Do not brown them, but keep them crisp.) Remove vegetables from pan.

Add more oil if necessary and stir-fry meat until thoroughly browned. Return peppers and onion to pan and add the drained bean sprouts. Heat over low heat for a few minutes, adding liquid if necessary. Serve over chow mein noodles. .

Preparation: 1 hour   **Easy**   Serves: 3 - 4
                                           Can do ahead   *Mrs. William I. Jack*

MEXICALI STACK-UP

"A good choice for a casual buffet dinner party."

2 bags Fritos
1 avocado, sliced
tomatoes, cut in bite-size
  pieces
lettuce, shredded
2 cups grated Cheddar cheese
black ripe olives, chopped
1 bunch green onions,
  chopped
Sauce:
1 lb. ground beef
1 small onion, chopped
1 6-oz. can tomato paste
1 small can tomato sauce
3 tomato paste cans of
  water
2 tsp. sugar
2 garlic cloves, minced
1 tbsp. each, Accent, chili
  powder, oregano, whole
  cumin seed, salt
1 cup cooked rice

Place vegetable garnishes and Fritos in small bowls.

Sauce: Brown meat and onion, add remaining ingredients and simmer 40 minutes. Place sauce in casserole-style dish.

Have each person layer his dinner in this order: Fritos - meat sauce - cheese - lettuce - tomatoes, olives, green onions, avocado.

Mrs. Jack Diederich

Preparation: 30 min.   Sauce can be   Serves: 6
Cooking: 40 min.   done ahead

LOBSTER STUFFED TENDERLOIN OF BEEF

"Terribly elegant."

3-4 lbs. whole beef
  tenderloin
2 4-oz. frozen lobster tails
1 tbsp. melted margarine
1½ tsp. lemon juice
6 slices bacon, partially
  cooked
½ cup sliced green onion
½ cup margarine
½ cup dry white wine
⅛ tsp. garlic salt

Cut tenderloin lengthwise to within ½" of bottom. Place frozen lobster tails in boiling salted water to cover, simmer 5 minutes. Remove lobster from shells. Cut in half. Place lobster end to end inside beef. Combine melted margarine and lemon juice. Drizzle on lobster. Close meat around and tie roast together with string. Place in roasting pan on rack. Roast 425° for 30 minutes. Place bacon on top, roast 5 minutes longer. Sauté onion in margarine in saucepan, add wine and garlic salt and heat. Slice roast. Spoon on wine sauce. Tenderloin can be stuffed and tied ahead of time and then refrigerated until ready to serve.

Preparation: 20 min.   Easy   Serves: 8
Baking: 35 min.   Can do ahead
                                         Mrs. John M. Webb

LIVER WITH ONIONS
"Delicately seasoned with sage."

2 cups sliced onion
1 stick butter
¼ tsp. sage
1 lb. calves liver, cut in
  strips
seasoned flour
1 tbsp. parsley
3 tbsp. beef broth
3 tbsp. white wine

Sauté onions in butter and sage in a large skillet for about 10 minutes. Shake liver in bag of seasoned flour. Add liver to onions and cook until done as you like it. Stir constantly. Remove liver and onions; place in warm bowl in warm oven. Add remaining ingredients to drippings in skillet.

Cook 1 minute. Pour over liver. Serve immediately.

Preparation: 15-20 min.   Easy   Serves: 3-4
Cooking: 20 min.   Serve immediately

Mrs. Frederic L. Cook

TAGLIARINI

1 lb. ground beef
1 onion
1 clove garlic
mushrooms, fresh or canned
½ tsp. ground pepper
1 tsp. salt
2 cans tomato sauce
1 can cream-style corn
tomato juice
1 pkg. wide noodles — cooked
½ lb. sharp cheese — grated
ripe olives — sliced

In a large skillet, sauté beef, onion, garlic, mushrooms and seasonings. Add the tomato sauce, corn and tomato juice until desired thickness is reached. Pour over noodles, cover with grated cheese. Bake at 325° for 45 minutes. Garnish with sliced ripe olives.

Preparation: 15 min.   Easy   Serves: 4 - 6
Baking: 45 min.   Can do ahead   Easily doubled

Mrs. Edwin A. Booth

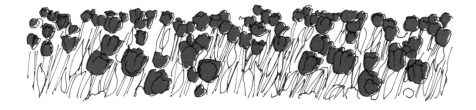

DON'S SPAGHETTI SAUCE WITH LOTS OF MUSHROOMS

8 small pork sausages
½ lb. sliced fresh mushrooms
1 large green pepper
1 tbsp. Italian salad dressing
  (Wishbone)
1 lb. ground chuck
dash salt
dash lemon pepper
1 qt. jar marinara sauce
  (Buitoni's) or 2 cans tomato
  sauce, or 2 cans tomato
  paste & 2 cans water
½ cup water

Fry the sausages until brown. Pour off most of the grease and slice the sausages into small pieces. Set aside. Simmer the mushrooms, peppers and salad dressing in the leftover grease. Add the ground chuck, salt, lemon pepper and diced sausage. Cook over low heat until all is brown and has simmered for about 30 minutes. Pour the marinara sauce in a large saucepan. Add the water, then the mushrooms, peppers, ground chuck and sausage. Simmer 10 minutes. Serve on spaghetti, seashells or gnocchi.

Preparation: 1 hour

Don Brockett

ITALIAN CASSEROLE

"This is a good family casserole."

1½ lb. ground beef
1 tbsp. chopped onion
salt and pepper to taste
1 can cream of mushroom
  soup
1 can cream of chicken
  soup
1 pkg. Uncle Ben's Long
  Grain and Wild Rice
1 cup cut-up celery
½ cup water
¼ cup milk
1 tbsp. parsley
mushrooms, if desired

Brown meat and onion. Add salt and pepper to taste. Combine remaining ingredients, add meat. Place in casserole. Bake at 350°, uncovered, for 2 hours.

Preparation: 20 min.	**Easy**	**Serves: 6 - 8**
Baking: 2 hours	**Can do ahead**	**Can freeze**

Mrs. William F. Millar

LAMB

EASY MOUSSAKA

"For eggplant lovers, it's a real treat."

3 med. sized eggplants
1 cup butter or margarine, divided
3 large onions, finely chopped
2 lbs. ground lamb or beef
3 tbsp. tomato paste
½ cup dry red wine
½ cup chopped parsley
¼ tsp. cinnamon
salt to taste
freshly ground pepper to taste
6 tbsp. flour
1 qt. milk
4 eggs, beaten until frothy
nutmeg to taste
2 cups ricotta cheese
1 cup fine bread crumbs
1 cup freshly grated Parmesan cheese

Peel eggplants and slice ½" thick. Brown slices quickly in a large, heavy skillet in 4 tablespoons butter (more as needed). Set aside. Heat 4 tablespoons butter in same skillet. Cook onions until lightly browned. Add ground meat. Cook 10 minutes. Combine tomato paste with wine, parsley, cinnamon, salt and pepper; stir into meat. Simmer, stirring frequently, until all liquid has been absorbed. Remove from heat. Preheat oven to 375°. Melt 8 tablespoons butter in a large saucepan; blend in flour with wire whisk. Meanwhile bring milk to boil; add gradually to butter-flour mixture, stirring constantly. When mixture is thickened and smooth, remove from heat. Cool slightly; stir in beaten eggs, nutmeg and ricotta cheese. Grease an 11 x 16" oven-proof pan, at least 2½" deep. Sprinkle bottom lightly with bread crumbs. Arrange alternate layers of eggplant and meat in the pan. Sprinkle each layer with Parmesan cheese and bread crumbs. (About 2 layers each of meat and eggplant). Pour ricotta cheese sauce over the top. Bake 1 hour or until golden. Remove from oven; cool slightly before cutting into squares to serve.

Preparation: 1 hour 15 min.   Can do ahead
Baking: 1 hour

Serves: 8 - 10
Can freeze

Mrs. Francis J. Sullivan

ROAST RACK OF LAMB

2 racks of lamb (7 or
  8 ribs each)
2 cups fresh bread crumbs
1 cup chopped parsley
4 cloves garlic, crushed
2 tsp. salt
1 tsp. rosemary
½ tsp. pepper
½ cup olive or salad oil

Trim off fat from racks and trim ends of bones. Check that backbone is cracked so racks can be carved into chops. In medium bowl combine bread crumbs, parsley, garlic, salt, rosemary and pepper. Toss to mix well, then add oil and toss again. Place racks with ribs down and pat half the mixture over meat side of each rack, pressing to hold in place. Wrap and refrigerate overnight. One hour before roasting, unwrap and place with ribs on rack in shallow roasting pan, and let stand at room temperature. Roast 10 - 12 minutes per pound until 147 - 150°.

Preparation: 15 min.   Easy   Serves: 7 - 8
                         Can do ahead

Mrs. Roger S. Brown

COMPANY LAMB

3½ lbs. lamb, cubed
¼ cup oil
1 lb. mushrooms
½ cup chopped onions
2 cans mushroom soup
1 tsp. oregano
1 cup sour cream
salt & pepper to taste
1 tbsp. sugar
1 cup red wine, burgundy
  preferred
1 tsp. cornstarch (optional)

Sauté lamb in oil. Add mushrooms and onions, cook slowly about 5 more minutes. Grease baking dish and add remaining ingredients. Cover. Bake slowly at 325° for 2 hours. If it seems runny, add cornstarch during the last 15 minutes. Serve on rice or noodles with corn muffins and salad.

Preparation: 20 min.   Easy   Serves: 8
Baking: 2 hours   Can do ahead

Mrs. James H. Rock

STUFFED LEG OF LAMB

6 lb. leg of lamb, <u>with skin</u>
1 small white onion, diced
3 tbsp. chopped parsley
3 tbsp. chopped dill
1 tbsp. salt
½ tsp. pepper

With a sharp knife, make an incision ¼" deep running lengthwise from top to bottom of lamb. Peel back the skin from incision laying meat open. Mix together rest of ingredients. Place stuffing between meat and skin. Replace skin over meat and secure with small skewers. Place in roasting pan and bake at 350° for 1 hour 50 minutes for pink lamb. Stuffing can be made several hours ahead and set aside.

Preparation: 30 min.   Serves: 6
Baking: 1 hour 50 min.

Mrs. W. Lukens Ward

LAMB NAVARIN

"A delicious lamb stew for winter buffet."

1 tbsp. olive oil
2 tbsp. butter
6-8 lbs. lamb shoulder,
 cut in 1½" pieces
2 large onions, chopped
2 cloves garlic, minced
¼ cup all-purpose flour
1 tsp. salt
¼ tsp. pepper
2 cups dry white wine
2 8-oz. cans tomato sauce
1 13¾-oz. cans chicken
 broth
¼ cup chopped parsley,
 stems reserved
1 bay leaf
½ tsp. leaf thyme,
 crumbled
2 cups fresh or frozen
 peas, cooked & drained
2 1-lb. cans small carrots,
 drained
2 1-lb. cans small white
 onions, drained

Heat oil and butter in large skillet over medium heat. Brown meat in batches, adding more oil or butter to the pan if necessary. Transfer meat to large Dutch oven when browned. Add onion to fat left in skillet. Cook 2 to 3 minutes, stirring occasionally. Add garlic, cook 1 minute. Sprinkle with flour, salt and pepper. Mix well. Add wine. Bring to boil. Stir until all brown bits are dissolved. Add tomato sauce, chicken broth, parsley stems, bay leaf and thyme. Bring to boil. Pour sauce over meat and cover. Simmer 1 hour 15 minutes or until meat is tender. Discard parsley stems and bay leaf. Add vegetables. Simmer until heated through. Sprinkle with parsley.

Preparation:	30 min.	Easy	Serves: 12
Cooking:	1 hour 30 min.	Can do ahead	Can freeze

The Committee

ARNI PSITO

Leg of Lamb, Greek Style

5 or 6-lb leg of lamb
4 cloves garlic
salt & pepper
¼ cup butter, softened
 at room temperature
1 large lemon
1 cup water

Wash roast. Dry. Place in roasting pan. Make several incisions in lamb. Insert cloves of garlic into them. Cloves may be cut in several parts. Rub salt, pepper, butter and juice of lemon over entire roast. Cover roasting pan. Roast 1 hour in 350° oven. Remove cover, add cup of water to gravy, and baste roast until meat is well browned or done to taste.

Preparation:	10 min.	Easy	Serves: 6 - 8
Baking:	2 hours		

James A. Boumbouras

LEG OF LAMB WITH ANCHOVY MINT SAUCE

6 lb. leg of lamb
3 cloves of garlic, slivered
  into 20 pieces
½ tsp. salt
½ tsp. pepper
1 tbsp. rosemary
1 tsp. ginger
2 tbsp. flour
1 cup white wine

Wipe lamb with paper towels. Use skewer to make holes in leg and insert slivers of garlic cloves. Mix salt, pepper, rosemary, ginger and flour. Rub over leg. Place leg with fat side up on rack in shallow pan. Insert meat thermometer. Roast uncovered 1 hour at 350°. Add wine and baste

Continue to bake and baste until thermometer registers desired doneness. Let stand 20 minutes before carving.

Anchovy Sauce:

pan of drippings from lamb
6 anchovy filets, chopped
2 tbsp. dried mint
1 tbsp. fresh lemon juice

Anchovy Sauce — Take pan drippings from lamb. Measure 1 cup. Skim off excess fat. Add water or beef broth if drippings are less than cup. Add filets, mint and lemon

juice and heat. Serve with lamb. Lamb can be prepared and ready for baking a day ahead.

Preparation: 15 min.
Baking: 2½ - 3 hours

Serves: 8 - 10

Mrs. Patrick C. Kopnicky

LAMB CURRY
"The condiments are in the sauce!"

2 tbsp. butter, melted
4 chopped onions
2-2½ lbs. diced uncooked
  lamb, trimmed
1 tbsp. salt
2 crushed bay leaves
1 clove garlic, crushed
dash thyme
2-3 tbsp. curry powder
1 qt. stock or water
2 tbsp. tomato sauce
2 tbsp. grated coconut
3 tbsp. chopped chutney
1 green apple, peeled &
  chopped
3 tsp. arrowroot or corn-
  starch mixed with a little
  water
½ cup cream
dash salt

Melt butter in saucepan, add onions, sauté until lightly browned. Add lamb and season with salt. Add bay leaves, garlic, thyme and curry. Mix well and add stock or water and tomato sauce. Bring to a boil and cook slowly over low heat for about 2 hours, until meat is tender. When done, remove it to serving dish. To the sauce in the pan, add coconut, apple and chutney. Thicken with cornstarch or arrowroot. Bring to boil, stirring constantly. Add cream, correct seasoning with salt, and pour sauce over lamb.

Preparation: 30 min.   Easy
Cooking: 2 hours 15 min.

Serves: 4

Mrs. Robert H. Bartlett

LAMB ON THE GRILL

6½ lbs. lamb
1¼ cup olive oil or Crisco
¾ cup soy sauce
¼ cup Worcestershire sauce
2 tbsp. dry mustard
2¼ tsp. salt
1 tbsp. ground pepper
¼ cup red wine vinegar
1½ tsp. dried parsley flakes
⅓ cup fresh lemon juice
2 garlic cloves, crushed

Have the butcher butterfly your lamb. Mix the rest of the ingredients together. Marinate the lamb in the mixture overnight in a roasting pan. Cook the lamb on a gas grill at medium heat, covered, for about 1 hour, basting occasionally.

Preparation: 5 min.
Cooking: 1 hour

Easy
Must do ahead

Serves: 6

Mrs. F. Gordon Kraft

BAKED LAMB SHANKS

4 lamb shanks
salt and freshly ground
  pepper
2 cloves garlic, finely
  minced
2 small carrots, cut in
  thin strips
1 large onion, thinly
  sliced
2 ribs celery,
  thinly sliced
2 bay leaves broken
1 tsp. oregano
½ tsp. thyme
1 cup tomato sauce,
  fresh or canned
½ cup red wine
1 cup water
8 or more new potatoes,
  peeled

Preheat oven to 375°. Sprinkle the lamb shanks with salt and pepper to taste and rub with garlic. Sprinkle the bottom of a roasting pan large enough to hold the shanks with the carrots, onion, celery, and bay leaves. Add the lamb shanks and sprinkle with oregano and thyme. Add the tomato sauce diluted in water and the red wine. Cover tightly and bake 1½ to 2½ hours, depending on the size of the shanks. During the last half hour of cooking, raise the temperature of the oven to 400° and uncover the roasting pan. Add the potatoes and continue cooking uncovered, basting the potatoes and meat with the pan drippings. Serve the shanks surrounded by the potatoes. Skim the fat off the strained sauce. Serve the sauce separately. (Note: If the shanks seem to be cooking too quickly, reduce the oven heat to 350° at the end of the first hour of cooking.

Preparation: 15 min.
Cooking: 1½-2½ hours

Easy
Can do ahead

Serves 4

Mrs. W. Lukens Ward

PORK & HAM

ORANGE PORK CHOPS

"Absolutely delicious and very appetizing in appearance."

4 center-cut pork chops, 1" thick
salt, pepper & paprika
2 to 4 tbsp. water
5 tbsp. granulated sugar
1½ tsp. cornstarch
¼ tsp. salt
¼ tsp. cinnamon
10 whole cloves
2 tsp. grated orange rind
½ cup orange juice

Season chops with salt, pepper and paprika. Brown well in hot fat in a skillet. Turn down heat, add water and simmer 45 minutes turning once (adding more water if necessary).

Orange glaze: In a sauce pan cook sugar, cornstarch, salt, cinnamon cloves, orange juice and rind stirring until thickened and clear. Serve over chops. Good with rice

Glaze can be doubled to serve over both chops and rice. Glaze can be done ahead and reheated.

Preparation: 10 min.   Easy   Serves: 4
Cooking: 55 min.

Mrs. William I. Jack

SWEET AND SOUR PORK CHOPS

"Very good, with a different taste."

1 tsp. ginger
1 tsp. paprika
1 tsp. salt
¼ cup flour
½ tsp. pepper
6 pork chops
1 tbsp. shortening
1 cup pineapple juice
2 tbsp. vinegar
3 tbsp. brown sugar
2 medium tomatoes

Mix first five ingredients. Coat both sides of chops in mixture. Brown chops in well-melted shortening. Pour in pineapple juice and vinegar. Sprinkle with brown sugar. Cook over low heat 40 minutes at least. The longer it cooks, the thicker the sauce. Serve with sliced tomatoes on top. Good over rice.

Preparation: 15 min.   Easy   Serves: 6
Cooking: 1 hour   Can do ahead Can freeze

Mrs. James Smith

DENVER PORK CHOPS

"Really crisp and good."

6 center cut pork chops
  (fat trimmed off)
salt & pepper
sour cream
corn flake crumbs

Season pork chops.
Coat both sides with sour cream
and then corn flake crumbs.
Place on cookie sheet and bake
in 325° oven 45 minutes or
until done.

Preparation:	10 min.	Easy	Serves: 6
Baking:	45 min.		

Mrs. Jon E. McCarthy

BAKED SOUTHERN HAM

"Great for the holidays."

10-15 lb. ham, pre-cooked
1 cup brown sugar
½ cup yellow mustard
3 tsp. cloves
pineapple
maraschino cherries
beer or fruit juice

Place ham in roaster filled
half full of water. Place in
350-375° oven for 1½ hours
to steam. Remove ham and
let cool. Trim off all excess
fat. Mix together brown sugar,
mustard and cloves. Spread

over ham. Decorate with pineapple and cherries. Bake 20 minutes
more at 325°. While baking, the ham may be basted with beer or
fruit juice.

Preparation:	20 min.	Easy	Serves: 16 - 20
Baking:	1½ hours + 20 min.	Must do ahead	

Mrs. William Randolph

MOTHER-IN-LAW CASSEROLE

2 lbs. mild sausage
cooking oil
4 or 5 green onions and tops
1 large piece of celery with
  leaves, chopped
4½ cups water
2 pkg. dry chicken noodle
  soup mix
1 pkg. (6 oz.) wild, herb or
  brown rice
2 small cans water chestnuts,
  chopped

Fry sausage to crumble. Drain
off fat. Use a small amount of
oil and sauté onions and tops.
Add celery, water, soup mix,
rice and chestnuts. Simmer 15
minutes. Combine with sausage.
Bake covered, 1½ hours at
350°.

Preparation:	15 min.	Easy	Serves: 12
Baking:	1½ hours	Can do ahead	Can freeze

Mrs. John A. Nave

HAM LOAF

"Try this for company."

1 lb. pork⎫ground & mixed
1 lb. ham ⎭
½ cup minute tapioca
1 cup milk plus one egg
1 chopped onion
¼ tsp. Worcestershire sauce
¼ tsp. pepper

Basting sauce:

1½ cups brown sugar
½ cup vinegar
½ cup water
1 tbsp. dry mustard
flour for thickening

Mix first 7 ingredients together. Shape into a loaf pan. Invert into a larger pan for baking. Bake 1 hour at 350°.

Mix basting sauce ingredients to a smooth paste and baste loaf while baking.

Mrs. Joseph B. Griffith

Preparation:	10 min.	Easy	Serves: 6
Baking:	1 hour	Can do ahead	

TOAD IN THE HOLE & YORKSHIRE PUDDING

¾ to 1 lb. sausage*
Yorkshire Pudding batter
add margarine or fat if required

*(Instead of sausage you may use frankfurters, kidneys, tomatoes, fingers of steak or a selection of these.)

Put sausage in a 13 x 9 x 2" oven-proof dish. Cook for about 10 minutes at 450°. If necessary, add fat or margarine and get this very hot too. Make pudding batter, pour it in and return to very hot oven (450° - 475°) for approximately 30 minutes. Lower heat slightly after 10 to 15 minutes so the batter does not get too brown before being cooked.

Yorkshire Pudding

4 heaped tbsp. flour
  (preferably plain)
pinch of salt
1 egg
just over 1 cup milk

Sift flour and salt together in a bowl. Drop in egg and beat mixture well. Gradually beat in just enough liquid to make stiff, smooth batter. Be sure there are no lumps. Allow to stand a few minutes, then gradually whisk or beat in the rest of the liquid. It is best if the mixture is put in refrigerator to stand some time before cooking. Melt 1 tbsp. margarine in 13 x 9 x 2" baking pan and allow fat to get hot. Give final beat to the batter and pour in pan. Bake at 400° for approximately 30 minutes. (The mixture should turn golden brown, rise on the sides and sink slightly in the middle. If preferred, use a muffin pan for individual puddings.) Serve immediately. Traditional with roast beef.

Preparation:	30 min.	Should do ahead	Serves: 6
Baking:	30 min.	Serve immediately	

Mrs. Geoffrey J. Bicknell

CHEEZY HAM AND RICE

"Splendid for a buffet. Serve in a chafing dish."

½ cup green peppers, diced
½ cup celery, diced
½ cup onion, diced
2 tbsp. butter
2 tbsp. flour
2 cups evaporated milk
1½ cups grated sharp
 Cheddar cheese
2 cups ham, cooked & cut
 in julienne strips
1 tsp. dry mustard
1 tsp. garlic salt
¼ tsp. red pepper
1 tsp. Worcestershire sauce
3 cups cooked rice

Sauté green pepper, celery and onion in butter over low heat until tender. Blend in flour. Add milk and cook until sauce is thick and smooth, stirring constantly. Add cheese and heat until melted, stirring constantly again. Add ham, mustard, salt, Worcestershire and red pepper. Spoon over cooked rice.

| Preparation: | 30 min. | Easy | Serves: 6 |
| Cooking: | 25 min. | Do ahead | |

Mrs. Charles C. Zatarain, Jr.

SWEET AND SOUR PORK

"Well worth the extra effort."

1 lb. loin pork
1 tbsp. dry sherry
2 tbsp. soy sauce
1 tbsp. cornstarch
2 tbsp. flour
3 green peppers, quartered
  & seeded
1 medium onion, quartered
1 carrot, cut in small pieces
  & boiled 4 min.
6 tbsp. sugar
1 tbsp. sherry or white wine
4 tbsp. soy sauce
2 tbsp. vinegar
4 tbsp. tomato sauce
1 tbsp. cornstarch mixed with
  ½ cup water

Cut pork in 1½ inch cubes and mix with next four ingredients. Fry pork in deep oil until crisp and golden (about 10 minutes). Drain on paper toweling. Sauté peppers, onion and carrots. Hold. Mix next 5 ingredients, add peppers, onion and carrots. Bring to a boil and add cornstarch, stirring constantly until it thickens. Add pork and mix well. Serve hot with rice.

Preparation: 30 min.
Cooking: 30 min.

Serves: 4

Mrs. Scott Sawhill

MAPLE BAKE

"Children love ham served this way."

1 ham slice, 1¼ to 1½" thick
cloves
1 cup maple syrup

Cut off excess fat. Stud the meat with cloves every inch or two. Place in greased baking pan the same size as ham slice.

Pour syrup over. Bake uncovered in 300° oven for 1 hour or until meat is very tender. Baste occasionally.

Preparation: 3 min.   Easy   Serves: 2 - 3
Baking: 1 hour

Mrs. Edward A. Montgomery, Jr.

VEAL

BIRDS OF VEAL

1 egg, slightly beaten
¼ tsp. salt
¼ tsp. black pepper
¼ tsp. allspice
1 tbsp. fine white bread
  crumbs
2 tbsp. grated Parmesan
  cheese
2 tbsp. chopped parsley
1½ lbs. veal, pounded to less
  than ⅛ "
1 small onion, minced
1 tbsp. olive oil
1 tbsp. butter
2 8-oz. cans tomato sauce
salt, pepper, basil
1 10-oz. pkg. frozen peas

To make stuffing, combine egg, salt, pepper, allspice, bread crumbs, cheese and parsley. Take veal slices, spread evenly with stuffing, fold over sides, then roll up, starting from one end. Tie with cooking twine. In a saucepan, sauté onion in olive oil and butter until golden. Add veal birds and brown well on all sides. Add tomato sauce, seasoning, simmer, covered for 1½ hour. Remove cover after 1 hour to permit sauce to thicken. Fifteen minutes before done, add frozen peas and cover again. Before serving remove twine. The dish may be accompanied by mashed potatoes.

Preparation:	30 min.	Easy	Serves: 4-6
Cooking:	1½ hours	Can do ahead	Can freeze

Mrs. Anthony Renda

VEAL IN LEMON SAUCE
"A delicious last minute dish."

1 lb. veal scallops
¼ cup flour
1½ tsp. salt
¼ tsp. pepper
2 tbsp. oil
2 tbsp. butter
2 tbsp. fresh, minced
  parsley
2 tbsp. lemon juice

Pound veal thin. Dip slices in mixture of flour, salt and pepper. Heat oil and butter in frying pan and brown veal on both sides. When tender remove, pour off fat and add lemon juice and parsley. Return veal to heat and coat well with lemon and parsley.

Preparation:	25 min.	Easy
Cooking:	10 min.	Serve immediately

Serves: 2

Mrs. Roger S. Brown, Jr.

BLANQUETTE DE VEAU

2 lbs. boneless veal shoulder
1 qt. water
1 small onion stuck with 2
  cloves
1 tsp. salt
1 sliced carrot
2 sprigs parsley
1 bay leaf
½ tsp. thyme
1 lb. small mushrooms
lemon juice
4 tbsp. butter
4 tbsp. flour
1 can small onions

Sauce:

2 egg yolks
2 tsp. lemon juice or sherry
½ cup cream

Combine in heavy pan, veal, water, onion, salt, carrots and herbs. Bring to a boil; skim, cover and simmer gently for 1½ hours. Remove all from stock. Strain stock, simmer mushrooms in it adding a few drops of lemon juice. Remove mushrooms, melt butter, blend in flour. Add stock, cook and stir until thickened. Add mushrooms and onions; add to veal, keep warm.

Sauce: Blend together egg yolks, lemon juice and cream. Warm with a little veal sauce, stir back into veal. Be careful not to curdle yolks. Can be made early and reheated carefully. Good over rice.

Preparation: 2½ hours   Can do ahead   Serves: 4-6
Cooking: 2 hours

Mrs. James Borden

OSSO BUCCO

4 or 5 slices veal shank, 1"
  thick
flour for dredging
3 tbsp. fat
2 diced onions
2 diced carrots
salt & pepper
1 tsp. oregano
boiling water
flour
2 tbsp. sherry
3 ripe tomatoes, peeled
  & chopped
chopped parsley
grated lemon rind

Dredge meat in flour mixed with salt and pepper. Brown in fat or margarine. Remove meat and brown onions and carrots quickly in same fat. Place onions and carrots in bottom of a baking dish. Sprinkle with salt, pepper and oregano. Place meat on top of vegetables. Sprinkle with oregano. Half fill the pan with boiling water. Cover pan with aluminum foil. Place in hot (420°) oven for 45 minutes. Remove from oven. Remove meat to an oven-proof serving dish. Strain liquid.

Thicken liquid with a little flour and add 2 tablespoons sherry. Pour sauce over meat. Place tomato pieces on top of meat. Bake in 400° oven for 30 minutes uncovered until brown. Sprinkle with chopped parsley and grated lemon rind before serving.

Preparation: 20 min.   Serves: 4
Baking: 1 hour 15 min.

Mrs. William H. Riley

ESCALOPES OF VEAL

"A super way to fix veal."

veal scallops
flour
butter
rosemary
chopped scallions
chopped parsley
thin slices of lemon
½ cup dry vermouth
1 can undiluted beef broth
1 can mushrooms

Season tender pieces of veal. Dust with flour and sauté quickly in butter. Place sautéed veal in a shallow pan and sprinkle with rosemary, chopped scallions and parsley. Add thin slices of lemon. In the pan that you have sautéed the veal add vermouth, beef broth and mushrooms. Stir and bring to a quick boil.

Pour sauce over veal and cook for about 5 minutes on top of stove to thicken the sauce. Serve with rice.

Preparation: 45 min.   Easy
Cooking: 20 min.   Do ahead

Mrs. Theus J. Sheil

VEAL SCALOPPINI

"What a wonderful flavor."

2 lbs. veal, thin slices
½ cup butter
½ cup sherry
1-2 tbsp. Wondra Flour
½ cup milk
½ cup water
1 beef bouillon cube or
  MBT beef packet
dash nutmeg
pepper
½ lb. thin sliced Swiss cheese

Pound veal lightly, brown in 6 tablespoons butter. Add sherry, cook a few seconds, remove from heat. Melt remaining butter in saucepan; stir in flour. Bring water and milk to boil. Dissolve bouillon. Add all at once to butter and flour mix. Stir vigorously until smooth and thick. Add nutmeg and pepper. Arrange a single layer of veal in shallow baking dish. Scrape pan and pour drippings over meat. Pour sauce over; arrange Swiss cheese slices over meat and sauce. May be refrigerated several hours. Bake at 425°, until cheese melts and turns brown.

Preparation: 15 min.   Easy   Serves: 4
Baking: 30 min.   Can do ahead

Mrs. Gilbert L. Dailey, Jr.

VEAL AND WATER CHESTNUTS IN CREAM

¼ lb. butter
2½ lbs. veal, preferably shoulder, cut into 1½" cubes
1 med. onion, finely chopped
1 clove garlic, minced
1 tsp. salt
½ tsp. M.S.G. (optional)
¼ tsp. coarsely ground black pepper
1 lb. fresh mushrooms, sliced
1 cup beef broth
2 8-oz. cans water chestnuts, drained and quartered
2 bay leaves
2 cups heavy cream
¼ cup brandy
¼ cup chopped parsley

Preheat oven to 375°. Melt half the butter in an oven-proof casserole and sauté the veal lightly until gray. Remove the veal and sauté the onion, garlic, adding the salt, M.S.G. and pepper. Return the veal to the casserole and remove from the heat. Melt the remaining butter in a skillet and sauté the mushrooms. Add the mushrooms, beef broth, water chestnuts and bay leaves to the veal. Place in the oven and cook, covered, 1½ hours. (All of this can be done ahead and refrigerated.) When ready to use, add the cream and simmer on top of the stove 15 to 20 minutes. Just before serving, add the brandy and parsley. Reheat quickly and serve immediately.

Preparation: 20 min.   Can do ahead   Serves 6
Cooking: 1½-2½ hours

Mrs. W. Lukens Ward

SCALOPPINE OF VEAL

"Marvelous flavor."

2 lbs. veal, thinly sliced
salt & pepper
2 tbsp. flour
2 tbsp. corn or peanut oil
3 oz. sliced mushrooms
1 med. green pepper, previously cooked & peeled
½ cup sherry or marsala wine
2 tbsp. water
2 tbsp. tomato sauce

Cut veal in 5" square, very thin slices. Season with salt and pepper. Flour lightly. Brown veal well on both sides in large frying pan, using corn or peanut oil. Add sliced mushrooms and green pepper. Drain oil. Add sherry or wine. Simmer 3 minutes longer. Add water and tomato sauce. Simmer for 5 minutes.

Preparation: 20 min.   Easy   Serves: 4
Cooking: 20 min.   Can freeze

Mrs. John M. Webb

POULTRY & GAME

CHICKEN SAUTERNE
"Great buffet idea — just add salad."

3 whole chicken breasts
1½ tsp. salt
1 pkg. frozen peas with onions
1 lb. small mushrooms
butter or margarine
3 tbsp. flour
1 tbsp. instant minced onion
½ tsp. celery salt
½ tsp. paprika
½ tsp. oregano
½ tsp. Worcestershire sauce
¼ tsp. Tabasco sauce
½ cup sauterne wine
1 cup light cream
hot fluffy rice

Simmer chicken breasts in water to cover with 1 tsp. salt, covered until tender, 30 minutes. Then remove skin and bones, leaving chicken in large pieces. Reserve 1 cup chicken broth.

Meanwhile, cook peas with onions as package directs. Stem mushrooms and sauté until golden brown; remove. In same skillet melt 3 tbsp. butter, stir in flour, instant onions, ½ tsp. salt, celery salt, paprika, oregano, Worcestershire sauce, Tabasco. Stir in chicken broth and wine. Stir over low heat until thickened. Cool slightly; stir in cream, mushrooms, peas, and chicken, reheat (do not boil). Serve over rice.

Preparation: 2 hours
Cooking: 45 min.

Can do ahead

Serves: 6
Can freeze

Mrs. Frederick J. Kellinger

CHICKEN

"An original masterpiece."

4 large breasts of chicken,
  boned (2 breasts split)
4 oz. cream cheese
1 tbsp. lemon juice
3 or 4 scallions
flour
salt & pepper
butter, margarine or oil
Gravy:
1 tbsp. flour
salt & pepper
1 cup water

After boning, flatten with side of knife. Mix cheese, juice and scallions, spread on each breast. Roll or pull together with string. Coat with mixture of flour, salt and pepper. Sauté in butter, margarine or oil, turning until done (20-25 minutes). Remove and make gravy, if desired. Add flour, salt, pepper, and water to pan drippings; stir until thickened.

Preparation:	15 min.	Easy	Serves: 3 - 4
Cooking:	20 - 25 min.	Can do ahead	

Mrs. Charles W. Dithrich

CHICKEN-WILD RICE CASSEROLE

"Great party dish — all the men had seconds."

4-5 lb. fowl
salt
pepper
thyme
bay leaf
onion
cubed celery
  or
leftover turkey or
  boned turkey roll
1 lb. wild rice
  or
1 pkg. Uncle Ben's Long
  Grain & Wild Rice
  mixture
large onion, chopped
6 tbsp. butter
6 tbsp. flour
2 cans cream of mushroom
  soup
2 cans chicken stock, strained
  from cooking chicken or
  2 cans milk
¾ lb. sharp cheese, grated
paprika

Cook fowl with seasonings and vegetables, or use turkey or turkey roll. Soak wild rice overnight and cook, or use Uncle Ben's — without the seasoning if you cook your own chicken, or with the seasoning if you use turkey roll. Sauté large onion in butter until soft, but not brown. Stir in flour, soup and stock or milk. In casserole layer sauce, rice, chicken, cheese, sauce, rice, chicken, sauce, cheese. Top with paprika. Bake in 350° oven, 30-40 minutes.

Preparation:	45 min.	Can do ahead	Serves: 10 - 12
Baking:	40 min.		

Mrs. Richard Webster

CHICKEN BURGUNDY

"A simple recipe with a subtle flavor."

2 frying chickens, cut up
½ cup seasoned flour
⅓ cup salad oil
1 lb. tiny white onions
2 whole cloves
1 bay leaf
⅛ tsp. marjoram
pinch rosemary
pinch mace
1 cup red wine
1 cup water
2 3-oz. cans sliced
  mushrooms

Dredge chicken in seasoned flour. Brown in oil. Put in casserole. Sprinkle with remaining flour. Add onions. Put spices, wine and water in separate pot and bring to boil. Strain over chicken. Cover and bake at 325° for 1 hour. Add mushrooms and liquid. Bake 1 hour again at 325°.

Preparation: 20 min.   Easy   Serves: 8
Baking: 2 hours   Can do ahead

Mrs. Robert H. Bartlett

CHICKEN CASSEROLE

2 med. onions sliced
6 chicken breasts split,
  boned & skinned
salt & pepper
2 cans cream of chicken soup
1 can golden mushroom soup
½ cup sherry
½ lb. fresh mushrooms
butter
paprika (optional)
toasted almonds (optional)

Spread sliced onions on bottom of 9 x 13" baking dish. Roll up chicken breasts and place on top of onions; salt and pepper. Mix soups, sherry and mushrooms sautéed in butter. Pour over top of chicken. Bake 2 hours at 350°; cover last half hour. Optional — sprinkle paprika and toasted almonds over top.

Preparation: 15 min.   Easy   Serves: 6-8
Baking: 2 hours   Can do ahead

Mrs. Gilbert Dailey

CHICKEN BREASTS IN SOUR CREAM

"Husbands go for this."

4 tbsp. flour
½ pt. sour cream
1 can cream of
  mushroom soup
1 cup white wine
  or sherry
pepper
garlic salt (optional)
4 chicken breasts

Mix flour with sour cream. Combine with all other ingredients except chicken. Place chicken breasts in a baking dish and pour mixture over them. Bake at 350° for 1½ hours.

Preparation: 15 min.   Easy   Serves: 4
Baking: 1½ hours   Can do ahead

Mrs. Charles H. Weaver

CHICKEN ROLLS

"Serve with mushroom wine sauce."

6 boned & split chicken
  breasts (allow 1½ per
  person)
for each half breast:
  1 thin slice prosciutto ham
  1 thin slice Muenster cheese
  ½ tsp. butter in wedge form
seasoned bread crumbs
lightly beaten egg

Remove skin from breast halves and pound thin between sheets of waxed paper. Place 1 slice ham and 1 slice cheese on each one and dot with butter. Roll up, tucking in ends and tie with string. Dip in beaten egg and then roll in bread crumbs. Place on cookie sheet with seam side down and freeze until firm. Remove and put into heavy plastic bag and return to freezer. To bake: Place, not touching, in shallow baking dish which has been greased. Bake at 350° for 1¼ hours. (If you haven't had time to freeze them — place for 4-6 hours in refrigerator and then bake without bringing to room temperature at 350° for 45 minutes.) Put on heated platter, or serve from baking dish, garnished with parsley.

Mushroom Wine Sauce

2 tbsp. butter
2 tbsp. flour
1 cup rich chicken stock
½ cup dry white wine
½ tsp. tarragon
salt & pepper to taste
4 oz. can mushroom pieces
  (or ¼ lb. fresh sliced &
  sautéed for 5 min. in butter)
½ cup half and half
1 egg yolk

Melt butter in saucepan and add flour and cook, without browning, stirring constantly for several minutes. Slowly add stock, wine and spices. Simmer several minutes and add mushrooms and simmer for 5 minutes. Remove from heat and stir in cream mixed with egg yolk, and cook, stirring, until heated through. Do not let boil. May be made a day ahead of time and reheated.

Preparation: 30 min. each recipe Must do ahead   Can freeze
Baking: 1 hour 15 min.

Mrs. Edward A. Montgomery, Jr.

PLANKED CHICKEN

Take one dead chicken and one oak tree. Cut the oak tree in small pieces and put one on top of and one on the bottom of the chicken. Add two tablespoons of soy sauce, one-half cup of Coca-Cola, four pieces of wilted lettuce and three teaspoons of chocolate buttermilk.

Empty this into the chicken and oak boards. Place under a broiler with the heat on for fifteen minutes until the planks catch on fire.

When the Fire Department comes, and you can see the dinner has been ruined, go to the restaurant and enjoy a good hamburger, or bury the chicken and eat the planks!!!

Jack Bogut

LEMON CHICKEN

"Try this on your grill."

3 chicken breasts, split (6 halves)
¼ lb. butter
⅓-½ cup lemon juice
1½ tbsp. poultry seasoning
1 pkg. long grain and wild rice

In small saucepan, combine butter, lemon juice and poultry seasoning. Heat until boiling. Place chicken breasts, bone side up, towards fire of broiler or charcoal grill. Baste liberally on both sides. Broil 20-25 minutes watching carefully not to char it too much. Turn breasts over and rebaste. Broil 5-10 minutes or until golden brown. Prepare rice according to package. Serve next to chicken using remaining lemon butter mixture on both.

Preparation: 10 min.	Easy	Serves: 6
Cooking: 40 min.	Can do ahead	Can freeze

Mrs. William J. Devlin

CHICKEN DIVAN

"Always a Favorite"

6-8 chicken breasts
1 large bunch of
  broccoli
Sauce:
4 tbsp. butter
4 tbsp. flour
2 cups chicken stock
½ cup thick cream,
  whipped
3 tbsp. sherry
salt, pepper
¼ cup grated
  Parmesan cheese

Wrap chicken breasts individually in foil and bake in the oven until thoroughly done. When they are cool, slice in large thin pieces. If you have purchased cut-up fryers, use the backs, necks, and gizzards to make the required chicken stock. Wash and drain broccoli. Cook it in boiling salted water for about 10 minutes or until it is just tender. Drain and keep hot.

Sauce: Melt butter in saucepan, blend with flour and gradually add chicken stock, stirring constantly until thick and smooth. Cook over low flame for about 10 minutes, stirring frequently. Fold into the sauce the whipped cream and sherry. Season to taste with salt and pepper. Place cooked broccoli on a hot oven-proof platter and pour over it half the sauce. To the remaining sauce, add the Parmesan cheese. Over the sauce-covered broccoli, arrange 18 (all you have) thick slices of cooked chicken. Cover the chicken slices with the remaining sauce and sprinkle with grated Parmesan. Set the dish under the broiler until the sauce bubbles and is lightly browned. "I have found it necessary to make 1½ times the sauce recipe to make it juicy enough to my liking. This dish can be prepared in advance and put in the freezer for several days. It takes only about 30-45 minutes in a hot oven to get it to bubble on the sides and be brown on top."

Preparation: 30 min.	Can do ahead	Serves: 6-8
Cooking: 10 min.		Can freeze

Mrs. Wesley Posvar

CHICKEN RICE DIVAN

"An excellent one-dish meal."

2 10-oz. pkgs. frozen broccoli
  spears
½ cup shredded Parmesan cheese
6 large slices cooked chicken or
  2 cups cubed chicken
salt & pepper
1 cup cooked rice

White Sauce:

2 tbsp. butter or margarine
2 tbsp. flour
1 cup milk
1 tbsp. lemon juice
1 cup dairy sour cream

Cook broccoli according to directions; drain. Arrange in 11½ by 7½ by 1½" baking dish. Sprinkle with half the cheese. Top with chicken. Season with salt and pepper. Spoon on cooked rice.

Prepare white sauce: Melt butter, blend in flour, add milk all at once. Cook over medium heat, stirring constantly, until mixture thickens and bubbles. Remove from heat. Stir in lemon juice; gently fold in sour cream, and pour over chicken. Sprinkle with remaining cheese. Bake at 400° for 15-20 minutes or until lightly browned.

Preparation:	20 min.	Easy	Serves: 6
Baking:	20 min.	Can do ahead	

Mrs. Robert Bartlett

SWISS CHICKEN-HAM BAKE

"Superb — perfect for a ladies lunch."

½ cup chopped onion
2 tbsp. butter or margarine
3 tbsp. all-purpose flour
½ tsp. salt
¼ tsp. pepper
1 3-oz. can sliced mushrooms
1 cup light cream
2 tbsp. dry sherry
2 cups cubed cooked chicken
  or turkey
1 cup cubed cooked ham
1 5-oz. can water chestnuts,
  drained & sliced
½ cup shredded process Swiss
  cheese
1½ cups soft bread crumbs
3 tbsp. butter or margarine, melted

Cook onion in the 2 tablespoons butter until onion is tender, but not brown. Blend in flour, salt and pepper. Add undrained mushrooms, cream and sherry. Cook and stir until thickened. Add chicken, ham and water chestnuts. Pour into 1½-quart casserole; top with cheese. Mix crumbs and melted butter and sprinkle around the edge of casserole. Bake in hot oven (400°) until lightly brown, about 25 minutes.

Preparation:	30 min.	Easy	Serves: 6
Baking:	25 min.	Can do ahead	Can freeze

Miss Veronica M. Quigley

"SHEERIN" (SWEET CHICKEN PILAF)

Rice

4 cups cooked rice, drained
¼ lb. (1 stick) butter or margarine, melted

Chicken

¼ lb. (1 stick) butter or margarine
1   4 lb. frying chicken, disjointed
2 tsp. salt
½ tsp. freshly ground black pepper
1½ cups orange juice
3 tbsp. sugar
1 cup blanched, sliced almonds
⅓ cup pistachio nuts
¾ cup chopped pitted dates

While rice is still hot, pour melted butter or margarine over it. Stir well.

Melt 3 tablespoons butter in Dutch oven or deep skillet; brown chicken pieces in it. Sprinkle with salt and pepper, and add ¼ cup of the orange juice. Cover and cook over low heat 1 hour, adding enough orange juice from time to time to keep the chicken from burning. Remove the chicken from the bones and cut it into small pieces. To the pan juices, add the sugar, almonds, pistachios, dates, remaining orange juice, and remaining butter or margarine. Cook over medium heat 20 minutes. Then return the chicken to the pan. In a casserole, arrange alternating layers of rice, chicken, rice, and chicken. Scrape the bottom of the rice pan and sprinkle on top. Cover casserole and place it in a 400° oven for 10 minutes.

Preparation & Cooking:	Easy	Serves: 4 - 6
1 hour, 45 min.	Can do ahead	

Mrs. John A. Nave

CHICKEN-BROCCOLI CASSEROLE
"Excellent for a crowd."

3 pkgs. frozen broccoli (spears or chopped), or asparagus, or use fresh
6 chicken breasts, cooked
3 cans condensed cream of chicken soup
1½ cups Hellmann's mayonnaise
2 tsp. lemon juice
6 tbsp. sherry (or more)
¾ cup shredded sharp Cheddar cheese
¾ cup soft bread crumbs
2 tbsp. melted butter

Arrange cooked broccoli in 9 x 13" pan or large flat casserole. Cut chicken in large bitesize pieces and place over broccoli. Mix together soup and mayonnaise, lemon juice and sherry and pour over broccoli and chicken. Then sprinkle with cheese, then crumbs and drizzle the melted butter over the top. Bake covered at 350° about 1 hour, until bubbly and very hot.

Preparation:	1 hour	Easy	Serves: 8
Baking:	1 hour	Can do ahead	

Mrs. W. Ralph Green

REAL HONEST-TO-GOODNESS SOUTHERN FRIED CHICKEN

"Best fried chicken ever!"

1 fresh fryer, cut-up
beaten egg (optional)
milk (optional)
flour
salt & pepper
grease (Crisco & bacon fat)

Wash the chicken well. The chicken can either be dipped in beaten egg or milk and then floured, or just floured. To flour, shake it in a brown paper bag containing flour, salt and pepper. Heat about 1" of grease in a skillet (preferably cast iron) and brown the chicken on both sides. Reduce heat and cook, uncovered, about 30 minutes, depending on the thickness of the chicken. Remove from skillet and place on paper towels to drain.

Preparation: 10 min.   Easy   Serves: 4
Cooking: 30 min.

Mrs. Monro B. Lanier, II

CHICKEN BREASTS

"Try this with fruit salad."

4 whole boned, skinned breasts
8 pieces dry chipped beef
1 cup Cheddar cheese, shredded
8 slices bacon
Sauce:
1 can mushroom soup
½ pt. heavy cream
2 jiggers dry vermouth
1 can sliced mushrooms

Flatten and halve breasts. Stuff each with chipped beef and shredded cheese. Roll and wrap with bacon. Secure with toothpicks. Bake in sauce at 350° for 1 hour covered, ½ hour more uncovered. Turn each piece once to brown bacon slightly. Do not freeze. Serve with rice cooked with bouillon cubes, or herbed rice.

Preparation: 45 min.   Easy   Serves: 4 - 6
Baking: 1½ hours   Can do ahead

Mrs. Robert H. Snow

NO PEEK CHICKEN

"Easily expandable."

1 box Uncle Ben's Long Grain
 & Wild Rice with herbs
1 can cream of mushroom soup
1 can cream of celery soup
1 can cold water
1 tsp. parsley
dash of curry powder
6-8 pieces of chicken
1 pkg. Lipton onion soup mix

Lightly grease casserole. Mix first 6 ingredients and place chicken on top. Sprinkle chicken with onion soup, seal with foil and bake at 350° for 2½ hours. Don't peek!!

Preparation: 5 min.   Easy   Serves: 6
Baking: 2½ hours   Can do ahead

Mrs. Samuel Caldwell

GOLFER'S CHICKEN

"Try this zesty sauce on spareribs next time."

4 chicken quarters
1 env. Lipton's dry onion soup
1 small bottle red Russian
  dressing
8 oz. apricot jam

Combine dry soup, Russian dressing and jam. Mix well until there are no lumps. Wash chicken and pat dry. Slightly overlap in flat pyrex dish. Spoon and spread 1 tablespoon sauce on each piece. Bake at 225° for 4-5 hours, or however long your game takes. Be careful to place well below heating element if using electric oven. This can be done in 1 hour at 375° if you're not playing golf. Sauce keeps in refrigerator for months.

Preparation:	15 min.	Easy
Cooking:	1 hour	Can do ahead

Serves: 4

Mrs. Robert A. Schmidt

EASY CHICKEN TETRAZZINI

"A snap to prepare."

½ pkg. fine noodles
1 can mushroom soup
¼ small jar Parmesan cheese
1 4-oz. can mushrooms,
  drained
2-3 cups shredded chicken
½ pt. sour cream
3 tbsp. sherry

Boil noodles in salted water for 8 minutes. Combine noodles, soup, cheese, mushrooms and chicken in a bowl. Stir in sour cream. Place in a greased baking dish and bake at 350° for 30 minutes. Before serving, stir in sherry and some more cheese.

Preparation:	15-20 min.	Easy
Baking:	30 min.	Can do ahead

Serves: 4-6

Mrs. Richard M. Johnston

ROAST DUCKLING

Place on rack in shallow pan. Roast in slow oven, 325°, allowing 2 to 2½ hours. Serve with cherry sauce separately or pour a portion of the sauce over the duckling the last 30 minutes. Pour off excess fat several times during cooking.

Cherry Sauce:

½ cup sugar
1 tbsp. cornstarch
few grains salt
2 tbsp. tarragon vinegar or
  wine vinegar
⅔ cup juice from cherries
1½ cups bing cherries
2 tbsp. lemon juice

Combine sugar, cornstarch and salt in saucepan. Stir in vinegar and juice from cherries. Cook over low heat, stirring constantly until mixture is thickened and clear. Add cherries and lemon juice. Heat through just before serving. (If you make the sauce early in the day, cool uncovered and store in refrigerator.)

Preparation:	15 min.	Easy
Baking:	2½ hours	Can do ahead

Mrs. Scott Sawhill

PHEASANT

"A Gourmet's Recipe."

2 large or 3 small pheasants
½ cup milk
salt
fresh pepper
2 to 3 thin slices of onion
3 tbsp. (approx.) butter
2 to 3 cups sour cream
 (1 cup per bird)
giblets & blood if any

Brush birds inside and out with milk. Season inside and out with salt and pepper. No stuffing necessary. Sauté onion lightly in butter in deep flame-proof casserole. Brown birds lightly in this fat and remove from heat. Smooth sour cream over top and sides of birds. Put in giblets. *Cover Casserole.* Cook one hour at 375°, no basting needed. When done, sour cream will be curdled. Scrape from the birds into the casserole and remove the birds to carve. Pour giblets and liquid into blender and blend until smooth and creamy, about 2 minutes. Pour into casserole. Meanwhile, dissect the birds. (Rubber gloves are helpful in protecting against scalded hands and in this way you can slice and tear all possible meat from carcass.) Put meat into sauce. Can be refrigerated for a day or two or just left alone if using in several hours. Cover with aluminum foil with steam vents poked in it for reheating. Be careful not to recurdle the sour cream by using too high a heat. Stir frequently.

Preparation: 45 min.   Can do ahead   Serves: 2-3 persons
Baking: 1 hour   per Pheasant

Mrs. Albert C. Muse

ROCK CORNISH GAME HENS WITH WILD RICE STUFFING

4 1¼ lb. Rock Cornish
 Game Hens
½ lemon
salt & pepper
2 tbsp. butter
½ pkg. Uncle Ben's
 Wild Rice
chicken bouillon cube
¾ cup chopped mushrooms
¼ cup baked ham,
 cut in thin strips
¼ cup shelled
 pistachio nuts
8 strips bacon

Preheat oven to 350°. Rub hens with lemon half inside and out, and sprinkle salt and pepper inside and out. Prepare rice according to directions, adding the chicken bouillon cube to the water. In skillet, sauté mushrooms quickly in butter. Add ham, rice and nuts. Stuff hens. Close with skewers and tie legs with string. Place bacon on top — 2 pieces per bird. Roast for 45 minutes to 1 hour. Can be served hot or cold.

Birds can be stuffed early in the afternoon to be served that evening, but make certain the stuffing is cool.

Preparation: 30 min.   Can do ahead   Serves: 4
Baking: 45 min. - 1 hour

Mrs. W. Lukens Ward

FISH & SEAFOOD

CRAB FLORENTINE CASSEROLE
"Is so good people eat more than they should."

2 tbsp. butter, melted
2 pkg. frozen chopped spinach,
   thawed and drained
1 can (10½ oz) mushroom soup
1 can (10 oz.) white sauce
1¼ cup shredded Swiss cheese
2 tbsp. sherry or 1 tbsp.
   lemon juice
1½ lb. crabmeat
1 can (6 oz.) water chestnuts,
   sliced
3 tbsp. Parmesan cheese

Cook spinach in butter until liquid is evaporated. Stir in soup (undiluted).

Combine white sauce, Swiss cheese and sherry. Cook until cheese melts and add crabmeat and water chestnuts.

In a casserole, make a layer of half spinach mixture, top with half crab mixture. Repeat layers. Sprinkle with Parmesan cheese. Bake uncovered at 300° for 1 hour.

| Preparation: | 30 min. | Easy | Serves: 6 |
| Baking: | 1 hour | Can do ahead | |

Mrs. William I. Jack

CRAB-SPINACH SOUFFLÉ
"Elegant and easy!"

1 pkg. frozen chopped spinach
   soufflé, defrosted
2 lbs. small curd cottage cheese
6 tbsp. flour
6 eggs
1 stick butter, diced
½ lb. sharp Cheddar cheese,
   diced
1 can crabmeat, 7½ oz.

Mix everything together and bake for 1 hour at 350° in a 13 x 9" greased pan.

| Preparation: | 15 min. | Easy | Serves: 10 - 12 |
| Baking: | 1 hour | Can do ahead | |

Mrs. R. Allen Moulton, Jr.

CRAB-SHRIMP CASSEROLE

"Real company fare."

1 cup mayonnaise
2 tsp. Worcestershire sauce
2 tbsp. prepared mustard
½ cup sherry (the better the
   sherry the better the result)
1 tsp. salt
dash of cayenne pepper
1 tsp. curry powder
2 tbsp. parsley
½ cup onion, chopped
½ cup celery, chopped
2½ cups soft shredded bread
1 can mushroom soup
1 lb. King Crab, cooked
2 lbs. shrimp, cleaned & cooked

Combine all ingredients in baking dish. Bake at 350° for about 30 minutes. It can be served plain, in patty shells, or on toast points. My favorite is with a slice of cornbread underneath. (I sometimes add lobster as well as the shrimp and crab, and if I know the tastes of my guests, I will increase the amount of curry.)

| Preparation: | ½ hour | Easy | Serves: 10 - 12 |
| Baking: | ½ hour | Can do ahead | |

Mrs. Charles H. Weaver

ALASKA KING CRABMEAT TETRAZZINI

4 tbsp. butter or margarine
½ lb. mushrooms, thinly sliced
   (reserve 4 for garnish)
5 tbsp. flour
2 cups milk
1 cup light cream or evap. milk
½ tsp. salt
1 tsp. prepared mustard
1 tsp. chopped parsley
1 tsp. Worcestershire sauce
few grains of cayenne
2 pkg. (6 oz.) frozen Alaska
   King Crabmeat, defrosted or
   1 lb. fresh crabmeat
½ lb. thin spaghetti, cooked
   & drained
¼ cup grated Parmesan cheese

In a skillet, melt the butter. Add the sliced mushrooms and cook until golden brown. Sprinkle the flour over the mushrooms, stirring until blended. Gradually add milk and light cream. Add salt and prepared mustard, parsley, Worcestershire sauce and cayenne. Cook, stirring, until thickened.

Reserve a few pieces of crabmeat for garnish. Mix half the sauce with the crabmeat. Arrange the cooked spaghetti in a greased (2-quart) casserole, making a well in the center. Fill the well with the creamed crabmeat. Pour the remaining sauce over the spaghetti. Sprinkle the Parmesan cheese on top. Bake in a quick oven (400°) until golden brown on top. Garnish with crabmeat and mushrooms. Serve from casserole.

| Preparation: | 25 min. | Can do ahead | Serves: 4 |
| Baking: | 25 min. | | |

Mrs. J. Brandon Snyder

CRABMEAT QUICHE

"Real guest pleaser."

½ cup mayonnaise
2 tbsp. flour
2 eggs, beaten
½ cup milk
2 6-oz. pkg. Alaska crabmeat
8 oz. Swiss cheese, shredded
1/3 cup green onion, chopped
¼ cup green pepper, diced
small can mushrooms, drained
4 strips cooked bacon, crumbled

Mix together mayonnaise, flour, eggs and milk. Add crabmeat, Swiss cheese, onion, pepper, mushrooms and bacon. Put in a pastry shell and bake at 350° for 40 - 45 minutes.

Preparation:	30 min.	Easy	Serves: 6 - 8
Baking:	40 - 45 min.	Serve immediately	

Mrs. Robert S. Grigsby

CRABMEAT IN A ROLL

"Delightful for a summer luncheon."

10 finger rolls
2 cups flaked crabmeat
1½ cups diced celery
2 hard cooked eggs, chopped
½ tsp. salt
¼ tsp. pepper
3 - 4 tbsp. lemon juice
½ cup mayonnaise
dash Tabasco
lettuce

Cut center of each roll lengthwise. Pull apart and remove the inside. Mix crabmeat, celery, eggs, salt, pepper, Tabasco sauce and lemon juice. Add mayonnaise and mix together. Fill center of rolls. Place rolls on crisp lettuce and serve with your favorite beverage. May be served for lunch or hors d'oeuvres.

Preparation:	15 min.	Can do ahead	Serves: 4 - 6

Mrs. William Randolph

BAKED HADDOCK AU GRATIN

2 tbsp. butter or margarine
2 tbsp. flour
½ tsp. salt
1 cup milk
½ cup grated sharp cheese
2 tsp. lemon juice
1 lb. haddock fillet
bread crumbs

Melt butter in saucepan. Add flour and salt. Stir until blended. Slowly add milk and bring to a boil, stirring constantly. Remove from heat. Blend in cheese and lemon juice.

Arrange haddock in a greased shallow baking dish. Pour cheese sauce over top. Sprinkle with bread crumbs. Bake at 350° for 30 minutes.

Preparation:	20 min.	Easy	Serves: 3
Baking:	30 min.	Can do ahead	

Mrs. Henry Navratil

FLOUNDER STUFFED WITH CRABMEAT

"The wine and the cheese make this really special."

¼ cup onion
¼ cup butter
1 3-oz. can mushrooms,
   drained, save juice
1 7½-oz. can crabmeat
½ cup saltine cracker
   crumbs
2 tbsp. parsley
½ tsp. salt
8 flounder fillets

Sauce:

3 tbsp. butter
3 tbsp. flour
¼ tsp. salt
milk
⅓ cup dry white wine
4 oz. (1 cup) shredded Swiss
   cheese
½ tsp. paprika

In skillet, cook onion and butter until tender. Stir in drained mushrooms, crabmeat, cracker crumbs, parsley, salt and dash of pepper. Place flounder fillets skin side down; spread above mixture in middle; bring both ends up and overlap. Put in 12 x 7½ x 2 inch baking dish seam side down.

Sauce: In saucepan, melt butter. Blend in flour and salt. Add enough milk to mushroom juice to make 1½ cups. Add wine and cook until thickened. Pour over fillets. Bake 25 minutes at 400°. Sprinkle cheese and paprika over fillets and return to oven for 10 more minutes.

Preparation:	30 min.	Easy	Serves: 6 - 8
Baking:	35 min.		

Mrs. James Michael Stevens

FLOUNDER ROLL-UPS WITH BLUE CHEESE STUFFING

"Elegant and easy."

½ cup butter
¼ cup minced fresh parsley
1 medium fresh tomato,
   chopped
½ cup minced celery
¼ cup firmly packed blue
   cheese
3 cups soft bread crumbs
1 egg well beaten
½ tsp. salt
1½ to 1¾ lbs. flounder fillets
juice of 1 lemon

Melt ¼ cup butter in 10" skillet. Add parsley, tomato and celery; cook, stirring often, for 10 minutes. Remove from heat.

Crumble cheese into mixture. Add crumbs, egg and salt, mixing well. Spread mixture on fillets; roll up, fasten with toothpicks.

Butter an oblong 1½ quart baking dish. Melt remaining ¼ cup of butter; mix with juice of 1 lemon. Pour over fish rolls. Bake in 350° oven until fish flakes easily — about 30 minutes. Serve with rice pilaf.

Preparation:	½ hour	Easy	Serves: 6
Baking:	½ hour	Can do ahead	Can freeze

Mrs. Hugh V. Cochrane

BAKED STUFFED FISH
"Makes ordinary fish into something special."

Any good sized fish pre-
pared for stuffing
Pepperidge Farm Stuffing
Mix (the amount depends
on the size of fish)
water
sauterne
fresh chopped parsley
bacon strips
drawn butter
lemon wedges

Prepare the stuffing mix, according to package directions,
using half sauterne and half
water. Add plenty of fresh
chopped parsley. Stuff the
fish and place in a greased
baking pan. Lay strips of bacon
on top. Add a little more water
and sauterne for basting.

Bake in 350° oven, about 15
minutes to the pound. Baste
frequently. Serve with drawn
butter and lemon wedges.

Preparation:	15 min.	Easy	Serves: 2 persons
Baking:	15 min. per pound	Can do ahead	per pound

Mrs. Mary Cooper Robb

COLD BAKED SALMON WITH MUSTARD MAYONNAISE SAUCE
"Marvelous summer buffet dish."

1   7-10 lb. salmon, cleaned
¾ cup dry white wine
¼ tsp. thyme
½ tsp. basil
¼ tsp. dried tarragon
¼ tsp. dried rosemary
3 minced shallots or 1 small
onion
3 slices of lemon with peel
salt

Leave salmon whole. Rinse
under cold water and dry with
paper towels. Place wine and
remaining ingredients, except
salt, in saucepan. Let simmer
uncovered ½ hour without
boiling. Preheat oven to 375°.
Place fish lengthwise on long
sheet of foil, bringing up edges,
and pour wine mixture over
fish. Sprinkle with salt. Com-
pletely enclose fish, crimping foil tightly. Place in large baking pan
and bake about 2 hours or until fish flakes easily when tested with
fork. The fish can also be put in a large baking bag (plastic type).
When done remove center bone. Chill salmon and make mustard
mayonnaise in blender.

Mustard Mayonnaise Sauce

1 whole egg
2 tsp. wine vinegar
½ tsp. salt
2 tsp. dry mustard
1 tbsp. Dijon mustard
1 cup oil

Place egg, wine vinegar, salt
and mustard in blender. Turn
blender to high and gradually
dribble oil through top of
blender until mixture emul-
sifies and thickens (Takes about
1 minute).

Preparation:	1 hour	Must do ahead	Serves: 12
Baking:	2 hours		

Mrs. W. Lukens Ward

SALMON MOUSSE WITH GREEN MAYONNAISE

"For an elegant summer luncheon."

1 envelope plain gelatin
¼ cup cold water
½ cup boiling water
1 lb. cooked salmon; or
  1 large can of salmon
1 tbsp. grated horseradish
salt & pepper to taste
Tabasco to taste
1 tbsp. lemon juice
1 cup heavy cream, whipped

Soak gelatin in cold water, add boiling water. Flake the fish, then add the horseradish and other seasoning. Fold in the whipped cream. Place in a mold and chill 4 - 6 hours. Serve with Green Mayonnaise.

Green Mayonnaise

1 cup mayonnaise
2 tbsp. finely chopped
  parsley
⅓ cup finely chopped
  watercress
drop or so of green food
  coloring

Mix all ingredients together. Let stand for 1 hour.

Mrs. B. F. Jones, III

Preparation: 40 min.	Easy	Serves: 8 - 10
	Must do ahead	

FRUITS de Mer en COQUILLE (Mixed deviled seafood)

"Nice for a luncheon."

2 tbsp. melted butter
2 tbsp. dry green pepper
2 tbsp. dry minced onion
1 tbsp. butter
2 tbsp. flour
1 cup milk
1 tbsp. dry green onion
1 tbsp. brown mustard
1 tsp. Worcestershire sauce
dash of Tabasco
dash of salt
½ tsp. M.S.G.
1 cup buttered crumbs
1 8-oz. can clams with juice
1 6½-oz. can tuna in oil,
  drained
1 4½-oz. can shrimp, drained,
  washed and chopped
buttered crumbs

Rehydrate pepper and onion and cook in butter until tender. Add additional butter and flour, blend. Remove from heat. Add milk, blend until smooth, return to heat and cook slowly until thick. Stir in seasonings and crumbs. Add seafood. Blend with a big spoon until somewhat smooth. Pile into buttered shells or shallow baking dish. Cover with buttered crumbs. Bake 20 to 25 minutes at 400°.

Preparation: 35 min.	Can do ahead	Serves: 4 - 6
Baking: 20 - 25 min.		Can freeze

Mrs. George Heintzleman

FISH WITH YOGURT SAUCE

"Low cal fish."

½ stick butter or margarine
½ medium red onion, sliced thin
1 lb. fish fillets — flounder or sole
1 carton plain yogurt
parsley & lemon wedges

Sauté onion in butter in large skillet over low heat, until transparent. Add fish, sauté over medium low heat until done. Pour yogurt over fish and heat. Garnish with parsley and serve with lemon wedges.

Preparation: 10 min.   Easy   Serves: 2 - 3
Cooking: 10 - 15 min.

Mrs. Charles W. Dithrich

TUNA-CASHEW CASSEROLE

"Unusual fare."

1 4-oz. can chow mein noodles
1 can mushroom soup
¼ cup milk
1 large can tuna fish, drained
¼ lb. cashew nuts
1 cup diced celery
¼ cup chopped onions
salt & pepper to taste

Heat oven to 325°. Save ½ cup noodles. Combine rest of ingredients. Place in 1½ quart casserole. Sprinkle remaining noodles on top. Bake for 25 minutes.

Preparation: 10 min.   Easy   Serves: 4
Baking: 25 min.   Can do ahead

Mrs. Nathan W. Pearson

TUNA STUFFED CABBAGE

"A tasty variation of stuffed cabbage."

8 cabbage leaves
2 tbsp. butter
¼ cup chopped onion
½ cup diced celery
2 7-oz. cans tuna in vegetable oil
1 cup cooked rice
1 tbsp. prepared mustard
2 tsp. parsley, chopped
1 egg, beaten
2 8-oz. cans tomato sauce
1 cup sour cream

Cook cabbage leaves in boiling water about 5 minutes and drain well. Melt butter in skillet, add onions and cook until tender but not brown. Remove from heat and add celery, tuna, rice, mustard, parsley and egg. Mix well. Spread cabbage leaves flat, divide tuna mixture among leaves. Roll up. Place close together in baking dish. Pour tomato sauce over all. Cover. Bake at 350° for 30-35 minutes. Remove rolls to serving platter, keep warm.

Combine sour cream with tomato liquid in baking dish. Heat to serving temperature. Do not boil. Spoon sauce over cabbage rolls and serve.

Preparation: 30 min.   Can do ahead   Yield: 8 rolls
Cooking: 30 - 35 min.

Mrs. Helen Gordon

TUNA FISH CAKES
"Children love these."

1 large can tuna
½ cup chopped onion
½ cup chopped celery
3 slices of chopped bread
juice of a whole lemon
2 eggs
¼ cup of milk
salt & pepper
crushed saltine crackers

Flake tuna. Add onion, celery, bread and lemon juice and mix. Beat eggs with milk and add salt and pepper. Add to tuna mix. Form into patties. Roll in crushed saltine crackers. Refrigerate 2 hours. Fry in butter. Can also be served as a sandwich filling.

Preparation: 20 min.   Easy   Serves: 6 - 8
Cooking: 15 - 20 min.   Must do ahead

Mrs. Peter Flaherty

BROILED SHRIMP ANAFÉ
"For the grill. Have plenty of paper napkins on hand!"

4-5 uncooked shrimp
 per person
1 cup olive oil
juice of 2 lemons
¼ cup soy sauce
½ cup dry red wine
¼ cup chopped parsley
3 tbsp. fresh or dried
 tarragon or other herbs

Cut down back of shrimp and remove black vein, but not the shell. Wash and place in large bowl. Over them pour the remaining ingredients. Marinate the shrimp for at least 2 hours. Arrange in basket grill and cook over hot coals for 5 to 6 minutes. They should be tender and moist with slightly charred shells.

Preparation: 10 min.   Easy
Cooking: 5-6 min.   Must do ahead

Mrs. Henry Chalfant

SHRIMP ELEGANTE

2 tbsp. minced onion
2 tbsp. butter
1 lb. cleaned fresh shrimp
¼ lb. fresh sliced mushrooms
1 tsp. salt
⅛ tsp. pepper
3 tbsp. chili sauce
1⅔ cup water
1⅓ cup minute rice
1 cup sour cream
1 tbsp. flour
1 tbsp. chopped chives

Sauté onion in butter until golden. Add shrimp and mushrooms; sauté and stir until shrimp are pink. Combine salt, pepper, chili sauce and water. Add to shrimp mixture. Bring to boil. Stir in minute rice, cover, and simmer for five minutes. Combine sour cream and flour. Add to rice mixture and heat gently. Sprinkle with chives.

Preparation: 20 - 25 min.   Easy   Serves: 4
Cooking: 10 min.

Mrs. Edward E. Stalling, Jr.

SHRIMP NEWBURG

"A great luncheon or supper dish."

2 tbsp. butter
1¾ tbsp. flour
1 cup cream or half and half
3 tbsp. chili sauce
1 tbsp. Worcestershire sauce
1 tsp. dry mustard
1 lb. cooked shrimp
salt & pepper to taste
2 tbsp. sherry

Make cream sauce with butter, flour and cream. Stir until it thickens. Add chili sauce, Worcestershire, mustard, shrimp and salt and pepper to taste. Just before serving, add 2 tbsp. sherry. Serve hot. Serve on rice. Reheat in top of double boiler.

Preparation:	10 min.	Easy	Serves: 3 - 4
Cooking:	10 min.	Can do ahead	Can freeze

Mrs. John G. Zimmerman, Jr.

SHRIMP AND MUSHROOM CURRY

"Great company recipe."

¾ cup all-purpose flour
1½ tsp. curry powder
2 tsp. salt
½ tsp. ginger
2 tsp. granulated sugar
1 cup minced onions
1 cup diced, pared green apples
¾ cup butter or margarine
1 qt. chicken broth
2 cups milk
1½ - 2 lbs. cooked shrimp
8-oz. can button mushrooms
tbsp. lemon juice

Day before: Mix together first 5 ingredients. In large kettle, sauté onion and apple in ¾ cup butter until tender. Blend in flour mixture. Slowly stir in chicken broth and milk; cook, stirring often, until thick. Remove from heat. Add cooked shrimp to curry sauce. Add lemon juice and mushrooms to curry sauce. Refrigerate.

About ½ hour before serving: Reheat curry. Cook 3 cups rice (or amount desired). Garnish rice with minced parsley. Offer condiments — chutney, coconut, raisins, chopped peanuts.

Preparation:	45 min.	Must do ahead	Serves: 8
Cooking:	30 min.		

Mrs. Joh̶ ̶ ̶ner

SCALLOPED SCALLOPS

2 lbs. scallops
2 cups white sauce, using ½
  cup broth from scallops as
  part of liquid
1 can mushroom soup
buttered bread crumbs

Parboil scallops 10 minutes, do not cook. Drain, reserving ½ cup liquid. Make white sauce. Mix scallops with soup and white sauce. Place in greased casserole, sprinkle with buttered bread crumbs. Bake at 350° for 45 minutes.

Preparation:	½ hour	Easy	Serves: 4 - 6
Cooking:	45 min.		

Mrs. Robert H. Bartlett

SHRIMP AND SCALLOP CASSEROLE

"A very elegant casserole, and not too rich."

1 lb. raw cleaned shrimp
½ lb. raw cleaned bay scallops
½ cup soy sauce
¼ lb. butter
1 tbsp. fresh chopped parsley
6 cloves garlic, crushed
½ lb. fresh mushrooms,
  thinly sliced
1 can water chestnuts, sliced
½ can bean sprouts

Marinate seafood in soy sauce 15 minutes. While seafood is marinating, melt butter in saucepan. Add parsley and crushed garlic. Remove seafood from sauce. Place in a shallow casserole or baking dish. Top with mushrooms, water chestnuts and bean sprouts. Pour butter mixture on top. Bake at 350° for about 25 minutes. (Test shrimp for doneness.)

Preparation:	30 min.	Easy	Serves: 4
Cooking:	20 - 25 min.	Can do ahead	

Mrs. Eva Damianos

BAKED STUFFED FILLETS

"Rich and delicious."

¼ cup butter
2 tbsp. chopped onion
⅓ cup chopped celery
1 tbsp. chopped parsley
¼ tsp. dried sage
1 cup soft bread crumbs
½ cup coarsely shredded
  Cheddar cheese
salt & pepper
1½ lbs. fillet of sole

Sauce:
3 tbsp. butter
3 tbsp. flour
¾ tsp. salt
¼ tsp. pepper
¾ cup milk
¾ cup light cream

Heat oven to 375°. Melt butter. Add onion and celery, and cook until tender. Remove from heat and stir in parsley, sage, bread and cheese.

Sprinkle fillets with salt and pepper. Spoon some stuffing over each fillet. Roll up and secure with toothpick. Place in buttered, shallow baking dish. Bake 30 minutes. While baking, prepare sauce.

Sauce: Melt butter, blend in flour, salt and pepper. Gradually add milk and cream. Cook, stirring constantly, until thickened.

Place fillets in serving platter. Stir any liquid left in baking dish into sauce. Pour sauce over fish. Place under broiler for 3 to 5 minutes.

May be completely made the day before, then reheated.

Preparation:	20 min.	Easy	Serves: 4 - 6
Baking:	35 min.	Can do ahead	

Mrs. Richard M. Johnston

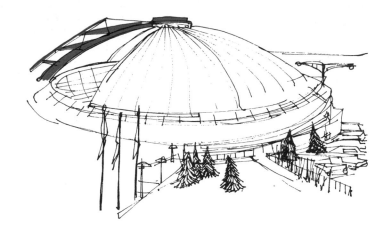

SANDWICHES

BROILED CRAB OPEN-FACERS

"A marvelous sandwich spread, which also may be served on toast points for cocktails."

1 can crab meat, drained and
  flaked or ½ lb. fresh crab
  (do not use Alaskan King
  Crab).
¼ cup mayonnaise or salad
  dressing
3 oz. pkg. cream cheese,
  softened
1 egg yolk
1 tsp. finely chopped onion
¼ tsp. prepared mustard
1 tsp. chili sauce or BBQ
  sauce
dash salt
3 English muffins, split
  and toasted
2 tbsp. butter, softened

Stir crab and mayonnaise together — set aside. Beat together cream cheese, egg yolk, onion, mustard, chili sauce, and salt until smooth and creamy. Spread toasted muffin halves with butter, then with crab mixture. Top with cream cheese. Place on baking sheet; broil 5 - 6 inches from heat for 2 - 3 minutes until top is bubbly and golden.

| Preparation: | 10 min. | Easy | Serves: 3 |
| Cooking: | 3 min. | Can do ahead | |

Mrs. Jack Diederich

CHICKEN SALAD BUNS

2 cups diced cooked chicken
1 cup chopped celery
1/3 cup chopped sweet
  pickles
1/4 tsp. salt
dash of pepper
dash of onion powder
2/3 cup mayonnaise
chili sauce
1/2 cup shredded American
  cheese
4 hamburger rolls, halved

Combine all ingredients, except chili sauce and cheese. Toast rolls. Spread with chicken mixture. Sprinkle with shredded cheese. Dot center with chili sauce. Place under broiler 5-7 minutes to melt cheese.

Mrs. Kenneth Johns, Jr.

Preparation:	15 min.	Easy	Yield: Serves 8
Cooking:	5 - 7 min.		

HAM AND CHEESE BRUNCH SANDWICH

16 slices sandwich bread, crusted
8 slices sharp cheese
8 slices boiled ham
6 eggs
3 cups milk
1/2 tsp. dry mustard
1/2 lb. sautéed mushrooms
  (or 1 small can)
1 cup crushed cornflakes
1/2 cup melted butter

Put 8 slices buttered bread on bottom of well-greased 13 x 9" baking dish. Top each slice with cheese and ham. Put other 8 slices of bread on top-buttered side up. Mix eggs, milk and mustard. Pour over all. Refrigerate overnight. Place mushrooms on top, then sprinkle cornflakes mixed with melted butter on top of all. Bake 45 minutes at 350°.

Preparation:	30 min.	Easy	Serves: 8
Baking:	45 min.	Must do ahead	

Mrs. Edward I. Sproull, Jr.

HAM AND CHEESE ROLLS

1/2 lb. soft butter
3 tbsp. prepared mustard
1 1/2 tbsp. poppy seed
1 tsp. Worcestershire sauce
1 onion, grated
12 hamburger rolls
1 lb. chipped ham
12 slices Swiss cheese

Mix first 5 ingredients. Spread mixture on both sides of roll.

Place ham and cheese on rolls. Wrap in foil. Heat 10 minutes at 400°.

Can be stretched to make 16 sandwiches. May be made ahead and refrigerated. If so heat 15 minutes instead of 10 minutes.

Preparation:	20 min.	Easy	Serves: 12
Baking:	10 min.	Can do ahead	Can freeze

Mrs. Kenneth Johns, Jr.

McINTOSH SANDWICH

slices of white bread
mayonnaise
mustard
thinly sliced or chipped ham
thinly sliced McIntosh apples
slices of American cheese

Coat slices of bread with a combination of mayonnaise and mustard. Pile on several slices of ham and spread a little more mayonnaise on top of ham, if desired. Add apples and cover with a slice of cheese. Bake at 375°, 5-10 minutes or until cheese has melted, and browned slightly. You want all layers to be thoroughly hot.

If McIntosh apples are not in season, use Winesap, Roman Beauty or some other tart apple.

Preparation: 10 min.   Easy
Baking: 10 min.

Mrs. Roger S. Brown, Jr.

TUNA TEMPTATIONS

6½ or 7 oz. can tuna
¼ lb. American cheese, cubed
2 tbsp. green pepper
2 tbsp. minced onions
2 tbsp. sweet pickles, chopped
½ cup mayonnaise
salt & pepper
6 hot dog buns

Flake tuna and combine with other ingredients. Add salt and pepper to taste. Split hot dog buns and fill. Wrap in foil. Place in shallow pan and bake in moderate oven (350°). If frozen, heat at 400°, 30 minutes.

Preparation: 15 min.   Easy   Serves: 6
Baking: 15 min.   Can do ahead   Can freeze

Mrs. W. Kendall Jones

BERNIE'S QUICK PIZZA

fat for browning
1 lb. ground chuck
¼ cup chopped onion
½ clove garlic, minced
  (optional)
1 can refrigerator
  biscuits (10)
10 slices Mozzarella cheese
chili sauce
grated Parmesan cheese
garlic powder
oregano
salt & pepper

Brown ground chuck in fat with onion and garlic. Using a floured rolling pin, roll each biscuit to a 4-inch diameter. Top each of 10 biscuits with a layer of browned meat, one slice of Mozzarella cheese, a little chili sauce, some grated Parmesan, and a sprinkle of garlic powder, oregano, salt and pepper.

Bake in preheated 550° oven for 8 minutes or until brown at edges.

Preparation: 15 min.   Easy   Yield: 10 small pizzas
Baking: 8 min.   Can do ahead

Mike Levine

PIZZA

*"Add Mozzarella, mushrooms and pepperoni, and
they'll eat every crumb."*

Pizza Sauce:

1 #2½ can tomatoes
1 small can tomato paste
3 tbsp. oil
3 tsp. oregano
1 tsp. garlic salt

Crust:

1 box Hot Roll mix
1 cup warm water

Combine ingredients and cook for one hour or until rather thick. Makes enough sauce for 2 large pizzas.

Combine to form dough. Do not let rise. Press into 2 greased cookie sheets or 2 large pizza pans. Cover with sauce and your choice of toppings. Bake at 425° for 20 - 25 minutes.

Preparation:	20 min.	Easy	Yield: 2 large
Cooking:	1 hour (sauce)	Can do ahead	Can freeze
Baking:	20 min.		

Mrs. Thomas R. Wright

MONTE CARLO SANDWICH

"A perfect Saturday lunch sandwich."

3 slices sandwich bread
mayonnaise
white turkey or chicken slices
sliced Gouda cheese
sliced ham
1 egg
½ cup milk
butter

Cut crusts from bread.

On first slice of bread spread:
1st layer — mayonnaise, white turkey or chicken slices, sliced Gouda cheese. Cover with slice of bread.

2nd layer — mayonnaise, sliced ham, sliced Gouda cheese. Top with third slice of bread.

Tie with cotton string, like a present.

Can be prepared to this point, hours in advance, cover and refrigerate.

Beat egg and milk with fork, dip tied sandwich in French toast batter (egg and milk.)

Fry in butter turning to fry all six sides. Snip string with scissors and remove it before serving. Eat with knife and fork.

Preparation:	10 min.	Easy	Serves: 1
Cooking:	10 min.	Can do ahead	

Mrs. Upton Hudson

BAKED CHEESEBURGER SANDWICH

"Good for a quick family meal."

8 slices white bread
½ lb. ground beef
¼ cup chopped onion
2 tbsp. chopped celery
1 tbsp. prepared mustard
½ tsp. salt
1 egg, well beaten
¾ cup milk
½ tsp. salt
⅛ tsp. dry mustard
1 cup shredded American
cheese

Toast bread and butter both sides.

Brown ground beef. Add onion and celery, cook 5 minutes. Stir in prepared mustard and salt, remove from heat.

Combine next 4 ingredients.

Place 4 slices of buttered toast in a 9" square pan. Top with meat and then cheese. Place 4 remaining toast slices on top. Pour egg mixture over all. Bake 30-35 minutes at 350°.

Preparation:	45 min.	Easy	Serves: 4
Baking:	30 min.		

Mrs. Kenneth Johns, Jr.

HOT SAUSAGE ON A BUN

"Shop at your local ethnic grocery for hot sausage."

3 lbs. hot sausage
1 green pepper, chopped
1 med. onion, chopped
1 clove garlic, chopped
1 No. 2 can whole tomatoes
1   12-oz. can tomato paste
oregano, parsley
thyme & bay leaf
6-8 Italian buns

Place sausage, cut in lengths to fit buns, in water to cover.
Boil 35-40 minutes.
Drain all but 5 tbsp. of juice.
Sauté chopped pepper, onion and garlic in juice until soft.
Add tomatoes with juice, tomato paste and spices to taste.
Simmer 15-20 minutes and serve on buns.

Preparation:	15 min.	Easy	Serves: 6 - 8
Cooking:	1 hour		

Mrs. William J. Devlin

SONORA MEXICAN TACOS

1   16-oz. can whole
   tomatoes
1   10-oz. can tomato-green
   chili mix
1 finely chopped small onion
salt & ground pepper
   to taste
¾ lb. ground beef
2 tsp. Chili Con
   Carni seasoning
1 head lettuce,
   finely shredded
½ lb. Texas Longhorn
   style cheese
1 pkg. of 12 Taco shells

Mash tomatoes, tomato-green chili mix, finely chopped onion, salt and pepper. Simmer briefly and keep hot. Fry hamburger in small amount of cooking oil, breaking into smallest possible pieces. Drain oil completely, add chili con carni seasoning, salt and pepper; set aside. While tomato-green chili mixture and hamburger are cooking, shred lettuce and grate cheese. Arrange taco shells in suitable large baking tin (with sides).

Divide and spoon hamburger mix into taco shells, add grated cheese atop hamburger in taco shells. Bake in 250° oven for 5 to 10 minutes until cheese melts. Remove and stuff generous amount of shredded lettuce into taco shells, spoon 2 tablespoons tomato-chili sauce over lettuce and serve immediately. The tomato, chili-onion mixture should be quite watery, not thick at all. Eat tacos with fingers. Heated canned Frijoles Refritos make an excellent accompaniment. Leftover sauce can be reheated and splashed over breakfast eggs to make "Huevos Rancheros".

Preparation: 25 min.	**Easy**	**Yield: 12**
Baking: 5-10 min.	**Serve immediately**	*Ralph Benz, Jr.*

SAUCES, PICKLES & RELISH

TOMATO CHUTNEY

"A delicious relish served cold on pork, meat loaf, hamburger, etc."

1 cup chopped green pepper
4 cups peeled ripe tomatoes, chopped
2 cups green tomatoes, chopped
4 cups tart apples, peeled & chopped
½ cup chopped onions
2 tbsp. white mustard seed
2 tsp. celery seed
1 tsp. salt
2 cups sugar
1 tsp. cinnamon
1 tsp. ground cloves
4 cups vinegar

Preparation: 1 hour
Cooking: 2½ hours

Chop first five ingredients, separately, through the medium blade of a food chopper. Then drain and measure to get the amounts called for. Add rest of ingredients. Mix all and cook at simmer in a large pot (uncovered) for 2 hours or until cooked down. Pour into jars and seal. No need to process.

Yield: 6 - 9 pts.

Mrs. William H. Riley

SAUCE BERCY FOR CALVES' LIVER

"This transforms liver into something really special."

¾ cup dry white wine
3 finely minced shallots
½ cup undiluted beef
  bouillon
salt
freshly ground pepper
2-3 oz. softened butter
juice of ½ lemon
5-6 sprigs parsley, minced
1 tsp. cornstarch

Put wine and shallots in saucepan, bring to a boil and reduce by half. Stir in beef bouillon, salt and pepper. Take off the heat and stir in butter, lemon juice and parsley. When well combined, add cornstarch to thicken. If afraid of having it lump, put into a little white wine first. Pour over 4-5 thin slices of calves' liver. May be reheated. Easily doubled.

Preparation:	15-20 min.	Easy	Serves: 2
Cooking	10 min.	Can do ahead	

Mrs. Edward A. Montgomery, Jr.

BEEF MARINADE FOR BROILING

"This really zips up flank steak."

¼ cup soy sauce
¼ cup oil
1 lemon, squeezed
2 garlic cloves,
  sliced or split
fresh ground pepper

Mix ingredients and pour over flank steak or 3 pound steak. Marinate overnight or at least 4 hours, turning meat a few times. Best if beef is broiled or charcoaled, rare.

Preparation:	5 min.	Easy	Serves: 4-6
		Must do ahead	

Mrs. Dennis Leonetti

BREAD AND BUTTER PICKLES

6 cups thinly sliced
  cucumbers, unpeeled
1 lb. onions, sliced thinly
1 green pepper
¼ cup salt
2 cups white sugar
¼ tsp. ground cloves
1 tbsp. mustard seed
½ tsp. celery seed
  (or more if desired)
2 cups cider vinegar

Mix cucumbers, onion and green peppers. Cover with cold water in large bowl. Add salt, cover and let stand 3 hours. Mix remaining ingredients, bring slowly to boiling point and boil 5 minutes. Drain the vegetables thoroughly in a colander — rinse well with cold water. Add them to the hot syrup and heat slowly to just below boiling point, stirring occasionally. Pour in sterilized jars.

Yield: 4 pts.

Mrs. John A. Shoener

BREAD AND BUTTER PICKLES

30 cucumbers 1 to 1½"
  diameter
10 onions, small-medium
4 tbsp. salt
7½ cups white vinegar
6 cups sugar
3 tsp. celery seed
3 tsp. ground ginger
1½ tsp. turmeric
3 tsp. white mustard
  seed

Scrub and clean cucumbers and onions and slice into large bowl. Use 4 tablespoons salt to sprinkle in layers and let stand for 1 hour. Drain well. Mix in large kettle, vinegar, sugar, celery seed, ginger, turmeric and mustard seed. Bring to boil and add cucumbers and onions. Bring again to boil and simmer 10 minutes. Put in jars. Will keep 6 months

in refrigerator. Can also be sealed and processed.

Preparation:	1 hour	Easy	Yield: 8-10 pints
Cooking:	10 min.	Must do ahead	*Mrs. James Rock*

PLUM SAUCE

1 cup red plum preserves
½ cup apricot preserves
½ cup applesauce
2 tbsp. honey
4 tbsp. cider vinegar
few drops garlic juice
1 clove

Combine all ingredients in a saucepan. Bring to boil over medium heat. Cook, stirring constantly, 5 minutes — until well blended. Remove clove after cooking. Cool. Pour into sterilized jars and seal. Keeps a long time. Serve with

barbecued pork, spareribs, fried shrimp, egg rolls and fried wonton.

Preparation:	5 min.	Easy	Yield: 2½ cups
Cooking:	15 min.	Must do ahead	*Mrs. Richard B. Lord*

"BETTER-&-QUICKER-THAN-BOUGHT BARBECUE SAUCE!"

1 cup cooking oil or
  2 sticks margarine or
  ½ cup oil & 1 stick
  margarine
1 pt. ketchup
1 tbsp. Tabasco sauce
1 small bottle
  Worcestershire sauce
½ cup brown sugar
2 tbsp. grated onion
2 tbsp. salt, or less to taste
1-2 cloves garlic (optional)
2 lemons thinly sliced

Bring all ingredients to a boil and simmer until lemons look cooked (only rind remains) —about 10 minutes. Great for chicken or pork, on or off the grill.

Mrs. Joseph B. Griffith, Jr.

Preparation:	10 min.	Easy	Yield: 1 qt.
Cooking:	10 min.	Can do ahead	

ONION SAUCE

3 tbsp. butter or margarine
2 cups thinly sliced onions
¼ cup cider vinegar
1 can consomme
1 tbsp. flour
salt
pepper

Melt 2 tbsp. butter in small pan. Add onion and cook until golden. Add vinegar, cook 1 minute. Add consomme and bring to boil. Mix flour and remaining butter. Simmer 5 minutes, stirring until thickened. Serve warm. For meat fondue.

Preparation:	5 min.	Easy	Yield: 2 cups
Cooking:	20 min.	Can do ahead	

Mrs. Kenneth Johns, Jr.

NATRONA HEIGHTS BAR-B-QUE SAUCE

3 tbsp. butter
small onion, minced
3 tbsp. brown sugar
1 chicken or beef bouillon
  cube, dissolved in ¼ cup
  hot water
2 tbsp. vinegar
2 tbsp. lemon juice
1 cup ketchup
  (I use hot ketchup)
salt, pepper, dash of
  Tabasco
1 tsp. prepared mustard

Melt butter, add chopped onion and brown. Add brown sugar and stock and then rest of ingredients. Simmer about 20 minutes, covered. Good for ham Bar-B-Ques, etc.

Mrs. J. Baird Atwood

Preparation:	30 min.	Easy	
Cooking:	20 min.	Can do ahead	

MUSTARD SAUCE FOR HAM
"A must for a party ham."

2 tbsp. flour
½ cup butter
½ cup vinegar
½ cup sugar
2 beef cubes (extract)
2 egg yolks, well beaten
2½ tsp. prepared mustard

Cream flour and butter together in a double boiler.
Add vinegar, sugar, beef cubes, egg yolks and mustard.
Cook until it thickens.

Preparation: 15 min.   Easy   Yield: 2 cups
Cooking: 15 min.

Mrs. James Harris

BAKED PEACH HALVES
"Terrific as a garnish for baked ham."

1 large can peach halves (11)
½ stick butter
1 cinnamon stick
½ peach syrup from can
⅓ cup brown sugar (more
  if desired)
maraschino cherries

Bring butter, cinnamon stick, syrup and brown sugar to boil. Place peach halves in buttered baking dish, putting a maraschino cherry in center of each. Pour syrup mixture over peaches and bake at 350° for ½ hour. May remain in oven at low temperature until dinner is ready. Garnish with parsley.

Preparation: 10 min.   Easy   Serves: 8
Baking: 30 min.

Mrs. Thomas M. Garrett

PINEAPPLE CASSEROLE
"A nice side dish with ham."

½ cup sugar
3 tbsp. flour
3 eggs
No. 2 can Dole unsweetened
  crushed pineapple
4 slices cubed bread
1 stick melted butter

Beat sugar, flour and eggs with a spoon. Add pineapple *with juice.* Pour into buttered casserole. Stir melted butter into bread cubes until bread is soaked with butter. Sprinkle bread cubes on top of casserole. Bake 1 hour at 350°.

Preparation: 15 min.   Easy   Serves: 8
Baking: 1 hour

Mrs. David N. W. Grant, Jr.

HOT MUSTARD SAUCE

1 beaten egg
¼ cup brown sugar
3 tbsp. granulated sugar
2 tbsp. hot mustard
½ cup vinegar
1 tbsp. melted margarine

Combine and blend first 4 ingredients. Blend in vinegar, then margarine. Cook, stirring constantly, until thickened. Suitable for ham, franks, chicken fondue.

Preparation: 5 min.
Cooking: 20 min.
Easy
Can do ahead
Yield: ½ to 1 cup

Mrs. Kenneth Johns, Jr.

LEMON BUTTER

2 eggs, beaten
1 cup sugar (scant)
1 tsp. butter
juice of 1 large lemon

Cook all ingredients over low heat, stirring constantly, until thick. Serve warm or cold over hot biscuits, rolls, English muffins, etc.

Preparation: 1-2 min.
Cooking: About 10 min.
Easy
Can do ahead
Yield: 1 cup

Mrs. Robert Y. Kopf, Jr.

HEAVENLY PEACH JAM

3 oranges
1 or 2 lemons
1 med. jar maraschino
  cherries
3 lbs. cut-up peaches
3 lbs. sugar

Quarter the oranges and lemons and seed them. Then grind fruit quarters (peel and all) in food chopper. Cut up cherries by hand. Add fruit to cut-up peaches; add sugar and let stand overnight. Next day boil 45 minutes to 1 hour. Pour mixture into sterilized jars. When cool, cover with paraffin.

Preparation: 1 hour
Cooking: 45 min.-1 hour
Easy
Yield: 6 half pints or 7-8 jelly glasses

Mrs. Allen T. Shoener

TANGERINE MARMALADE

"Great to give as Christmas gifts."

12 tangerines
6 cups sugar

Wash tangerines well. Drain, peel, reserving peels. Section, remove pits, and run sections and peel through the blender. Combine puree and sugar in a large pot. Bring slowly to a boil over moderate heat, stirring frequently, until it reaches 220° (jelly stage) — about 35 minutes. Remove from heat, skim any foam, and pour into hot, clean jars. Seal immediately, turn upside down for a few seconds, then stand upright to cool.

Preparation: 15 min.
Cooking: 45 min.
Easy
Yield: 4-6 small jars

Mrs. Edward I. Sproull, Jr.

VEGETABLES

HEINZ HALL

On September 8, 1927, the Loew's Penn Theater opened its doors, billing itself as "the most opulent movie palace between New York and Chicago." Forty-four years later, new excitement returned with the theater's reopening as Heinz Hall. Addressing the inaugural concert was Henry J. Heinz II who personally supervised the design and execution of the new Hall. Special efforts were made to salvage the baroque elegance of the old theater while incorporating an acoustical system that renders some of the best natural sound in the country.

Additional illustrations in this section:

RETICULATED DISH WITH PEAS — English, Minton, c. 1825 — Ailsa Mellon Bruce Collection.

The world-renowned Pittsburgh Symphony, under the direction of William Steinberg, can be enjoyed during the season at Heinz Hall.

The formidable portal of the Manchester Bridge; built in 1874 over the Allegheny River.

Allegheny County Seal.

"Argus", "Tulip," "Pear," "Excelsior," "Loop" and "Bell Flower" are designs of Bakewell & Co. glass. Established in 1808 by Benjamin Bakewell, father of American flint glass work, the company was the first to make cut glass wares, and counted the White House among its customers. From the collection of E. Holl Gordon.

Chef Brockett from Mister Rogers' Neighborhood. This well-known children's program originates from Pittsburgh's educational television station.

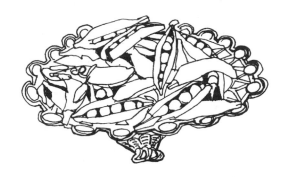

VEGETABLES

ARTICHOKES PIQUANT
"A Special Treat!"

2 pkgs. frozen artichoke hearts
¼ cup mayonnaise or salad dressing
¼ cup milk
2 tbsp. chopped parsley
2 tbsp. lemon juice
1 tbsp. grated onion
¼ tsp. Worcestershire sauce
2 hard-cooked eggs, chopped

Cook artichoke hearts as directed on package. Drain. Heat mayonnaise or salad dressing, milk, parsley, lemon juice, onion and Worcestershire sauce just until hot. Add eggs. Pour over hot artichoke hearts.

Preparation: 10 min.   Easy
Cooking: 15 min.

Serves: 5

Mrs. W. H. Krome George

SAUTÉED ASPARAGUS

asparagus
2 or more tbsp. butter
salt
garlic powder

Break off tough ends of asparagus, and julienne the tops. Melt butter in a frying pan. Add the asparagus, salt and garlic powder to taste. Cover and shake the pan, while cooking, so that the asparagus cooks evenly and is well-coated. Be careful not to overcook, they should be slightly crisp.

Easy

Mrs. Roger Brown, Jr.

BROCCOLI CASSEROLE
"Perfect party pleaser!"

2 pkg. frozen chopped
  broccoli, cooked and
  drained
1 can cream of mushroom
  soup
2 eggs
4 oz. sharp cheese, grated
¾ cup mayonnaise
1 med. onion, chopped
½ cup Ritz cracker crumbs

Mix all ingredients except
cracker crumbs. Pour into
a square, *well-buttered,*
baking dish. Sprinkle top
with crumbs and dot with
butter. Bake at 350° for
30 minutes.

Preparation: 25 min.   Easy   Serves: 6
Baking: 30 min.   Can do ahead

Mrs. Michael F. Ragan

BROCCOLI VINAIGRETTE
"A delicious salad or summer vegetable."

1 lb. fresh broccoli
1 cup clear French dressing
  with herbs & spices, or
  garlic
¼ cup finely chopped dill
  pickle
¼ cup minced green pepper
2 tbsp. snipped parsley
2 tbsp. capers (optional)
2 hard cooked eggs, diced

Trim broccoli. Cook in 1 inch
of salted water until barely
tender. Drain. In jar, combine
French dressing, pickle, green
pepper, parsley and capers.
Shake vigorously to blend.
Stir in diced egg. Place drained
broccoli in low dish. Pour dressing over broccoli. Chill for
several hours or overnight. Serve
garnished with sliced hard
cooked eggs.

Preparation: 20 min.   Easy   Serves: 4
Cooking: 20 min.   Must do ahead

Mrs. H. Alan Speak

SPECIAL BAKED BEANS
"Wonderful dish for a crowd — doubles or triples well!"

6 slices bacon
1 onion, sliced
3 green peppers, sliced
2 1-lb. cans baked beans, drained
1 tbsp. molasses
1 tbsp. mustard
2 cups red wine

Fry bacon and crumble. Sauté
sliced onions and pepper in
bacon fat. Combine everything
in bean pot and bake at 350° for
1 hour, uncovered. Stir occas-
sionally. This will hold in oven
longer, if necessary. Can be made
ahead, stores well refrigerated for
several days, and reheats well.

Preparation: 10 min.   Easy   Serves: 6 - 8
Baking: 1 hour   Can do ahead

Mrs. William Becque

GREEN BEAN CASSEROLE
"Tangy and flavorful."

2 No. 2 cans French cut
  green beans
1 med. onion, cut in rings
8 strips bacon
½ cup slivered almonds
6 tbsp. sugar
6 tbsp. vinegar

Drain beans and put in 1½-quart casserole dish. Place separated onion rings over beans. Fry bacon strips and save drippings. Cut the strips in halves or quarters and lay over onion rings. Sprinkle almonds over bacon. Add sugar and vinegar to bacon drippings and heat. Pour over casserole. Marinate several hours or overnight. Bake 45 minutes at 350°.

Preparation: 25 min.   Easy   Serves: 6
Baking: 45 min.   Must do ahead   *Mrs. Robert G. Morrell*

GREEN BEANS WITH CHERRY TOMATOES
"Eye-appealing dish."

1½ lbs. fresh green beans
scant stick butter
¾ tsp. garlic salt
1 tbsp. sugar
½ tsp. basil
salt & pepper to taste
½ pt. cherry tomatoes

Cook beans 30 minutes in 1 cup water. In fry pan melt butter. Add garlic salt, sugar, basil, salt and pepper. Swish cherry tomatoes around until barely soft and heated but *not* squishy. Add to beans and mix well.

Preparation: 45 min.   Easy   Serves: 6 - 8
                                          Mrs. James Cavalier

ARROZ & HABICHUELAS (BEANS)

1 tsp. olive oil
1 med. onion, minced
¼ lb. ham, diced fine
1 clove garlic, minced
½ green pepper, minced
¼ tsp. salt
1 tsp. each stuffed olives
  & capers
1 8-oz. can tomato sauce
2 17-oz. cans red kidney
  beans
½ cup water

Place oil in sauce pan and slowly sauté onion, ham, garlic, green pepper and salt. Add the olives, capers and tomato sauce. Let simmer for 5 minutes over low heat. Add beans with ½ cup water. Cover and let cook 8-10 minutes until it becomes thick. Serve over rice.

Preparation: 15 min.   Easy   Serves: 8
Cooking: 15 min.   Can do ahead

*Mrs. Roberto Clemente
(Published with permission of the Pittsburgh Baseball Club, from the Pirate Wives' Cookbook.)*

BEETS WITH ORANGE
"Best beets ever."

½ cup sugar
1 tsp. salt
2 tbsp. beet juice
1 tbsp. cornstarch
½ cup vinegar
3½ cups small canned beets
grated rind and juice of
  1 orange
3 tbsp. butter
dash nutmeg

In saucepan, mix sugar, salt, cornstarch, vinegar, beet juice, and orange juice.

Bring to a boil and stir until clear. Stir in orange rind and beets. Heat gently, and before serving add butter and nutmeg.

Mrs. D. Edward Stouffer

Preparation:	10 min.	Easy	Serves: 6 - 8
Cooking:	10 min.	Can do ahead	

CARROTS VICCHY
"These delicious carrots cook in no time."

¾ cup boiling water
¼ cup butter
2 tsp. salt
¼ tsp. nutmeg
⅛ tsp. pepper
1 tbsp. sugar
5 cups carrots, sliced
  diagonally, ¼" thick
1 tbsp. lemon juice
½ tsp. monosodium
  glutamate
¼ cup snipped parsley

Combine water, butter, salt, nutmeg, pepper and sugar with carrots. Simmer covered, 8-10 minutes, or until tender crisp. Stir in lemon juice, monosodium glutamate, and parsley before serving.

Jane Cricks

Preparation:	15 min.	Can do ahead	Serves: 6
Cooking:	12 min.		

CAULIFLOWER AND ONION IN CHEESE SAUCE

1 large head cauliflower
1 large can onions, drained
  (or better yet, same amount
  of fresh)
4 tbsp. butter
4 tbsp. flour
1½ cups milk
salt & pepper
Worcestershire sauce
1 lb. grated American cheese

Break cauliflower in bite-sized pieces, and cook 10 minutes. Cook fresh onions 10 minutes also. Make a cream sauce of butter, flour and milk. Add seasonings to taste and grated cheese. Place in casserole in layers of cauliflower, onions, cheese sauce. Bake 30 minutes in 350° oven.

Chunks of sliced leftover ham can be added to the above casserole for a main dish.

Preparation:	30 min.	Easy	Serves: 8
Baking:	30 min.	Can do ahead	

Mrs. Robert Kopf, Jr.

CAULIFLOWER SAUTERNE
"Unique Treat!"

1 large head cauliflower
¼ cup butter
¼ cup flour
1 cup rich milk
½ cup sauterne
½ cup water
½ cup shredded blanched
  almonds
salt & pepper
¼ cup grated Cheddar
  cheese

Wash and separate cauliflower into flowerets. Drop into boiling salted water. Cook 10-15 minutes.

Prepare sauce: Melt butter and stir in flour. Add milk, wine and water. Cook, stirring, until thick and smooth. Add almonds, salt and pepper. Drain cauliflower carefully. Place in greased baking dish. Pour sauce over and

sprinkle with grated cheese. Bake in 375° oven, 20 minutes.

Preparation: 45 min.	Easy	Serves: 4 - 6
Baking: 20 min.	Can do sauce ahead	

Mrs. Jon McCarthy

CORN FRITTERS
"Family Favorites."

2 eggs
1 cup flour
2 tsp. baking powder
1 can creamed corn
¼ cup sugar
powdered sugar

Mix first 5 ingredients together and drop by spoonful into hot oil, until brown. Turn over to brown other side.

Sprinkle powdered sugar over them and serve.

Preparation: 10 min.	Easy	Yield: 30 fritters
Cooking: 15 min.		Can freeze

Miss Laverne Woytek

EASY CORN PUDDING

2 cups cream style corn
4 tbsp. flour
2 tbsp. sugar
salt & pepper to taste
¼ cup melted butter or
  margarine
3 or 4 beaten eggs
1 cup milk

Mix all except eggs and milk in a 2-quart souffle or baking dish. Add eggs and milk. Bake 1 hour at 350°, uncovered.

Preparation: 10 min.	Easy	Serves: 6
Baking: 1 hour	Can do ahead	

Mrs. William H. Riley

EGGPLANT AND RICE PROVENCALE

"This is really special!"

large eggplants, about 2 lbs.
4 tbsp. olive oil
3 cups finely chopped onion
1 green pepper, cored, seeded, cut into 1" cubes
2 finely minced cloves garlic
1 tsp. chopped fresh thyme or ½ tsp. dried
1 bay leaf
3 tomatoes, peeled, cored & chopped
1 cup raw rice
3¾ cups chicken broth
salt & freshly ground black pepper
½ cup grated Parmesan cheese
2 tbsp. butter

Preheat oven to 400°. Trim off ends of eggplants and cut them into 1" cubes. Heat the oil in a large skillet and add eggplant cubes. Cook over high heat, shaking the skillet occasionally. Add the onion, green pepper, garlic, thyme and bay leaf, stirring. Stir in the tomatoes and lower the heat. Simmer 5 minutes or until most of the liquid in the skillet is evaporated. This is important — the ingredients must be stewed until fairly thickened. Stir in the rice and chicken broth. Season with salt and pepper. Spoon the mixture into a baking dish, and sprinkle with cheese. Dot with butter and bake, uncovered, 30 minutes.

Preparation: 45 min.   Serves: 8
Cooking: 30 min.

Mrs. Irwin S. Terner

PEANUT TOPPED EGGPLANT

"Try something different."

1 eggplant, peeled
margarine
salt & pepper
chopped onions, fresh or frozen
1 can tomato sauce or Hunt's herbed special tomato sauce
Mozzarella or Swiss cheese
2 handfuls of dry roasted peanuts

Slice peeled eggplant ½" thick into flat baking dish. Put small dab of margarine and salt and pepper on each slice. Sprinkle onions over all. Cover with canned tomato sauce. Spread grated or shredded cheese over all this. Put 1 or 2 handfuls of peanuts in blender and turn to chop. Spread peanuts over ingredients in casserole and put in 350 - 375° oven for 30 to 40 minutes.

Preparation: 20 min. Easy
Baking: 30 - 40 min. Can do ahead

Mrs. Charles Dithrich

CHAMPIGNONS A LA BOURGUIGNONNE

"Delicious accompaniment to broiled beef or lamb."

18 - 24 large mushrooms (keep in mind that they shrink some during cooking)
½ lb. butter
3 tbsp. finely chopped parsley
2 tbsp. finely chopped shallots
1 clove garlic, crushed
¼ tsp. salt
freshly ground pepper

Wash mushrooms, remove stems (being careful not to break caps) and save for another purpose. In a small bowl, cream butter until soft, using a wooden spoon. Add remaining ingredients and mix well. Fill each mushroom cap with mixture, arrange in single layer on buttered ovenproof baking dish. Add about 2 tablespoons water, cover closely with foil, and bake at 350° for about 10 minutes.

Be careful not to spill butter out when serving.

Preparation:	30 min.	Easy	Serves: 6
Cooking:	15 min.	Can do ahead	*Mrs. James W. Wilcock*

MUSHROOM SUPREME

"A marvelous dish for that special dinner party."

1 lb. whole mushrooms
2 beef bouillon cubes
½ cup hot water
½ stick butter
2 tbsp. flour
½ cup cream
⅛ tsp. salt
dash pepper
½ cup bread crumbs
½ to 1 cup Parmesan cheese

Sauté mushrooms in butter. Dissolve beef cubes in water. Melt ½ stick butter and blend with flour. Add cream, salt and pepper, and beef broth. Top with cheese and bread crumb mixture before baking. Bake in buttered casserole for 30 minutes at 350°.

Preparation:	30 min.	Easy	Serves: 6 - 8
Baking:	30 min.	Can do ahead	*Mrs. Joseph J. Weibel*

FRENCH FRIED ONION RINGS

"Fabulous fries!"

3 large Spanish onions
ice water
1 egg, beaten
1 cup buttermilk
1 cup flour
½ tsp. salt
½ tsp. baking soda
fat for deep frying

Slice onions about ¼" thick, separate them into rings and soak in ice water for 2 hours. Drain, dry thoroughly. Dip into batter made by mixing the egg with the buttermilk and adding flour, sifted with salt and baking soda. Fry in deep fat at 375° until brown. Drain well on paper.

Preparation:	20 min.	Easy	Serves: 6 - 8
Cooking:	30 min.		*Mrs. Francis J. Sullivan*

SPINACH SOUFFLÉ

"Even nonspinach eaters go for this."

3 tbsp. butter
1 tbsp. finely chopped onion
3 tbsp. flour
½ cup milk & ½ cup cream
3 beaten egg yolks
salt & pepper, dash nutmeg
½ cup grated American
  cheese
1 cup chopped spinach (1 box
  frozen) drained
3 egg whites, beaten to peaks

Melt butter. Add onion and cook 1 minute. Blend in flour. Stir milk and cream in slowly and continue to stir until smooth and it comes to a slow boil. Add a little cream sauce to beaten yolks. Mix well. Add yolks to cream sauce and cook 1 minute. Add seasoning, cheese and spinach. Fold in beaten egg whites. Set casserole in pan of water and bake at 325° for 40 minutes.

Preparation:	20 min.	Easy	Serves: 5
Cooking:	40 min.	Can do ahead	Can freeze

Mrs. James E. Cavalier

SHEILA'S SPINACH CASSEROLE

3 pkgs. frozen, chopped
  spinach
1 cup sour cream
1 pkg. Lipton's onion
  soup mix
4 tbsp. margarine
½ cup bread crumbs
¼ cup grated Parmesan
  cheese

Cook and drain spinach. Mix sour cream and onion soup; toss it with spinach. Mix well. Put in casserole. Melt margarine, add crumbs and cheese and put on top. Bake at 325° for 30 to 40 minutes.

Preparation:	20 min.	Easy	Yield: Serves: 4-6
Baking:	30 - 40 min.	Can do ahead	*Mrs. James D. Seitzer*

SPINACH STUFFED TOMATOES

2 pkgs. frozen spinach, cooked,
  salted & drained well
2 oz. cream cheese
1 tbsp. butter or margarine
½ tsp. instant dried onion
4 large or 6 medium
  tomatoes
Parmesan to cover

Cook spinach, drain well, butter, toss with cream cheese, and onion. Take tops off, scoop out tomatoes and salt and pepper them. Fill with spinach mixture. Sprinkle with Parmesan. Will hold refrigerated at this point. Bake at 350° for 15 - 20 minutes.

Preparation:	20 min.	Easy	Serves: 4 - 6
Baking:	15 - 20 min.	Can do ahead	

Mrs. Edward I. Sproull, Jr.

VEGETABLE CASSEROLE
"A very tasty combination."

1 pkg. frozen broccoli cuts
1 pkg. frozen cauliflower
1 pkg. frozen mixed
  vegetables
1½ to 2 cans Cheddar cheese
  soup
bread crumbs or cubes

Cook vegetables separately and drain separately. Grease a 2-quart casserole with butter. Layer vegetables and between each layer spread ½ can or more of the soup. Top with crumbs or cubes and dot with butter. Bake at 350° until bubbly, about 30 minutes.

| Preparation: | 15 min. | Easy | Serves: 6 |
| Baking: | 30 min. | Can do ahead | |

Mrs. Michael F. Ragan

TAMALE RING

½ large can of tomatoes, strained
1 can of corn put through a grinder
1 green pepper, chopped
1 pt. ripe olives, chopped
1 clove garlic
1 cup white corn meal
1 large tbsp. chili powder
salt
2 eggs beaten separately

Mix first five ingredients; add remaining ingredients and mix well. Bake 1 hour in a buttered ring mold set in a pan of water at 350°. Serve with creamed chicken or shrimp.

| Preparation: | 30 min. | | Serves: 6 |
| Baking: | 1 hour | Serve immediately | |

Mrs. Robinson F. Barker

121

BARLEY CASSEROLE
"Something different."

1 cup medium barley
½ stick margarine
1½ cans onion soup
½ can water

Sauté barley in margarine until lightly brown. (5 minutes or so.) Add soup and water and bring to a boil. Cover. Bake at 350° for 45 minutes, or until liquid is absorbed.

Preparation:	10 min.	Easy	Serves: 8
Cooking:	45 min.	Can do ahead	Will freeze

Mrs. Richard Webster

ENGLISH PEA CASSEROLE

1 pkg. frozen peas
1 can (10½ oz.) cream
  of mushroom soup
¼ cup milk
¼ cup butter
⅓ cup diced celery
⅓ cup chopped onion
⅓ cup diced
  green pepper
1 can water chestnuts,
  sliced
cheese crackers, crumbled
¼ cup chopped pimiento

Cook peas according to package directions. Mix milk with mushroom soup and add to drained peas. Sauté celery, onion and green pepper; add to pea mixture. Add water chestnuts and pimiento and thoroughly combine all ingredients. Put mixture into a 1½ qt. casserole and *refrigerate overnight.* Cover with cheese crackers and bake uncovered in a 350° oven for 25 minutes.

Preparation:	20 min.	Easy	Serves: 4-6
Baking:	25 min.	Must do ahead	

Miss Cathern Riley

ZUCCHINI OR SUMMER SQUASH CASSEROLE

3 plus cups squash
2 carrots, shredded
1 small onion, grated
1 small jar pimientos
  (optional)
1 cup creamed chicken
  soup, undiluted
½ cup sour cream
½ pkg. Pepperidge Farm
  stuffing
⅓ cup melted butter

Cut unpared squash into bite-sized pieces. Lightly cook and drain. Mix dressing with butter. Mix all ingredients with ½ of the dressing mixture. Put in casserole and top with the balance of the dressing. Bake 25 minutes or until brown and bubbly at 350°.

Preparation:	25 min.	Easy	Serves: 8-10
Cooking:	25 min.	Can do ahead	Can freeze

Mrs. Robert D. Duggan

POTATOES

POTATO PUFF

1 5-oz. pkg. instant potatoes
¼ cup green onion
¼ cup pimiento
2 cups creamed, small curd
  cottage cheese
1 cup sour cream
1 tsp. salt
1 tsp. garlic salt
4 egg yolks
3 egg whites

Prepare potatoes as directed on package. Add onion, pimiento, cottage cheese, sour cream, salt, garlic salt. Mix thoroughly. Beat egg yolks and add to other ingredients. Beat egg whites until stiff and fold into first mixture. Bake in 2-quart buttered casserole for 1 hour at 350°.

Preparation: 20 min.	Can do ahead up Serves: 6 - 8
Baking: 1 hour	to adding egg whites

Mrs. Helen Jackson

POTATO LATKES (PANCAKES)

6 med. potatoes
1 small onion
2 eggs, lightly beaten
3 tbsp. flour
¼ tsp. pepper
1 tsp. salt
½ tsp. baking powder

Peel and grate potatoes and onion. Drain liquid. Stir in eggs. Add other ingredients. Mix well. Drop a spoonful at a time into hot greased skillet. Brown on both sides. Drain on paper towels. Serve with sour cream, sugar or applesauce.

Preparation: 20 min.   Easy   Serves: 6
Cooking: 10 - 15 min.

Potato Kugel

The mixture above can also be turned into a shallow, greased casserole and baked at 350° for 40 - 45 minutes. Cut like cake to serve.

Preparation: 20 min.   Easy   Serves: 6
Baking: 40 - 45 min.

Mrs. Sidney Selkovits

ROQUEFORT-STUFFED POTATOES

"For Roquefort Lovers!"

6 baking potatoes
4 tbsp. butter
3 tbsp. milk
1 cup sour cream
3 tbsp. crumbled
 Roquefort
2 tbsp. minced chives
1 tsp. salt
pepper to taste

Preheat oven to 450°. Wash potatoes, dry them, and rub skins with a little salad oil. Place in oven and bake until tender, about 45 minutes. Cut a slice from the top of each potato. Scoop out the pulp, being sure not to break skins, and mash. Beat in the butter, milk, and sour cream until light and fluffy. Stir in the cheese well. Add chives, salt and pepper. Put potatoes back in shells, mounding slightly. Return to oven for 8 - 10 minutes to heat through.

Preparation:	25 min.	Easy	Serves: 6
Baking:	45 - 50 min.	Can do ahead	

Mrs. John G. Zimmerman, Jr.

POTATOES CHANTILLY

4 cups mashed potatoes
½ cup heavy cream, whipped
 stiff
⅓ cup grated American cheese

Put mashed potatoes in a baking dish. Top with cream and sprinkle with cheese. Bake in hot oven until cheese is melted and topping is golden brown and bubbling.

Preparation:	20 min.	Easy	Serves: 6 - 8
Cooking:	10 min.	Can do ahead	Can freeze

Mrs. Francis J. Sullivan

SWEET-POTATO BALLS IN WALNUTS

"These are always a hit. Especially nice around a ham."

2½ cups mashed sweet
 potatoes
½ tsp. salt
dash pepper
2 tbsp. melted butter
1 cup chopped walnuts
⅓ cup honey

Combine mashed sweet potatoes, salt, pepper and butter; chill for easier handling. Shape in 2" balls — use about ¼ cup mashed potato for each. Heat the honey in a *small* heavy skillet. When hot, add potato balls, one at a time. With two forks carefully roll in glaze, coating completely. Roll in chopped nuts. Place sweet potato balls so they do not touch each other in a greased shallow baking dish or pan. Bake at 350° for 20 - 25 minutes.

Preparation:	30 min.	Easy	Serves: 10
Baking:	20 - 25 min.	Can do ahead	

Mrs. Thomas M. Garrett

LOUISIANA YAM, COCONUT AND ORANGE CASSEROLE

"This is as pretty as it is good!"

2 16-oz. cans Louisiana yams,
    drained
2 eggs
¼ cup butter, melted
½ cup brown sugar
½ cup pecans
¾ tsp. salt
¼ tsp. cinnamon
4 tbsp. rum
⅔ cup shredded coconut
1 tbsp. butter, melted
orange sections for
    garnish

Mash yams in large mixing bowl. Add eggs, ¼ cup butter, sugar, salt, pecans, cinnamon and rum. Beat until mixture is light and fluffy. Turn into a greased, shallow casserole or 1-quart baking dish. Bake at 325° for 35 minutes.

Toss coconut with 1 tablespoon butter. Sprinkle a border of coconut around edge of casserole. Arrange orange sections inside border. Bake 10 to 15 minutes until coconut is lightly browned.

Preparation:	10 min.	Easy	Serves: 6
Baking:	50 min.		

Mrs. Charles C. Zatarain, Jr.

SOUR CREAM POTATOES

4 med. size
    potatoes (boiled &
    mashed or riced)
2 tbsp. butter
½ pt. sour cream
⅓ cup minced onion
salt to taste
1 can french fried
    onion rings

Mix first 5 ingredients and beat until fluffy. Place in casserole and top with onion rings. Bake at 350° for 15 minutes.

Mrs. W. H. Krome George

Preparation:	30 min.	Easy	Serves: 4-6
Cooking:	15 min.	Can do ahead	

BAKED POTATO CASSEROLE

8 cooked, peeled &
    diced potatoes
1 lb. American cheese
    sliced in strips
1 cup mayonnaise
½ cup chopped onion
salt & pepper to taste
½ lb. partially fried
    bacon, chopped
¼ cup sliced stuffed olives

Combine first 4 ingredients. Place in a 9 x 13" pan. Top with bacon and olives. Bake 1 hour at 325°.

Preparation:	45 min.	Easy	Serves: 12
Baking:	1 hour	Can do ahead	

Mrs. Thomas R. Wright

RICE

FEATHERED RICE
"Has a delicious toasted flavor."

1½ cups raw white rice, unwashed
1½ tsp. salt
3½ cups boiling water
butter
curry powder (optional)

Spread rice in a shallow baking pan and bake in 400° oven for 30 minutes or until golden brown, stirring occasionally. (Don't worry if it smokes a bit.)

Put browned rice in a strainer and run cold water through it, then put it into a 1½-quart casserole. Add salt and boiling water. Cover. Bake in 400° oven for 25 minutes. Remove cover and fluff up with a fork. Just before serving add a generous amount of butter and a sprinkling of curry powder. Serve from casserole.

Preparation: 5 min.   Easy   Serves: 6
Baking: 55 min.

Mrs. Robert A. McKean, Jr.

VERY YUMMY RICE

¼ lb. butter
1 huge onion chopped fine
2 cups rice
2 cans beef consomme
½ lb. sharp cheese, grated
2 cans small mushrooms,
  with liquid
1 cup brown toasted almonds

Sauté onion in butter. Add uncooked rice and simmer 5 minutes. Pour all ingredients into casserole except almonds. Bake 1 hour at 325°. Stir in almonds when done.

Preparation: 10 min.   Easy   Serves: 8
Cooking: 1 hour   Can do ahead

Mrs. Holly W. Sphar, Jr.

OVEN STEAMED RICE

"Perfect rice every time."

1½ cups white or mixed rice
1½ tsp. salt
dash pepper
2 tbsp. butter
3½ cups boiling water
butter

In a 1½-quart ungreased casserole with tight-fitting lid (or use a piece of aluminum foil tightly fitted), combine rice, salt and pepper. Dot with butter and pour boiling water in and stir until butter is melted. Cover and bake 45 minutes in 350° oven. Do not peek or stir. Fluff up lightly before serving and mix generous amounts of butter through.

Can be doubled. Use a 3-quart casserole, but do not increase the cooking time.

Preparation: 15 min.   Easy   Serves: 6
Cooking: 45 min.   Can do ahead

Mrs. Edward A. Montgomery, Jr.

WILD RICE CASSEROLE

¼ lb. butter
1 cup wild rice
½ cup slivered toasted
  almonds
2 tbsp. each green onions,
  green peppers and chives
½ lb. mushrooms
3 cups chicken broth

Put all ingredients except broth in heavy frying pan and cook until rice turns a slight transparent color or yellow, stirring constantly. Place in a casserole with the broth. Cover tightly. Bake at 325° for 1 hour.

Preparation: 15 min.   Easy   Serves: 4-6
Baking: 1 hour   Can do ahead

Mrs. Frederick Lewis, Jr.

PASTA

WHITE CLAM SAUCE SPAGHETTI

½ stick butter
4 tbsp. olive oil
1 cup chopped scallions,
  including some green tops
½ tbsp. chopped parsley
½ tsp. oregano
½ tsp. basil
1 clove garlic
1 peeled tomato
salt & fresh ground
  pepper to taste
2 7½-oz. cans chopped
  or minced clams
1 16-oz. pkg. spaghetti
Parmesan cheese, grated

Heat butter and olive oil, and reserve 2 tablespoons of this melted mixture. Add chopped scallions and sauté briefly. Add parsley, oregano, basil, crushed garlic, chopped peeled fresh tomato, salt, pepper and clam juice drained from clams; simmer briefly. Add canned clams and then keep hot. Boil package spaghetti (al dente). Drain spaghetti and return to pan in which it was boiled. Add 2 reserved tablespoons olive oil and melted butter mixture, toss, add 4 tablespoons grated Parmesan. Toss, add ¼ of the sauce to spaghetti, toss again. Serve spaghetti on plate, spoon remaining sauce on top each spaghetti serving. Sauce should be consistency of regular tomato sauce. Add small amount of corn starch and water mixed if necessary for thickening. Serve as main course with Italian Bread and tossed salad.

Preparation: 20 min.   Easy   Serves: 4-6

Ralph Benz, Jr.

PASTERIE

"This is an unusual Italian recipe which can be used as an entree or as a meat accompaniment."

½ lb. spaghetti
6 large or 8 medium eggs
½-²/₃ cup milk
2/3 cup freshly grated Romano
  or Parmesan cheese
¼ tsp. salt
good dash pepper
1 lb. ricotta
about 3 tbsp. bacon drippings

Break spaghetti into fourths. Cook al dente. Mix together other ingredients except bacon drippings. Put 1½ tbsp. drippings on top of spaghetti. When it has melted, mix spaghetti into sauce. Grease a 9 x 13" pan with rest of bacon drippings. Can be assembled ahead of time and baked just before serving. Bake at 350° for 30 minutes or until set.

Preparation:	30 min.	Easy	Serves: 8
Baking:	30 min.	Can do ahead	Can freeze

Mrs. Foster A. Stewart

LASAGNE

Meat sauce

2 lbs. ground chuck
1 minced garlic clove
1 tbsp. salt
1 can tomatoes (1 lb.)
2 (6 oz.) cans tomato paste
10 oz. lasagne noodles
1 lb. Mozzarella cheese,
  sliced thinly

Cheese filling

3 cups cottage cheese
½ cup grated parmesan cheese
2 tbsp. parsley flakes
2 eggs, beaten
2 tsp. salt
½ tsp. pepper

Brown meat slowly. Spoon off fat. Add garlic clove, salt, tomatoes and tomato paste. Simmer, uncovered, 30 minutes, stirring occasionally.

Cook lasagne noodles in boiling salted water until tender. Drain. Rinse with cold water. (Add a little olive oil to noodles while cooking so they will not stick.)

While noodles are cooking, combine all ingredients for cheese filling and mix.

Arrange casserole with noodles first, then cheese filling, Mozzarella cheese slices, and meat sauce. Repeat layers. Use 13 x 9 x 2" baking dish. Bake at 375° for 30 minutes.

Let stand 15 minutes before cutting in squares.

Preparation:	1 hour	Easy	Serves: 6
Baking:	30 min.	Can do ahead	

Mrs. William A. Gordon, Jr.

CANNELLONI

48 entree crepes — (see note)*
  or 36   3" long manicotti tubes

Filling:

3 pkg. frozen chopped
  spinach
6 tbsp. olive oil
¾ cup finely chopped
  onion
3 tsp. finely minced
  garlic
6 tbsp. butter
3 lbs. ground chuck
9   chicken livers
15 tbsp. Parmesan cheese
6 tbsp. heavy cream
6 eggs slightly beaten
2 tsp. oregano
1 tsp. basil
salt and pepper

* (this recipe appears on page 48)

Bechamel Sauce:

12 tbsp. butter
12 tbsp. flour
3 cups milk
3 cups heavy cream
3 tsp. salt
½ tsp. pepper

Tomato Sauce:

6   15-oz. cans tomato sauce
3 tsp. basil
3 tsp. oregano

6 tbsp. grated Parmesan cheese
butter

Thaw spinach and drain it dry in a sieve. Heat oil in large skillet and cook onions and garlic over moderate heat for 7-8 minutes until soft, not brown. Add spinach and cook, stirring for 5 minutes. When all of the moisture is gone, transfer to large mixing bowl. Melt half of butter in skillet and lightly brown the chuck stirring constantly to break the lumps. Add to bowl. Melt rest of butter and cook livers until browned lightly and pink inside. Chop livers coarsely and add to bowl. Add Parmesan cheese, cream, eggs, and spices. Stir all together with wooden spoon until thoroughly blended. Fill crepes with about 2 tablespoons of filling each and fold sides over. Place seam side down in well-greased flat glass baking dish or lasagna pan.

Bechamel Sauce: Make as for a white sauce, using a whisk, and simmer after it comes to a boil and coats whisk wires. Pour Bechamel sauce over the filled crepes, dividing evenly among the casseroles. Spoon tomato sauce over the top, again dividing evenly among the casseroles. Scatter the Parmesan cheese over top of casseroles and dot with butter. Bake uncovered for 30 minutes in a 350° oven. Slide under broiler for 30 seconds to brown top.

Preparation:	3 hours	Can do ahead	Serves: 20-24
Baking:	30 min.		Can freeze

Mrs. Edward A. Montgomery, Jr.

SALADS & SALAD DRESSINGS

OLD ALLEGHENY POST OFFICE MUSEUM

Located on Pittsburgh's North Side is the handsome Pittsburgh History and Landmarks Museum, a fine example of Renaissance architecture. The inside houses a colorful exhibit of memorabilia featuring the restoration of residences and public buildings in Pittsburgh.

Additional illustrations in this section:

A stained glass window in the Frick Building entitled "Fortune", by John LaFarge.

Arts & Crafts Center of Pittsburgh, Mellon Park, Shadyside.

The stone marker over the doorway of the Fort Pitt Blockhouse.

SALADS

AVOCADO SALAD AND DRESSING
"Easy and different."

1 ripe avocado, peeled & sliced
lemon juice
salad greens, chilled
1 tomato, cut in wedges
1   3-oz. pkg. cream cheese
    cut in ½" cubes
1 cup thinly sliced zucchini, or
    cucumber
1 green pepper, chopped

Dressing

¼ cup salad oil
2 tbsp. cider vinegar
1 tbsp. minced onion
1 tsp. seasoned salt
¼ tsp. sugar
¼ tsp. chili powder
1/8 tsp. seasoned pepper

Sprinkle avocado with lemon juice. Place salad greens in bowl. Put avocado, tomato, cream cheese, zucchini, and green pepper on top.

Shake remaining ingredients in a jar. Pour dressing over salad — toss lightly.

Preparation: 15 min.   Easy   Serves: 8

Mrs. John G. Zimmerman, Jr.

FIVE BEAN SALAD

1 small can of each of the following (rinsed in colander & drained):
green string beans
cooked dry limas
green limas
kidney beans
yellow wax beans
chick peas (Garbanzos)
1-2 large green peppers, chopped
4 pieces celery, chopped
small can pimientos, cut in
  small pieces
1 bunch green onions, chopped

Syrup

2 cups vinegar
2 cups sugar
½ cup water
1 tbsp. salt

Mix and chill beans and vegetables.
Combine syrup ingredients and boil 5 minutes. Immediately pour over chilled beans and vegetables. Will keep 3-4 weeks in jars in refrigerator.

Mrs. Jon E. McCarthy

Preparation: 10 - 15 min.   Easy   Yield: 1½ qts.
                                    Must do ahead

BEET SALAD WITH APPLES
"Good with meat and fish."

1   1-lb. jar pickled sliced beets
2 med. tart apples
2 tbsp. mayonnaise
1 tbsp. sugar
⅛ tsp. salt
freshly ground pepper
2 tbsp. chopped parsley

Drain beets and cut into strips ¼ inch thick. Peel apples and dice finely. Mix beets, apples, mayonnaise, sugar, salt, and pepper to taste. Toss ingredients lightly together. Garnish with chopped parsley. Will keep one week.

Preparation: 15 min.   Easy   Serves: 4 - 6
                              Can do ahead

Mrs. John Gould

DON BROCKETT'S SALAD
"A thousand calories a bite!"

1 head lettuce
1 avocado
small jar of artichoke hearts
small can hearts of palm
cheese croutons
1 bottle Green
  Goddess dressing

Cut up the ingredients which will cut. Combine everything, toss, and serve.

Don Brockett

Preparation: 10 min.   Easy   Serves: 6-8

SESAME ASPARAGUS SALAD

¼ cup toasted sesame seed
1   10-oz. pkg. frozen cut
    asparagus
1 head Romaine, broken into
    pieces
2 pimientos, diced
1 green onion, chopped
¼ tsp. cracked pepper
¼ tsp. herb seasoning
2 tbsp. each of lemon juice
    & salad oil
salt to taste

Toast sesame seeds in oven.
Cook, drain, and chill asparagus.
Add to next 3 ingredients.
Mix pepper, herb seasoning,
lemon juice, and oil. Add to
first mixture; toss. Add salt.
Add sesame seed just before
serving.

Mrs. James Harris

Preparation: 10 min.	Easy	Serves: 4 - 6
	Can do ahead	

COLE SLAW

2 cups sugar
1 cup vinegar
1 tbsp. mustard seed
1 tbsp. salt
1 tsp. turmeric
2 qts. shredded cabbage
    (1 med. head)
2 grated carrots
4-6 stalks celery, chopped
1 green pepper, sliced very
    thin
1 onion, sliced thin

Boil first 5 ingredients until
sugar is melted. Let stand until cool. Mix vegetables and
cooled dressing well. Let
stand in refrigerator overnight. Will keep 1 week in
refrigerator.

Mrs. Richard P. Simmons

Preparation: 20 min.	Easy	Serves: 8
	Must do ahead	Can freeze

CURRIED CHICKEN SALAD

2-3 cups cooked chicken or
    turkey, cubed
1   4-oz. can water chestnuts,
    drained & sliced
½ lb. seedless grapes, halved,
    or 1   11-oz. can mandarin
    oranges
1 cup celery, chopped fine
1 cup mayonnaise
1 tsp. curry powder
2 tsp. soy sauce
2 tsp. lemon juice
salt to taste

Combine chicken, water chestnuts, grapes or oranges, and
celery.
Mix all remaining ingredients,
add to chicken, and toss well.
Chill several hours.
Serve on Bibb lettuce.

Mrs. Holly W. Sphar, Jr.

Preparation: 45 min.	Easy	Serves: 6
	Must do ahead	

SPECIAL CHAMPAGNE MOLD
"Wonderful for a wedding!"

Clear Layer:
2 envs. plain gelatin
2 cups cold water
¼ cup sugar
1 6-oz. can frozen
  lemonade concentrate,
  unthawed
½ cup champagne

Cream Layer:
3 envs. plain gelatin
1¾ cups cold water
½ cup sugar
2 6-oz. cans frozen
  lemonade concentrate,
  unthawed
1 cup champagne
2 cups heavy cream

Make clear layer:
Sprinkle gelatin over 1 cup cold water in pan. Place over low heat. Stir constantly, 2 or 3 minutes, until gelatin dissolves. Remove from heat. Add sugar and stir until dissolved. Add frozen lemonade and stir until melted. Add remaining water and champagne.

Pour into 12-cup mold. (I sometimes use a bundt pan) and chill until almost firm. Meanwhile begin preparing cream layer.

Make cream layer:
Sprinkle gelatin over water in 2½-quart pan. Place over low heat. Stir constantly until gelatin dissolves, about 3 or 4 minutes. Remove from heat. Add sugar and stir until dissolved. Add frozen lemonade. Stir until melted. Add champagne. Chill until mixture is consistency of unbeaten egg whites.

Whip cream until stiff. Fold into gelatin mixture. Turn into mold over almost firm clear layer. Chill until firm. Unmold onto serving platter. Serve with sweetened sliced strawberries, or leave whole and garnish with watercress and whole berries. (I have used blueberries when I couldn't get strawberries.) If you lightly grease the serving platter before unmolding gelatin the mold can then be moved and centered if necessary.

Preparation: 30 - 40 min.   Must do ahead   Serves: 12

Mrs. James Rankin Duncan

GREEK RICE SALAD

2 cups cooked rice
½ cup oil & vinegar dressing
½ cup raisins or currants
½ cup dry vermouth
½ cup slivered almonds
fresh chopped herbs,
  as desired

Mix rice while still warm with vinaigrette. Let chill. Poach raisins in vermouth until puffed and most of vermouth is absorbed. Chill. Add nuts and herbs, mix together and chill again.

Preparation: 30 min.   Easy   Serves: 8-10
Must do ahead

Mrs. James D. Seitzer

CAESAR SALAD

"This is absolutely fantastic."

⅓ cup lemon juice
⅓ cup olive oil
1 egg in shell
½ tsp. salt
olive oil
1 clove garlic
2 tomatoes
2 large heads of Romaine
½ cup Parmesan cheese
½ lb. bacon, fried & crumbled,
  or substitute Bacos
⅓ cup chopped scallions
snipped mint
½ tsp. ground pepper
¼ tsp. dried oregano
1 cup croutons

Mix lemon juice with ⅓ cup olive oil. Cover egg in shell with water — bring to boil — let stand 1 minute. Remove from water and refrigerate.

Sprinkle wooden bowl with salt and olive oil. Rub garlic around inside of bowl.

Place tomatoes, cut in eighths in bottom of bowl. Tear Romaine into pieces over tomatoes. Sprinkle with cheese, bacon, scallions, mint, pepper, oregano, and croutons.

Remove softly cooked egg from shell. Add egg to lemon juice and olive oil mixture, then blend together. Add Romaine, toss well.

Preparation: 1 hour   Easy   Serves: 6 - 8

Mrs. James D. Darby

ELEGANT CRAB SALAD

1 to 2 heads Bibb lettuce or
  Boston lettuce
2 med. tomatoes, cut up or
  sliced
¼ lb. fresh mushrooms, sliced
2 green onions, sliced with tops
2 oz. sharp Cheddar, cubed
10-12 black pitted olives,
  sliced
1 large can artichoke hearts,
  halved (not marinated)
1 6-oz. pkg. frozen crabmeat, thawed (2 pkgs. are
  better if you can afford it)
dressing — Kraft's Golden
  Caesar is great for this, or
  use your favorite
fresh ground pepper
salt if desired
garlic seasoned croutons

Select ingredients for freshness. Mix all ingredients, except croutons, with dressing.
Season with pepper and salt.
Garnish with croutons.
Cannot be made more than 1 hour ahead.

Preparation: 15 min.   Easy   Serves: 6

Mrs. John A. Nave

CORN RELISH SALAD

"A good summer buffet dish. Keeps about a month in tightly covered jar. Super easy."

1   12-oz. can whole kernel corn
½ cup coarsely chopped green
   pepper
½ cup diced celery
¼ cup chopped onion
1 small jar pimientos, diced
⅓ cup salad oil
3 tbsp. vinegar
1 tsp. salt
¼ tsp. pepper
¾ tsp. dry mustard

Combine all ingredients and chill.

Mrs. Foster Stewart

Preparation: 20 min.   Must do ahead   Serves: 4

CORN SALAD

"Easy and flavorful."

2   12-oz. cans whole kernel corn,
   drained
¾ cup diced unpared cucumber
¼ cup diced onion
2 small tomatoes, chopped
¼ cup sour cream
2 tbsp. mayonnaise
1 tbsp. vinegar
½ tsp. salt
¼ tsp. dry mustard
¼ tsp. celery seed
lettuce cups

Combine corn, cucumber, onion and tomatoes in salad bowl. Blend sour cream with mayonnaise. Add remaining ingredients. Add sour cream mixture to corn mixture; toss gently to coat vegetables. Chill thoroughly. Spoon into lettuce cups

Mrs. James Harris

Preparation: 15 - 20 min.   Easy   Serves: 6 - 8
                                Must do ahead

PINEAPPLE SOUR CREAM SALAD

1   3-oz. pkg. lemon jello
½ tsp. salt
1 cup boiling water
¼ cup cold water
2 tbsp. lemon juice
1 cup sour cream
1½ cups crushed pineapple,
   drained

Dissolve 1 package lemon jello and ½ teaspoon salt in 1 cup boiling water. Add ¼ cup of cold water, 2 tablespoons lemon juice and 1 cup sour cream. Beat until blended. Chill to thicken slightly. Set in ice and water. Whip until thick and foamy. Fold in 1½

cups of drained crushed pineapple. Chill.

Preparation: 20 min.   Easy   Serves: 6-8
                                Must do ahead

Mrs. Thomas R. Wright

138

TOMATO ASPIC

1 3-oz. pkg. lemon jello
1¾ cup hot water
1 8-oz. can tomato sauce
1 tsp. vinegar
Worcestershire sauce
salt & pepper

Dissolve lemon jello in hot water, add tomato sauce, stir. Add vinegar and several drops of Worcestershire sauce, salt and pepper, stir and chill.

Preparation: 10 min.   Easy   Serves: 4
                             Must do ahead

Mrs. W. O. Campbell

TOMATO CREAM CHEESE ASPIC

"Very rich and delicious."

1 can tomato soup
1 8-oz. pkg. cream cheese
1 3-oz. pkg. lemon jello
½ cup water
1 cup mayonnaise
chopped celery (optional)
chopped green pepper (optional)
grated onion (optional)
lettuce
hard boiled egg slices

Heat soup, stirring to keep from sticking. Add cheese and beat until smooth. Stir in jello which has been dissolved in ½ cup water. Add mayonnaise and stir until smooth. Add chopped celery, chopped green pepper, and grated onion in the amount you like. Chill. Serve, congealed, on lettuce, garnished with hard boiled egg slices. Shrimp or crab meat may be added to the gelatin mix if desired.

Preparation: 20 min.   Must do ahead   Serves: 10

The Committee

CUCUMBER MOLDED SALAD

"This is a rather unusual, elegant salad."

1 pkg. lime jello
1 cup boiling water
1 tsp. salt
1 tbsp. vinegar
1 tsp. onion juice
1 cup heavy sour cream
¼ cup mayonnaise
1 large cucumber, finely
  chopped

Dissolve jello in boiling water, mix with salt, vinegar, onion juice. Chill until slightly thick. Fold sour cream and mayonnaise into jello.

Pat chopped cucumber with paper towel to absorb excess water. Add to above mixture. Place in oiled ring mold and chill until ready to serve.

Fill center of mold with shrimp, chicken, lobster, or crabmeat salad (or anything you wish). I often fill with tomatoes, sliced.

Preparation: 30 - 40 min.   Easy   Serves: 4 - 6
               including   Must do ahead
               chilling

Mrs. Robert H. Bartlett

SPINACH WITH CRAB MEAT DRESSING

"Very tasty and good with beef or chicken main course."

3 pkgs. lime jello
3 cups boiling water
½ cup cold water
6 tbsp. vinegar
1½ cups mayonnaise
3 cups cottage cheese
4 tbsp. minced onion
3 pkgs. chopped spinach
(thaw, drain & squeeze out water)
1 cup diced celery

Crab Dressing:

3 cups mayonnaise
¾ cup chili sauce
6 tsp. horseradish
½ large onion, chopped
Tabasco sauce; if desired
2 cups crabmeat

Dissolve jello in hot water and add cold water and vinegar. Add all other ingredients and pour into mold.
Dressing: Mix all ingredients except crabmeat together. Fold in crabmeat. Serve spinach mold on lettuce and top with crabmeat dressing.

Mrs. N. D. Belnap, Jr.

Preparation: 30 min.   Easy   Serves: 12
                               Must do ahead

SPINACH SALAD

"A super recipe!"

2 slices crisply fried bacon
1 clove garlic
1   10-oz. pkg. fresh spinach
1 med. onion
1 carrot, grated

Crumble bacon. Rub salad bowl with cut of garlic clove. Wash and remove stems from spinach. Blot spinach very dry. Cut onion into thin slices. Break spinach into bite-sized pieces and put into salad bowl. Add half of onion slices and all of carrot. Top with 3 tablespoons salad dressing. Toss salad with 2 forks until all leaves are coated with dressing. Sprinkle salad with remaining onion rings and crumbled bacon.

Preparation: 20 min.   Easy   Serves: 6
                               Serve immediately

SPINACH SALAD DRESSING

⅓ cup tomato juice
2 tbsp. salad oil
1 tsp. salt
3 tbsp. vinegar
¾ tsp. dry mustard
1 tsp. grated onion

In a screw top jar, cup size or larger, put all the salad dressing ingredients, screw top tightly on to jar. Shake well.

Preparation: 5 min.   Easy   Yield: ¾ cup
                               Can do ahead   *Mrs. James Harris*

SPINACH SALAD MOLD

"Try this in a ring mold — garnish with tomato slices."

6 10-oz. pkgs. frozen chopped
  spinach, cooked & well drained
1 cup sour cream
1 large onion, chopped
½ cup chopped celery
1 tsp. lemon juice
2 tbsp. vinegar
1 tsp. chopped parsley
1 tsp. tarragon
1 tsp. salt

Mix all ingredients and pack
into 1-quart mold. Chill
several hours.

Preparation: 30 min.   Must do ahead   Serves: 10

Mrs. Joseph B. Griffith

SPINACH SALAD

1 lb. spinach, cleaned & drained
½ pt. sour cream
1 pkg. cheese & garlic dressing
  (Good Seasons)
bacon bits
chopped hard-boiled eggs
croutons

Mix together and let marinate.
You may add bacon bits or
chopped hard-boiled eggs or
croutons. Go a little lighter on
the Good Seasons — ½ package
might be plenty.

Preparation: 10 min.   Easy   Serves: 4 - 6

Mrs. Clifford Early

ALASKAN FRUIT SALAD

"Children love this and can even make it."

1 env. unflavored gelatin
1½ cups lemonade
1 3-3¼-oz. pkg. regular vanilla
  pudding mix
½ cup whipping cream
1 11-oz. can mandarin orange
  sections, drained
1 8¼-oz. can crushed
  pineapple, drained
½ cup maraschino cherries,
  quartered

Soften gelatin in ¼ cup of
lemonade. In medium saucepan, combine remaining
lemonade, pudding mix and
softened gelatin. Cook and
stir over medium heat until
mixture thickens and bubbles.
Chill until partially set.
Whip cream; fold into gelatin
mixture. Fold in oranges, pineapple and cherries. Chill until
mixture mounds; turn into 4-
cup mold. Chill 4 to 5 hours
or overnight. Unmold. Garnish with additional fruit, if desired.

Preparation: 10 - 15 min.   Easy   Serves: 6 - 8
Cooking: 10 min.   Must do ahead

Mrs. John M. Webb

CRANBERRY TUNA MOLD

"There is something different you can do with tuna!!
Tangy and terrific."

1 env. Knox unflavored gelatin
¼ cup cold water
¼ cup boiling water
2 cans tuna
1 cup mayonnaise
1 cup chopped celery
1 onion, chopped

Soften gelatin in cold water
and dissolve in boiling water.
Add all other ingredients
and spoon into 8 x 8" pan.
Chill until firm.

Topping

1 box lemon gelatin
¾ cup boiling water
1 can whole cranberry sauce
¼ cup orange juice

Topping:
Mix and spoon over chilled
tuna mixture. Chill overnight.

Preparation: 30 min.　　Must do ahead　　Serves: 8

Mrs. E. S. Henry, Jr.

RATATOUILLE SALAD

3 heads Bibb lettuce
1 head Romaine lettuce
2 med. zucchini,
 thinly sliced
½ lb. eggplant
olive oil
1-2 med. onions.
 thinly sliced
2 large tomatoes
½ raw green pepper,
 sliced
raw mushrooms
salt & pepper
favorite salad dressing

Shred the lettuce coarsely.
Cube the eggplant and sauté
quickly in olive oil. Slice the
tomatoes, and then quarter the
slices. Toss the lettuce and
vegetables together with salt,
pepper and your favorite salad
dressing. Serve immediately.

George C. Hayes, M. D.

Preparation: 15 min.　　Easy　　　　Serves: 6
　　　　　　　　　Serve immediately

NANNIE'S LUNCHEON SALAD

"Is easily expanded to serve an indefinite number."

¼ cantaloupe in wedge form, peeled
8-10 large shrimp, cooked & peeled
5-6 green grapes, halved
mayonnaise flavored with curry
 to taste

Place cantaloupe wedge on
lettuce bed. Arrange shrimp
on top of wedge and cover
with curried mayonnaise.
Garnish with halved grapes.

Preparation: 15 min.　　Easy　　　　Serves: 1
Assembly: 5 min.　　Can do ahead　　Serve immediately

Mrs. William J. Williamson, Jr.

VEGETABLES IN SOUR CREAM MOLD

1 3-oz. pkg. lemon flavored
  gelatin
2 bouillon cubes
½ tsp. salt
1 cup boiling water
2 - 4 tbsp. tarragon vinegar
1 cup sour cream
¾ cup diced celery
½ cup thinly sliced radishes
½ cup diced cucumber
¼ cup green pepper strips
2 - 3 tbsp. thinly sliced scallions
dash pepper

Dissolve gelatin, bouillon cubes, and salt in boiling water. Add vinegar. Chill until thickened. Blend in sour cream and add remaining ingredients. Pour into 1-quart mold or individual molds. Chill until firm. Unmold on crisp lettuce and garnish with water cress, if desired. May be served with French dressing or mayonnaise.

Preparation: 20 min.   Easy   Serves: 6
                             Must do ahead

Mrs. Richard Webster

SWEET-SOUR KRAUT

2 lbs. sauerkraut, washed
1 green pepper
1 med. onion
1 cup celery
1½ cups sugar
½ cup salad oil
⅔ cup vinegar
⅓ cup water

Add chopped vegetables to sauerkraut. Combine sugar, oil, vinegar and water. Heat and pour over sauerkraut. Marinate overnight.

Preparation: 15 min.   Easy   Serves: 6
                             Must do ahead

Mrs. Allan W. Beatty

CALICO MACARONI SALAD

"A different macaroni salad — tangy and very good."

2 cups cooked shell macaroni
2 tbsp. vinegar
1 tbsp. salad oil
2 tbsp. grated onion
1 cup diced celery
½ cup minced parsley
½ cup chopped stuffed olives
½ tsp. salt, dash of pepper
3 tbsp. sour cream
2 tbsp. chopped pimiento

Marinate macaroni in refrigerator overnight in vinegar and oil. Do not drain. Combine with other ingredients. Chill before serving.

Preparation: 30 min.   Easy   Serves: 4 - 6
Must do ahead

Mrs. Foster Stewart

HARD BOILED EGG RING

9 hard boiled eggs put
   through ricer
1 envelope Knox gelatin
¾ cup hot water
¼ cup cold water
1 cup mayonnaise
½ tsp. salt
½ tsp. paprika
3 turns pepper

Dissolve gelatin in ¼ cup cold water, filled to 1 cup with hot water. Mix all ingredients, including gelatin, and pour into ring mold. Chill overnight. Fill center with crab, shrimp, chicken, tuna or vegetable salad.

Preparation: 25 min.   Easy   Yield: Serves 6
Must do ahead

Mrs. Thomas M. Garrett

UNTOSSED SALAD

fresh, raw spinach,
   broken in pieces
salt, pepper, sugar
½ lb. crumbled,
   fried bacon
4-6 chopped hard-boiled
   eggs
chopped lettuce
salt, pepper, sugar
thawed, uncooked peas
sliced, sweet onion
mayonnaise
julienne strips Swiss cheese

Layer ingredients in the order given. Sprinkle the salt, pepper and sugar over the spinach and lettuce. The mayonnaise layer should coat the top like frosting. Cover and refrigerate for several hours.

Preparation: 15 min.   Easy   Serves: 8
Must do ahead

Mrs. Timothy Merrill

SALAD DRESSINGS

BLENDER CAESAR DRESSING

1 tsp. salt
½ tsp. pepper
¼ tsp. garlic powder
1 tsp. Worcestershire sauce
¼ cup salad oil
1 egg
another ½ cup salad oil
¼ cup lemon juice
¼ cup grated Parmesan cheese
anchovies

Put first five ingredients in blender. Coddle egg 1 minute. Put in blender and turn motor on. Immediately remove cover and add ½ cup more salad oil. Turn off and add lemon juice and cheese. Give the blender one more flick. Refrigerate. Add anchovies to the salad when you make it — will taste too strong if put in the dressing.

Should be done ahead to blend flavors. Do not double recipe — make twice instead.

Preparation: 5 min.   Easy   Yield: 1½ - 2 cups
Must do ahead

Mrs. Edward I. Sproull, Jr.

LEMON SALAD DRESSING

2 tbsp. lemon juice
2 tbsp. olive oil
4 tbsp. mayonnaise
freshly ground black pepper
a little salt
sliced black olives

Beat all ingredients together. Sliced black olives may be added. Serve on a salad of mixed greens.

Preparation: 5 min.   Easy   Yield: ½ cup
Can do ahead

Mrs. William I. Jack

OMAR KHAYYAM DRESSING

"This is especially good on Maurice Salad!"

2 eggs, raw
1 tbsp. sugar
1 tsp. salt
½ tsp. paprika
½ tsp. dry mustard
1 tsp. Worcestershire sauce
½ cup ketchup
2 cups salad oil
½ cup white or apple vinegar
¼ cup warm water
1 tbsp. mayonnaise

Blend all ingredients in blender until thoroughly mixed. Can be made ahead. However, if it is, replace in blender and mix before serving.

Mrs. David B. Oliver II

Preparation: 10 min.   Easy   Yield: 4 cups
Can do ahead

HONEY DRESSING FOR FRUIT SALAD

"This really perks up fruit salad."

½ cup vinegar
¼ cup sugar
¼ cup honey
1 tsp. dry mustard
1 tsp. paprika
1 tsp. celery seed
1 tsp. fresh onion juice
1 cup Wesson oil

Boil ingredients together and let cool.

Preparation: 5 min.   Easy   Yield: 2 cups
Cooking: 5 min.   Must do ahead

Mrs. Robert E. Weiss

SOUTHERN FRENCH DRESSING

"Stores in refrigerator for weeks."

1 tsp. paprika
1 cup sugar
2 tsp. salt
1 tsp. dry mustard
1 tsp. black pepper
1 tbsp. Worcestershire sauce
1 tsp. horseradish
1 med. onion, grated
1 can condensed tomato soup
1 cup cider vinegar
1 cup salad oil
1 clove garlic, skewered with
  a toothpick

Mix all dry ingredients in a bowl. Add everything else except garlic and beat thoroughly. Do *not* use blender. Pour into jar and add garlic, which may be removed after a few days if you wish.

Mrs. Richard D. Collins, Jr.

Preparation: 10 min.   Easy   Yield: 1 qt.
Can do ahead

SEATTLE SALAD DRESSING

1 cup oil
¼ cup vinegar
⅔ cup catsup
½ cup sugar
1 tsp. paprika
1 tsp. fresh lemon juice
1 tsp. fresh minced onion

Blend ingredients together.

Mrs. W. Kendall Jones

Preparation: 5 min.   Easy   Yield: 1⅔ cups
                         Can do ahead

SWEET MAYONNAISE — for Potato Salad
"Old family recipe."

3 whole eggs or 5 yolks,
  mixed well
¾ cup sugar
1 tbsp. flour
1 tsp. salt
dash of mustard & pepper
½ cup vinegar
½ cup milk

Combine all ingredients in saucepan and cook *slowly* until thickened. Chill. Can be done ahead and frozen.

Mrs. John Albert Nave

Preparation: 30 min.   Must do ahead   Yield: 1½ - 2 cups
Cooking: 15 min.   Can freeze

SWEET SALAD DRESSING
"Try this on fresh spinach leaves with mandarin oranges."

½ cup sugar
1 tsp. salt
1 tsp. dry mustard
1¼ tsp. paprika
generous tsp. onion flakes
1 cup salad oil
¼ cup vinegar
1 tsp. celery seed (or salt)

Mix ingredients and refrigerate. Serve with spinach salad and 1 can mandarin oranges, drained. Dressing will keep for 1 to 2 months. Put in blender if separates too much.

Mrs. Calvert G. de Coligny

Preparation: 5 min.   Easy   Yield: 1½ cups
                         Can do ahead

HERB MAYONNAISE
"Really yummy on chicken sandwiches, in potato salad, deviled eggs, etc."

1 pt. fine quality mayonnaise
2 tbsp. olive brine, juice from green
  or stuffed olives
2 tbsp. herb vinegar
chopped herbs

Combine all ingredients. Add combinations of chopped chives, parsley, basil or dill weed. Mix thoroughly. Store in refrigerator indefinitely.

Preparation: 10 min.   Easy   Yield: 1 pt.
                         Can do ahead

Mrs. Howard G. Wilbert

ROQUEFORT DRESSING

"Suitable for dip, as it is very thick."

1 3-oz. pkg. cream cheese
1/3 cup Roquefort or Blue cheese
1/4 tsp. salt
1/2 tsp. garlic powder
1/4 tsp. prepared mustard
1/2 tsp. Beau Monde Seasoning
   (optional)
1/2 cup mayonnaise
1/2 cup light cream
1/2 tsp. chives

Blend cheeses with the seasonings. Add the mayonnaise alternately with the cream. Whip until smooth. To make it thicker, substitute sour cream for light cream.

Preparation: 15 min.

Easy
Can do ahead

Yield: 2 cups

Mrs. James W. Wilcock

ROQUEFORT DRESSING

1/2 pt. sour cream
1/4-1/3 lb. Roquefort
1 cup mayonnaise
3 tsp. salad vinegar
1 tsp. Worcestershire sauce
1/2 tsp. parsley

Blend all ingredients together. Refrigerate.

Preparation: 5 min.

Easy
Can do ahead

Yield: 2 cups

Mrs. J. Sterling Davis, Jr.

PETITE MARMITE (salad dressing)

1 tbsp. oregano
4 eggs
2 tbsp. yellow mustard
2 tbsp. chopped parsley
2 tsp. garlic, chopped fine
1 tsp. salt
1 tsp. pepper
1 cup wine vinegar
1 qt. olive oil

In stainless steel or glass bowl, mix all ingredients except olive oil. Beat with a hard whip until well blended. Add olive oil, pouring very slowly, beating mixture constantly until it maintains a medium thickness. Dressing will separate in refrigerator, so shake before using.

Preparation: 30 min.

Can do ahead

Yield: 1½ qt.

Mrs. Joseph J. Weibel

SWEETS

CHILDREN'S ZOO

On any day from May until October, the Children's Zoo features the happy meeting of small children and small animals in a storybook setting with a White Mice City and a Jonah Whale they can walk through. In the Twilight Zoo, in six exhibits, small mammals live in their natural habitat — predator and prey coexisting peacefully. In the man-made miracle called the Aquazoo, marine life from the Arctic to the tropics thrives in beautifully illuminated tanks and pools, each adjusted to the natural water and temperature requirements of the inhabitants.

Additional illustrations in this section:

Early Pittsburgh Trolley — August 1891.

The University of Pittsburgh and the Syria Mosque viewed from a chemistry lab.

Puppets — Daniel & Henrietta Pussycat — Mister Rogers' Neighborhood.

A Pittsburgh Trolley Sign.

Gateway Center Tulips.

The Women's Committee, Museum of Art, Carnegie Institute, annually decorate Christmas trees with a theme. The Gershwin tree, part of the music composers' group, was designed by Mrs. A. Reed Schroeder.

Cornflakes and Lady Elaine — Mister Rogers' Neighborhood

Puppets — X the Owl & Grandpère — Mister Rogers' Neighborhood

Good Ship Lollipop — Children's Sightseeing Boat

CAKES

TEXAS HOT COCOA CAKE
"A rich and spicy chocolate cake."

3 heaping tbsp. cocoa
¼ lb. butter
½ cup vegetable oil
1 cup water
2 cups sugar
2 cups Wondra Instant flour
½ cup buttermilk
2 eggs
1 tsp. baking soda
1 tsp. cinnamon
1 tsp. vanilla

Frosting:
1 stick butter
3 heaping tbsp. cocoa
6 tbsp. milk
1 box confectioner's sugar
nuts (optional)

Combine in saucepan cocoa, butter, oil and water. Bring to boil. Let cool. Combine sugar and flour in a large bowl. Pour cocoa mixture, when *cooled*, over flour and sugar; and beat till smooth. Combine buttermilk, eggs, soda, cinnamon and vanilla; then beat into above mixture. Grease and flour a 9 x 13″ pan; bake at 400° for 35-40 minutes.

Frosting: Start 10 minutes before baking is done.

Combine frosting ingredients in a pan, except confectioner's sugar, and heat until butter melts. Add confectioner's sugar. Stir well, then beat until

thick. Spoon frosting over hot cake. Top with nuts if desired.

Preparation: 45 min.
Baking: 35 - 40 min.

Serves: 10 - 12
Can freeze

Mrs. Rose Amatos

151

SERBIAN FAST CHOCOLATE CAKE

⅔ cup vegetable
  shortening (Crisco)
2 cups granulated sugar
2 tbsp. lemon juice
2 tsp. vanilla
3 cups flour
1 tsp. salt
2 tsp. baking soda
2 cups water
3 tbsp. cocoa

Icing:

3 tbsp. flour
¾ cup water
¾ cup shortening or
  butter
1 cup sugar
1 tsp. vanilla
1 tsp. lemon juice

Combine shortening and sugar until light and fluffy. Mix in lemon juice and vanilla. Stir together flour, salt, and baking soda. Add alternately with water to creamed mixture, beginning and ending with flour. Stir in cocoa. Pour batter into well greased baking pan 8 x 12 x 2 inches. Bake in preheated oven at 350° for 1 hour. Cool in pan and ice.

Icing: Cook flour and water in pan until thick. Beat shortening with sugar and remaining ingredients. Add cooked mixture and beat until fluffy.

Preparation:	30 min.	Easy	Serves: 12
Baking:	1 hour	Can do ahead	Can freeze

Mrs. Mildred Spudich

RUM CAKE

"So lightly flavored with rum, that even children love it!"

1 pkg. (2 layer) yellow cake mix
1 pkg. (3¾ oz.) instant vanilla
  pudding mix
½ cup pure vegetable oil
⅔ cup water
4 eggs
⅓ cup light rum

Glaze: ⅓ cup sugar
  2 tbsp. water
  2 tbsp. light rum
  1 tbsp. grated orange rind

Heat oven to 350°. Grease and flour 10" Bundt pan or 10" tube pan. Combine cake mix, instant pudding mix, oil, ⅔ cup water, eggs and ⅓ cup rum in large bowl. Blend in ingredients together on low speed. Beat at medium speed for 4 minutes. Turn into prepared pan. Bake 45 to 50 minutes or until cake springs back when lightly touched with fingertip.

Cool in pan 10 minutes. Remove from pan. Cool.

Glaze: Combine sugar, 2 tablespoons water, 2 tablespoons rum and orange rind. Simmer 5 minutes. Brush over warm cake; repeat once or twice while cake cools.

Preparation:	15 min.	Easy	Serves: 16
Baking:	45 - 50 min.	Can do ahead	Can freeze

Mrs. John A. Shoener

CHEESE CAKE

"Serve plain fresh strawberries with this."

Crust:
1½ cups graham
  cracker crumbs
4 tbsp. ground almonds
  or walnuts
2 tbsp. sugar
1 tsp. ground lemon
  peel
½ cup melted butter

Filling:
1½ lbs. soft cream cheese
1 cup sugar
1 tsp. vanilla
3 tsp. lemon juice
1 tsp. lemon rind
4 eggs

Topping:
1 pint ice-cold
  sour cream
½ cup sugar
½ tsp. vanilla
cinnamon

Combine crumbs, nuts, sugar, lemon peel; stir in butter until thoroughly blended. Press mixture firmly against bottom of 9" spring form pan. Bake in 350° oven for 10 minutes. In large bowl, beat cheese until creamy. At medium speed add sugar gradually, then vanilla, lemon juice and rind and blend well. Add eggs one at a time, and beat at medium speed for 10 minutes, until fluffy. Pour into pan. Bake at 350° for 35 minutes. Turn off heat and cool for 30 minutes in oven with door open. Combine sour cream, sugar and vanilla and whip for 10 minutes until foamy. Spoon over top of cake. Bake in 250° oven for 10 minutes. Sprinkle with cinnamon. Cool. Wrap and freeze. (To serve without freezing, refrigerate for 2 hours or more before unmolding.) Serving day: Remove from spring form pan and thaw in the refrigerator for 4 or 5 hours.

| Preparation: | 35 min. | Easy | Serves: 16-18 |
| Baking: | 45 min. | Must do ahead | Can freeze |

Mrs. Douglas E. Cox

PISTACHIO CAKE

"Different and very good!"

1 pkg. Duncan Hines Butter Cake
  mix
½ cup oil
4 eggs
1 cup sour cream
1 pkg. Pistachio Instant
  Pudding (Royal)

Filling:
½ cup sugar
1 tsp. cinnamon
½ cup nuts, chopped

Mix first 5 ingredients 5 minutes on medium speed — very thick mixture. Combine the filling ingredients. In a greased and floured Bundt or angel food pan, layer from bottom to top: 1st, ½ of batter; 2nd, ½ of filling; 3rd, rest of batter and 4th, rest of filling. Place cake in cold oven. Set oven at 350° and bake 1 hour.

| Preparation: | 15 min. | Easy | Serves: 12 - 15 |
| Baking: | 1 hour | Can do ahead | Can freeze |

Mrs. Jon E. McCarthy

APPLE CAKE
"Very moist cake with great flavor!"

2 cups sugar
1½ cups corn oil
3 eggs
2 tsp. vanilla
3 cups unsifted all-purpose
flour
1 tsp. baking soda
1 tsp. salt
¼ tsp. ground cloves
1 tsp. cinnamon
5 cups diced apples
1 cup chopped walnuts

Cream together sugar and corn oil. Add eggs, one at a time, and vanilla. Sift together flour, soda, salt, cloves and cinnamon. Add dry sifted mixture to apples and walnuts. Then add to creamed mixture. It will be difficult to stir and the end result will be a stiff doughy mixture. Bake in greased 9x13x2" pan at 325° for 55-60 minutes. Sprinkle with confectioners sugar. Serve warm with whipped cream or plain.

| Preparation: | 30 min. | Easy | Serves: 12 - 16 |
| Baking: | 55 - 60 min. | Can do ahead | Can freeze |

Mrs. James E. Cavalier

BLACKBERRY CAKE
"Try this with caramel icing."

1 cup shortening
1½ cups sugar
3 eggs
1 tsp. soda
3 cups flour
2 tsp. nutmeg
1½ cups blackberries,
canned or frozen

Grease and flour 2 8" or 9" layer pans. Cream shortening; add sugar and eggs. Sift together flour, soda and nutmeg. Add blackberries to creamed mixture. Add dry ingredients. Mix well. Pour into pans. Bake in moderate oven (350°) for 35 minutes or until done. Very good with caramel icing.

| Preparation: | 15 min. | Can do ahead | Can freeze |
| Baking: | 35 min. | | |

Mrs. W. Kendall Jones

POUND CAKE
"From a grandmother neighbor's old recipe. My husband's favorite."

2 sticks butter
5 whole eggs
2 cups sugar
2 cups flour
1 tsp. rum, vanilla, or
almond flavoring

Soften butter. Beat 1 minute. Add eggs, one at a time, beating 1 minute or more after each addition. Add sugar gradually, continue beating, and add flour, then flavoring. Bake in a tube pan, buttered and sprinkled with sugar, at 300° for 1½ to 1¾ hours. Keep door closed until done.

| Preparation: | 20 min. | Easy | Serves: 12 - 16 |
| Baking: | 1½ - 1¾ hours | Can do ahead | Can freeze |

Mrs. Richard Webster

SOUR CREAM POUND CAKE
"A very rich, moist cake."

3 cups flour
3 cups sugar
1 tsp. baking powder
½ lb. butter
6 eggs
½ pt. sour cream
1-2 tsp. vanilla

Mix all ingredients thoroughly. Turn into greased tube pan and bake at 350° for 1 hour.

| Preparation: | 10 min. | Easy | Serves: 12 - 16 |
| Baking: | 1 hour | Can do ahead | Can freeze |

Mrs. James Harris

COLD OVEN POUNDCAKE
"Easiest pound cake ever."

3 sticks butter
2¾ cups granulated sugar
5 eggs
3¾ cups sifted flour
⅛ tsp. salt
¼ tsp. baking powder
1 cup milk
1 tsp. vanilla

Cream butter and sugar; add eggs, one at a time; add sifted dry ingredients, alternating with milk and flavoring. Beat 1 minute and pour into well-greased tube pan. Put cake into cold oven, then turn oven on to 325° and bake for 1½ hours or until knife inserted is clean. Turn out after 10 minutes. When cool, put in air tight container. Serve the next day. It's good the first day, but super the next.

| Preparation: | 20 min. | Easy | Serves: 12 - 16 |
| Baking: | 1½ hours | Can do ahead | Can freeze |

Mrs. A. Reed Harper, Jr.

ORANGE CAKE
"A very easy cake akin to a light fruit cake. Good family dessert."

1 large California orange
1 cup raisins
½ cup shortening
1 cup sugar
2 beaten eggs
2 cups flour
1 tsp. salt
1 tsp. baking soda
1 cup milk
chopped nuts
cinnamon
sugar

Squeeze juice from the orange and reserve. Grind the orange skin with the raisins through a food chopper.

Cream shortening, add sugar. Add eggs. Add flour, salt and soda, which have been sifted together, alternately with milk. Fold in raisin-orange mixture.

Bake in greased tube pan at 350° for 40 minutes. Remove from pan and cool. After the cake has cooled, pour the reserved juice over the top. Sprinkle with nuts, cinnamon and sugar.

| Preparation: | 15 min. | Easy | Serves: 12 |
| Cooking: | 45 - 50 min. | Can do ahead | Can freeze |

Mrs. Foster A. Stewart

GATEAU HELENE
"Great dessert for men."

2 eggs
¼ tsp. salt
1 cup sugar
1 tsp. rum flavoring
½ cup milk
1 tbsp. butter
1 cup flour, sifted
1 tsp. baking powder
apricot preserves
whipping cream
Coffee-Rum Syrup
1 cup sugar
1 cup strong, fresh coffee
¼ cup rum
Rum-Cream Filling
⅓ cup sugar
¼ cup flour
⅛ tsp. salt
1 cup milk
2 egg yolks or 1 whole
  egg, slightly beaten
1 tsp. rum

Beat eggs until thick and light. Beat in salt, sugar and rum flavoring. Heat milk and butter to boiling point. Add to creamed mixture. Sift flour and baking powder, and beat into above mixture. Turn into a greased and floured cake pan, 9 x 1½". Bake in a preheated 350° oven for 35-40 minutes. Remove from pan. Spoon all of the Coffee-Rum Syrup slowly over entire surface of the warm cake. Let stand until cold. Split carefully into 2 layers; fill with Rum-Cream Filling. Garnish top with apricot preserves and whipping cream (put through ribbon tip of pastry tube).
Coffee-Rum Syrup: In a saucepan, combine sugar and coffee over low heat until sugar dissolves. Boil 3 minutes; cool. Add ¼ cup rum.
Rum-Cream Filling: Combine sugar, flour and salt in top of double boiler. Add milk; stir over low heat until thickened. Cook over hot water, covered, for 10 minutes. Add a little of the hot mixture to egg; combine with remaining hot mixture. Cook 2 minutes longer, stirring constantly. Chill. Add rum.

Preparation: 2 hours   Can do ahead   Serves: 16
Baking: 35-40 min.

Mrs. A. M. Aksoy

STRAWBERRY JAM CUPCAKES
"Good enough without frosting."

1 cup sugar
½ cup butter or margarine
2 eggs, beaten
2 cups sifted flour
1 tsp. cinnamon
1 tsp. nutmeg
1 tsp. baking soda
½ cup sour milk
1 cup strawberry jam

Cream sugar and butter until fluffy, add eggs and blend. Sift flour and spices, add alternately with sour milk. Add strawberry jam. Put in buttered and floured muffin pan. Bake 20-25 minutes at 375°.

Preparation: 15 min.   Easy   Yield: 2 dozen
Baking: 25 min.   Can do ahead   Can freeze

Mrs. Allen T. Shoener

CALIFORNIA DATE CAKE
"Moist and delicious!"

1 cup chopped dates
1 tsp. soda
1 cup boiling water
½ cup shortening
1 cup sugar
2 eggs well-beaten
1½ cups sifted flour
¼ tsp. salt

Topping:
1 6-oz. pkg. chocolate
  chips
½ cup sugar
½ cup chopped pecans

Mix dates, soda and boiling water. Let stand to cool. Cream shortening and sugar. Add eggs. Sift flour and salt and add to creamed mixture. Blend in dates. Pour into 9 x 13" well-greased pan.
Combine topping and sprinkle on top before baking. Bake at 350° for 35 minutes.

Preparation: 30 min.	Easy	Serves: 12-15
Baking: 35 min.	Can do ahead	Freeze

Mrs. Richard B. Lord

FRUIT CAKE
"A marvelous white fruitcake, originally from Virginia."

1 lb. butter or
  margarine
2 cups sugar
1 dozen eggs
3 cups flour
1 tsp. baking powder
1 tbsp. vanilla
1 tbsp. lemon
1 tbsp. black walnut
  flavoring
1 tbsp. almond flavoring
1 tbsp. cinnamon
1 tbsp. nutmeg
1 No. 2 can crushed
  pineapple, undrained
1 cup flour
1 lb. white raisins
2 lbs. mixed fruit
1 lb. Brazil nuts
1 lb. English walnuts
¼ lb. almonds
¼ lb. green cherries
¼ lb. red cherries
1 slice red pineapple
1 slice green pineapple
English walnuts

Cream butter and sugar. Add eggs and flour sifted with baking powder. To the batter add the vanilla, lemon, black walnut, almond, cinnamon and nutmeg seasonings. Add the crushed pineapple and mix well. Add 1 cup flour to raisins, mixed fruit, Brazil nuts, walnuts, and almonds. Combine the batter and fruit mixture. Grease 3 pans well and line with wax paper. Divide the batter between the 3 pans and cover with wax paper to prevent burning during the baking. Bake at 250° for about 3 hours. During the second hour place a pan of water on the rack above the cakes. Trim the tops of the cakes with the red and green cherries and pineapple, and the walnuts.

The Committee

Preparation: 1 hour
Baking: 3 hours

Yield: 3 cakes
5¾" x 9½" x 3"

BRANDIED FRUIT CAKE

"A traditional dark fruitcake."

¾ lb. candied pineapple,
  shredded
¾ lb. golden raisins
½ lb. candied red cherries,
  halved
½ lb. candied green cherries,
  halved
½ lb. seeded raisins
½ lb. currants
5 oz. candied orange peel,
  chopped
5 oz. candied lemon peel,
  chopped
½ cup cognac
4 oz. slivered blanched
  almonds
4 oz. pecans, coarsely
  chopped
½ cup sifted flour
½ cup butter
1 cup dark brown sugar,
  packed
1 cup sugar
5 eggs
1 tbsp. milk
1 tsp. almond extract
1½ cups sifted flour
½ tsp. baking powder
½ tsp. ground cinnamon
¼ tsp. ground cloves
¼ tsp. ground mace
additional cognac
almond paste (optional)

Prepare all fruits and place in bowl. Pour ½ cup cognac over fruits. Cover bowl and let fruits stand 1 or 2 days. Add slivered almonds, chopped pecans and ½ cup flour. Mix thoroughly. Cream butter and beat in sugars gradually. Add eggs one at a time, beating well after each addition. Stir in milk and almond extract. Sift flour with baking powder, cinnamon, cloves and mace. Add to creamed mixture gradually, blending thoroughly. Pour batter over fruits and nuts in bowl. Blend mixture thoroughly with hands. Butter two 9 x 5 x 3" baking pans. Line with brown or waxed paper and butter again. Divide batter between 2 pans, pressing it down firmly in the middle and at the corners. Bake in 275° oven for about 3 hours, or until cakes test done. Cool in pans about 30 minutes. Remove cakes to racks. Peel off paper and cool thoroughly. Wrap in clean cheesecloth soaked with cognac. Store in tightly-covered containers in cool place. Sprinkle cheese cloth with additional cognac several times a week. Let cakes age at least 6 weeks. To serve spread top of cakes with almond paste if desired. Let paste dry and spread with confectioner's sugar glaze.

Must do ahead   **Yield: 2 loaves**

Susan Spengler

PUMPKIN CAKE WITH CREAM CHEESE ICING

"A rich cake for winter treats."

2 cups sugar
4 eggs
1 cup salad oil
2 cups pumpkin
2 cups all-purpose flour
2 tsp. cinnamon
2 tsp. baking soda
½ tsp. salt

Icing:

1 stick butter
1 box powdered sugar
8 oz. softened cream cheese
2 tsp. vanilla
1 cup chopped nuts to
  sprinkle on top

Combine all ingredients in large bowl. Turn into large 13 x 9" pan, greased and floured. Bake in 350° oven, 35 minutes or more.

Icing: Blend all ingredients in mixer and spread on top of cooled cake. Sprinkle nuts on top.

Preparation:	15 min.	Easy	Serves: 8 - 10
Baking:	35 - 45 min.	Can do ahead	Can freeze

Mrs. R. Allen Moulton, Jr.

PIES

DOWN-UNDER APPLE PIE

"The favorite apple pie in our house. Originally from Australia."

6 tart cooking apples
1 cup sugar
2 tbsp. flour
1 tsp. ground cinnamon
1 tsp. grated lemon peel
⅛ tsp. ground cloves
⅛ tsp. salt
a 9" pie plate, lined with
  your favorite pastry, the
  edges fluted

Topping:

½ cup flour
¼ cup sugar
⅛ tsp. salt
½ cup grated Cheddar cheese
¼ cup melted butter
sour cream

Peel, quarter, core and slice thinly the apples. Mix the sugar, flour, cinnamon, lemon peel, cloves and salt; and toss the apple slices lightly in this mixture. Arrange the apples, overlapping the slices, in the pastry-lined pan.

Topping: Combine the flour, sugar, salt and cheese. Mix in the melted butter. Sprinkle the cheese crumbs over the apples. Bake at 400° for 40 minutes, or until the topping and crust are golden brown. Let the pie cool on a wire rack and serve it warm, topping each slice with a generous spoonful of sour cream.

| Preparation: | 30 min. |
| Baking: | 40 min. |

Serves: 6-8

Mrs. Thomas M. Garrett

MER'S FAMILY PIE CRUST

"A flavorful old family recipe."

1 cup shortening
2½ cups flour
1 tbsp. sugar
1 tsp. salt
dash nutmeg
juice of ½ lemon
1 egg
about ⅔ cup milk

Cut shortening into flour, salt, sugar and nutmeg until it is in lima bean size pieces. (Add up to ½ cup flour extra, if needed.) Add juice of ½ lemon to dry ingredients.

In a measuring cup, break egg and add enough milk to make ⅔ cup. Beat with fork and add enough of this mixture to hold dry ingredients together. Do not overmix. Roll out.

Preparation: 30 min.   Can do ahead   Yield: 1 2-crust pie
                                         Can freeze

Mrs. Dennis Leonetti

SWEDISH COCONUT TARTS

pastry for 2 crust pie
3 beaten eggs
1½ cups sugar
½ cup butter, melted
1 tbsp. lemon juice
1 tsp. vanilla
1 can flaked coconut
  (3½ oz.)
whipped cream

Prepare pastry dough. For tart shells, roll ⅛" thick on lightly floured surface. Cut in eight 5 or 6 inch circles. Line eight fluted tart pans with pastry. Combine eggs, sugar, melted butter, lemon juice, coconut and vanilla. Pour into unbaked tart shells. Bake at 350° oven for 40 minutes, or until knife inserted in center comes out clean. Cool. Top each tart with sweetened whipped cream, if desired.

Preparation: 20 min.   Easy   Serves: 8
Baking: 40 min.   Can do ahead

Mrs. John W. Gould

CHOCOLATE MARSHMALLOW CREAM PIE

16 graham crackers
¼ cup butter, melted
32 large marshmallows
½ cup milk
½ large Hershey bar
  (7.25 oz.)
½ pt. whipping cream

Mix graham crackers and butter and put into pie plate. Refrigerate for 10 minutes. Melt marshmallows and milk in double boiler. Add Hershey bar, let cool. Whip cream, add marshmallow mix to it, and pour into pie crust. Chill for 2 hours.

Preparation: 30 min.   Easy   Serves: 6-8
Refrigeration: 2 hours   Must do ahead Can freeze

Mrs. L. J. Barnhorst

COFFEE TOFFEE PIE
"Rich and delicious."

1 cup flour
½ tsp. salt
½ cup shortening
¼ cup brown sugar, packed
¾ cup ground walnuts
1 tbsp. ice water
½ cup butter
½ cup sugar
1 sq. melted unsweetened
  chocolate
2 tbsp. instant coffee
2 eggs
2 cups heavy cream
2 tbsp. instant coffee
½ cup confectioner's sugar
1 tbsp. dark rum

Combine flour and salt in bowl, cut in shortening; lightly stir in brown sugar and walnuts. Sprinkle in the ice water and mix quickly. Pack mixture in 10" pie pan. Bake at 375° for 15 minutes, or until firm. Beat butter until creamy, add sugar and beat until fluffy. Blend in chocolate and coffee. Add 1 egg, beat 5 minutes; add second egg and beat 5 minutes more. Pour into pie shell. Refrigerate, covered, overnight. Combine the last 4 ingredients, refrigerate 15 minutes covered. Beat until stiff, swirl on pie. Chill 2 hours.

Preparation:	45 min.	Must do ahead	Serves: 8
Baking:	15 min.		

Mrs. Irwin S. Terner

LAYERED LEMON PIE
"An original masterpiece."

Crust:
20 chocolate wafers
¼ cup butter

Filling:
¼ cup butter
¹/₃ cup lemon juice
¾ cup sugar
dash salt
3 slightly beaten eggs
1 pt. vanilla ice cream

Crust:
Crumble chocolate wafers, or pulverize in blender. Mix with melted butter and pat into pie shell. Bake 8 minutes at 350°.
Filling:
Melt butter, stir in lemon juice, sugar, dash salt. Stir to dissolve. Pour ½ into 3 slightly beaten eggs. Return eggs to rest of butter mixture and cook over medium heat until thick. Chill.

Divide 1 pint vanilla ice cream in half. Put half into cookie crust. Pour half lemon mixture over. Freeze. Repeat layers. Freeze. Garnish with cookie crumbs or chocolate curls. Let stand 10 minutes at room temperature before serving.

Preparation:	45 min.	Easy	Serves: 8
Baking:	8 min.	Must do ahead	Freeze
Freezing:	30 min.		

Mrs. Philip Beard

CREME DE MENTHE PIE

24 Oreo cookies
¼ cup melted butter
1 pt. whipping cream
7 oz. jar marshmallow
  creme
¼ cup Creme de Menthe

Place cookies in 2 large baggies. Tie tightly and crush with rolling pin. Mix cookies with butter and press into large, flat, Pyrex baking dish. Put aside a handful, to sprinkle on top. Whip cream, set aside. Whip marshmallow and Creme de Menthe together. Fold into whipped cream. Pour into dish. Cover with Saran Wrap and freeze. Cut in small squares to serve. Remove 5 minutes ahead of time.

Preparation: 15 min.	Easy	Serves: 6-8
Freezing: 3 hours	Must do ahead	Must freeze

Mrs. John McLean, Jr.

STRAWBERRY PIE

2 8" pie shells, baked
2 qts. strawberries
sugar, to sprinkle
4 tbsp. cornstarch
juice of 1 lemon
1 tbsp. butter
2 cups sugar
½ pt. heavy cream, whipped

Bake 2 8" pie shells and cool them. Wash berries and drain on paper towels. Cover the bottom of the pie shells with ½ of the berries, sliced, if large. Sugar them lightly. Crush rest of the berries and mix with cornstarch, lemon juice, butter and 2 cups sugar. Cook until thick. Cool. Pour into shells and cover with whipped cream. Refrigerate.

Preparation: 30 min.	Must do ahead	Yield: 2 8" pies
Cooking: 10 min.		

Mrs. Richard Marsh

PEACH POLKA DOT PIE

"Excellent! Men ask for seconds!"

Pie Crust:
1 cup + 2 tbsp. flour
1 tbsp. sugar
¼ tsp. salt
⅓ cup salad oil
1½ tbsp. milk

Filling:
4-6 peaches
¼ cup flour
¾ cup sugar
2 tsp. cinnamon
1 cup whipping cream

Mix dry ingredients into a 9" pie plate. Mix oil and milk well with fork, then pour over flour mixture, mix well and pat around pie plate to form a crust. Bake at 425° for 5 minutes to set the crust. *Filling:* Peel peaches, cut in half, set on pie crust with cut side down. Mix 3 dry ingredients together and add unwhipped cream. Blend well and pour over peaches. Bake 45 minutes at 425° or until custard is set. Cool.

Preparation: 20 min.	Easy	Serves: 6-8
Baking: 50 min.		

Mrs. William S. Pampel, Jr.

LEMON PIE

4 eggs
¼ cup lemon juice
grated rind of 1 lemon
3 tbsp. water
½ cup sugar
another ½ cup sugar
baked pie shell

Separate eggs, putting whites into mixing bowl and yolks in top of double boiler. Beat yolks until thick. Add lemon juice, rind, water, and ½ cup sugar. Cook over water stirring until thick. Remove from hot water. Now beat whites until partly stiff. Add ½ cup sugar, gradually, and continue beating into a soft fine meringue. Fold the meringue into the cooked lemon mixture. When evenly blended, heap into baked pie shell. Put under broiler for a few minutes until light brown — carefully.

Preparation: 40 min.   Easy   Serves: 6-8
Baking: 3 min.   Can do ahead

Mrs. Scott Sawhill

PECAN PIE
"My grandmother's recipe!"

dough for 9" pie crust
4 eggs
1 lb. light brown sugar
¾ cup water
¼ cup soft butter or
  margarine
1 tsp. vanilla extract
pecan halves

Beat eggs in small mixing bowl until frothy. Set aside. Combine sugar and water in 2 quart saucepan. Place over moderate heat, stirring until sugar dissolves. Bring to a full boil and cook for 3 minutes. Gradually stir hot syrup into eggs. Blend butter and extract into mixture. Turn filling into pastry-lined plate. Arrange pecans on filling in desired pattern. Bake in moderate oven 350° about 1 hour until set. Remove to cooling rack.

Preparation: 10 min.   Easy   Serves: 10-12
Baking: 1 hour

Mrs. Jack M. Maxwell

MILLIONAIRE PIE
"Wow! Easy, too."

1 baked pie shell
8 oz. cream cheese, chilled
2 cups powdered sugar
1 cup drained crushed
  pineapple, chilled
1 box Dream Whip (1 env.)
  or 1½ cups Cool Whip
nuts (optional)

Combine chilled cheese, sugar, chilled pineapple and Dream Whip. Put in pie shell. Add nuts to top if desired. Chill.

Preparation: 10 min.   Easy   Serves: 6-8
                         Must do ahead

Mrs. Ralph Thorne

LIME PIE

"A favorite of the Associate Conductor."

1 tbsp. gelatin
½ cup sugar
¼ tsp. salt
4 egg yolks
½ cup lime juice
  (approx. 3 limes)
¼ cup water
1 tsp. grated lime peel
a touch of green food coloring
4 egg whites
½ cup sugar
1 cup whipping cream
1 9" pastry shell, baked

Mix gelatin, ½ cup sugar and salt in sauce pan. Beat yolks, juice and water together and blend with dry ingredients in pan. Cook over medium heat to boiling point. Remove from heat, add peel and coloring. Chill 1 hour, stirring occasionally, until mixture mounds. (Watch carefully, as once it starts to set it does so rapidly.) Beat egg whites into soft peaks, add sugar gradually and beat into stiff peaks.

Fold gelatin mixture into whites. Fold in whipped cream. Pour into pie shell. Chill. Before serving, you may decorate the pie with whipped cream, lime slices and grated lime peel.

Preparation: 20 min.   **Must do ahead**   **Serves: 6-8**

Mrs. Donald Johanos

WHIPPED CREAM ANGEL PIE

"Very easy, very pretty, very delicious."

4 egg whites
½ tsp. baking powder
pinch salt
¾ cup sugar
½ cup powdered sugar
1 tsp. vanilla
1 tsp. water
1 tsp. vinegar
½ pt. whipping cream
vanilla
sugar
½ square baking chocolate,
  grated

Beat egg whites until stiff, adding baking powder and salt. Sift sugars together and add very gradually to egg whites. Beat at high speed to very stiff peaks. Add vanilla, water and vinegar, and beat a few more minutes. Spread on the bottom of a 9" glass pie plate which has been well buttered. Bake at 275° for 1 hour. Remove from oven and let cool. Crust will crack, but do not be alarmed. When meringue crust is cold, add whipped cream flavored with vanilla and sugar. Spread on top of meringue. Then sprinkle chocolate on top and chill.

Preparation: 20 min.   **Easy**   **Serves: 6-8**
Baking: 1 hour   **Must do ahead**

Mrs. Richard K. Means

BLUEBERRY PIE

Crust
1½ cups flour
½ tsp. salt
½ tsp. grated lemon peel
½ cup shortening (Fluffo)
4 or 5 tbsp. water
1 tbsp. lemon juice

Filling
1 cup sugar
3 tbsp. flour
⅛ tsp. salt
½ tsp. grated lemon peel
1 tbsp. lemon juice
4 cups fresh blueberries
3-5 tbsp. margarine

Mix flour, salt and lemon peel. Cut in shortening with pastry blender. Add water and lemon juice by tablespoons. Mix until dough just adheres. Roll out on floured cutting board. Line pie pan. Combine sugar, flour and salt. Then add lemon peel, juice and berries. Fill pastry-lined pan with filling and dot with 3 to 4 tablespoons margarine. Adjust top crust. Bake at 450° for 10 minutes, then reduce heat to 350° for 30 minutes.

Preparation: 25 min.   Can do ahead   Serves: 6-8
Baking: 40 min.   Can freeze

Mrs. John M. Webb

FRENCH CHOCOLATE SILK PIE
"A never-fail dessert."

Crust:
½ box vanilla wafers,
  crushed in blender
1 cup chopped walnuts
3 tbsp. butter, melted

Filling:
½ lb. butter
1 cup confectioner's sugar
3 egg yolks, beaten
1½ squares unsweetened
  chocolate, melted
2 tsp. vanilla
3 egg whites, stiffly beaten
½ pt. whipping cream

Crust:
Combine ingredients and bake in 8" pie pan for 8 minutes at 375°. Cool.
Filling:
Cream butter and sugar. Beat in egg yolks, chocolate, and vanilla. Fold in whites. Fill cooled pie crust and refrigerate overnight.

Top with whipped cream. To make a "higher" pie, use the ingredients in the recipe 1½ times.

Preparation: 15 min.   Easy   Serves: 8-10
Baking: 8 min.   Must do ahead

Mrs. Peter E. Boorn

BRANDY ALEXANDER PIE

"Utterly delicious."

1 9" graham cracker crust,
  baked
1 env. unflavored gelatin
½ cup cold water
²/₃ cup sugar
⅛ tsp. salt
3 eggs, separated
¼ cup cognac
¼ cup creme de cacao
2 cups heavy cream,
  whipped
chocolate curls

Sprinkle gelatin over cold water in a saucepan. Add ⅓ cup sugar, salt and egg yolks. Stir to blend. Heat mixture over low heat, then stir in liqueurs. Cool. Refrigerate until partially set. Beat egg whites until stiff. Gradually beat in remaining sugar. Fold into gelatin mixture. Fold in half of whipped cream. Turn into crust; refrigerate several hours or overnight. Garnish with remaining whipped cream and chocolate curls.

Preparation: 40 min.

Easy
Must do ahead

Serves: 6-8

Mrs. Paul B. Reinhold

ANGEL PIE

"A favorite in Sewickley."

3 egg whites
1 tsp. baking powder
pinch of salt
1 cup sugar
1 cup chopped walnuts
½ cup cracker crumbs

Filling:

4 egg yolks
½ cup sugar
3 tbsp. lemon juice
2 tbsp. lemon rind, grated
1 cup whipped cream

Beat egg whites until stiff. Add baking powder, salt and sugar. Beat again. Fold in nuts and cracker crumbs. Spread in well-greased pie pan. Bake at 300° for 40 minutes.

Filling: Beat egg yolks. Combine with sugar, lemon juice and rind. Cook in double boiler until thickened. Cool. Whip the cream. Spread ½ of the cream on meringue, then put on filling. Top with remaining whipped cream. Chill for 24 hours.

Preparation: 30 min.
Baking: 40 min.

Must do ahead

Serves: 6-8

Lucille Smith

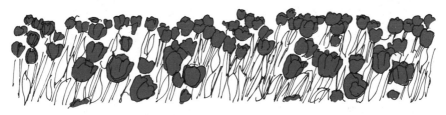

167

DESSERTS

APPLE CRUNCH

"Delicious and easy."

7-9 tart apples
1 cup granulated sugar
1 cup brown sugar
1 cup flour
½ cup butter
¼ tsp. salt
¼ tsp. vanilla
½ cup pecans (optional)

Slice apples and place in casserole. Stir sugar into sliced apples.

Combine remaining ingredients and pour over apples. DO NOT STIR.

Bake at 350° for 1 hour.

Preparation: 45 min.	Easy	Serves: 6
Baking: 1 hour	Can do ahead	

Mrs. Ray C. Singley

LEMON AMBROSIA
"Perfect dessert for a ladies luncheon."

6 eggs, separated
¾ cup sugar
juice & grated rind of
  2 lemons
1 small pkg. lemon jello
scant cup boiling water
¾ cup sugar
2 pkg. plain ladyfingers
½ cup heavy cream
vanilla
coconut, toasted

Put yolks in double boiler with sugar, lemon juice and grated rind. Cook until thick, stirring constantly. Cool. Meanwhile, dissolve jello in scant cup of boiling water. Cool. Add to egg yolk mixture. Beat egg whites with ¾ cup sugar. Fold into egg yolk mixture. Line 8" springform pan on sides and bottom with ladyfingers, split in half. Pour lemon mixture into pan. Refrigerate overnight. Before serving, whip cream with vanilla to flavor. Cover top of ambrosia with whipped cream and sprinkle with toasted coconut.

Preparation: 30 min.	Easy	Serves: 12
Cooking: 10 min.	Must do ahead	

Mrs. Ruth Proper

FRUIT DESSERT
"A wonderful combination of textures and flavors."

2 cups graham cracker crumbs
1 stick margarine
½ cup granulated sugar
8 oz. Philadelphia cream cheese
2 tbsp. milk
1 cup confectioner's sugar
1 pkg. Dream Whip
1 cup water
1 cup sugar
2 tbsp. cornstarch
1 pkg. strawberry jello
1 qt. fresh strawberries, cleaned
  & sliced

Crust: Blend cracker crumbs, margarine and granulated sugar. Spread in a 9 x 12" pan and bake for 10-12 minutes at 350°. Cool.

Cream filling: Blend cream cheese and milk, then fold in confectioner's sugar. Prepare Dream Whip as directed, and fold into cheese mixture. After graham cracker crust has cooled, spread cream cheese filling over crust.

Strawberry topping: Cook water, sugar and cornstarch until thick. Remove from stove and stir jello into it until it dissolves. Add fresh sliced strawberries. Pour on top of cream cheese filling and refrigerate until jelled. Any fruit may be used with this.

Preparation: 25 min.	Easy	Serves: 12
Cooking: 20 min.	Must do ahead	

Mrs. B. F. Jones, III

CHOCOLATE LADYFINGER DESSERT
"Everyone will want seconds."

2½ pkg. ladyfingers
8 oz. Baker's semi-sweet
chocolate
4 tbsp. boiling water
6 eggs, separated
3 tbsp. powdered sugar
2 tsp. vanilla
Topping — whipped cream
flavored with vanilla &
powdered sugar or Cool
Whip

Line a round, deep bowl with wax paper, then line with ladyfingers.

Melt chocolate with 4 tbsp. boiling water over very low heat. Cool a bit, then beat in the 6 egg yolks one at a time. Add sugar and vanilla.

Fold in the beaten egg whites.

Pour some of the chocolate mixture over the ladyfingers. Then put another layer of ladyfingers on top. Continue layers using remainder of chocolate mixture and ladyfingers, ending with ladyfingers. Cover with wax paper and a plate that will fit snugly. Leave in refrigerator overnight. To serve — turn out and cover with the whipped cream topping or Cool Whip.

Preparation: 25 min.   Easy   Serves: 10 - 12
                                Can do ahead

Mrs. Robert A. McKean, Jr.

MARVELOUS RICE PUDDING
"You may want to double this recipe."

½ cup seedless raisins
2 tbsp. rum
1 tsp. lemon juice
grated rind of 1 lemon
¼ cup rice
2 cups milk
¼ tsp. salt
2 tbsp. butter
2 eggs, separated
⅓ cup sugar
⅛ tsp. nutmeg

Soak raisins in rum, lemon juice and rind for at least 2 hours, preferably overnight.

Put rice, milk and salt in double boiler and cook 1 hour, stirring gently with a fork from time to time. When rice is done, take it off the stove and stir in butter. Beat egg yolks slightly and stir in a little of the hot mixture. Then combine the two mixtures and add sugar, nutmeg and raisins.

Set pan in cold water to cool. Beat egg whites until stiff. Mix in cooled rice mixture and pour into a greased casserole. Set casserole in a pan of hot water and bake at 325° for 30 minutes.

Preparation: 1 hour   Can do ahead   Serves: 4
Baking: 30 min.

Mrs. Foster A. Stewart

SIM'S DELIGHT

"Aptly named — a truly delightful old family recipe."

2 white cake layers
  or lady fingers
vanilla ice cream,
  softened
macaroons
eggnog laced with brandy
Angostura bitters (optional)

Put a layer of cake or lady fingers in a deep oblong or round mold. Put a layer of ice cream on top. Do this at least one more time, or more depending on the depth of the dish. Refrigerate 6 to 8 hours or store in freezer.

Remove before serving so that it can be sliced easily. Heat and pulverize macaroons to scatter over the top after unmolding. Pour eggnog over top when ready to serve. Pass additional eggnog separately. Angostura bitters may also be passed separately at table.

Preparation: 20 min.   Easy   Serves: 8-10
                               Must do ahead   Can freeze

Mrs. Henry Oliver

GALA GRASSHOPPER MOLD

"A frozen molded dessert."

2½ cups miniature marshmallows
1 1-lb. 4-oz. can pineapple
  chunks (drain & place juice
  in pan)
⅓ cup Creme de Menthe
green food coloring
2 egg whites
2 tsp. sugar
2 cups whipping cream or
  1 small container Cool
  Whip & 1 cup whipping
  cream
cherries & pineapple chunks

Add marshmallows to syrup drained from pineapple. Place over low heat until completely melted. Remove from heat and blend in the Creme de Menthe and 5 drops of green food coloring. Chill until mixture begins to thicken. Beat egg whites until they hold peaks, add the sugar and beat until stiff. Beat cream until stiff. Fold egg whites and cream into mixture, blending well, fold in pineapple chunks. Turn into a 2½-quart mold.

Freeze until firm. When ready to serve unmold and garnish with cherries and pineapple chunks.

Preparation: 45 min.   Must do ahead   Serves: 10
                                                      Freeze

Rose Amatos

171

CRANBERRY FRAPPE
"A light summer dessert."

1 pkg. plain gelatine
1 cup cold water
1 lb. fresh cranberries
2½ cups sugar
4 tbsp. lemon juice
few grains salt
1 beaten egg white

Soak gelatine in 1 cup cold water for 5 minutes. Cook cranberries in 3 cups water until soft. Force thru strainer. Add sugar, lemon juice and salt. Bring to boil, then cool and add gelatine. Partially freeze and then add 1 beaten egg white and freeze.

Preparation:	30 min.	Easy	Serves: 6
Cooking:	20 min.	Must do ahead	Freeze

Mrs. Allan W. Beatty

MIDSUMMER BERRIES
"Terrific summer dessert."

1 10-oz. pkg. Lorna Doones
¾ cup butter
1 cup confectioner's sugar
2 eggs
⅓ cup chopped walnuts
1 qt. fresh raspberries or
   blueberries
1 cup whipped cream
   (unsweetened)

Roll cookies into crumbs. Cover bottom of 9" pan with half the crumbs. Cream the butter and the sugar, and add eggs 1 at a time, beating after each addition. Spread the butter mixture over crumbs, then sprinkle with nuts and top with berries. Spread with whipped cream and top with remaining crumbs. Chill 2 hours or more. Cut into squares.

Preparation:	45 min.	Must do ahead	Serves: 9 - 12

Mrs. Kenneth E. Johns, Jr.

MIXED FRUIT CASSEROLE

1 orange
1 lemon
½ cup light brown sugar
¼ tsp. ground nutmeg
1 small can apricots
1 small can pineapple tidbits
1 small can sliced peaches
1 small can pitted black cherries
sour cream

Grate rind from lemon and orange. Add brown sugar with nutmeg. Cut orange and lemon in very thin slices. Drain and combine fruits. Butter 1-quart casserole and arrange fruits in layers, sprinkling each layer with some of the brown sugar mixture. Bake 30 minutes at 350°. Serve with spoonful of sour cream on top.

Preparation:	20 min.	Easy	Serves: 4 - 5
Cooking:	30 min.	Can do ahead	

Mrs. Thomas Debevoise

APRICOT ANNIE

"This looks and tastes like a lot more work."

1 small box dried apricots
1 cup sugar
1 cup heavy cream, whipped
1 package ladyfingers
1 tbsp. Grand Marnier (optional)
  (If used, add to pulp mix &
  fold into cream)

Cook apricots and strain. Leave 6 to 8 in strainer to dry out a bit to use for garnish. Mash enough for 1 cup pulp. Add sugar. Fold into cream which has been whipped. Line sherbet dishes or dessert dishes with ladyfinger halves. Fill with mixture. Garnish with reserved halves. Chill.

Preparation: 10 - 15 min.   Easy   Yield: 6
                                Must do ahead

The Committee

BENZ á l'ORANGE

"Keep this in your freezer for unexpected guests."

½ gal. vanilla ice cream,
  softened
12 oz. frozen orange juice
  concentrate, partially thawed
½ cup brandy or Cointreau

Stir all together and refreeze. Cover tightly.

Preparation: 5 min.   Must do ahead   Yield: ½ gal.
                                          Must freeze

Mrs. Ralph Benz, Jr.

FRENCH PUDDING

"An easy, cool summer dessert."

1½ cups vanilla wafer crumbs
½ cup butter
1½ cups powdered sugar
2 eggs
1 tsp. vanilla
½ pt. whipping cream
1 large can crushed pineapple
  (drain well)
1 cup chopped pecans

Butter 8" square pyrex dish — press 1 cup vanilla wafer crumbs on bottom. Cream butter and sugar, add eggs and cream until fluffy, add vanilla. Spread on top of crumbs for first layer. Whip cream (add a little sugar to sweeten slightly). Spread on top of first layer. Add layer of crushed pineapple. Sprinkle top with remaining ½ cup crumbs. Top with chopped nuts. Refrigerate overnight or until firm enough to cut into squares.

Preparation: 25 min.   Easy   Serves: 10 - 12
                          Must do ahead

Mrs. Charles Lang

BASIC HOMEMADE ICE CREAM

for a 1 gal. electric freezer:
3 eggs
2 qts. half & half
¼ tsp. salt
3 tbsp. vanilla
3 cups sugar (more if fruit
  is fresh)
1 pt. coffee cream
2 lbs. crushed canned
  pineapple in heavy syrup
  or 4-5 cups mashed strawberries or peaches

Beat the 3 eggs in a large bowl. Add 1 quart of the half & half and beat to homogenize. Add salt, vanilla and sugar. Stir. Pour into freezer container. Add 2nd quart of half & half, the coffee cream and the fruit. Taste and add more sugar if needed. The freezing lessens the sugar taste. Make it *very* sweet if fresh fruit is used. May be frozen but better eaten immediately.

Preparation: 45 min.

Yield: 1 gal.
Can freeze

John S. Liggett, M.D.

HOMEMADE CHOCOLATE ICE CREAM BASE

electric or hand freezer
5 cups milk
5 squares unsweetened
  chocolate, melted
2½ cups sugar
5 tbsp. flour
¾ tsp. salt
4 eggs, slightly beaten
5 cups cream (coffee cream,
  or 3 cups whipping cream & 2
  cups coffee cream)
2 tsp. vanilla

Scald milk over low heat. Stir in melted chocolate. Combine sugar, flour and salt in bowl. Add eggs and mix well. Pour hot milk over egg mixture carefully, stirring constantly. Cook over low heat until mixture coats a spoon. Chill in refrigerator. Follow the directions on your electric or hand freezer, using the cream and vanilla.

Preparation: 30-45 min.   Easy

Serves: 12-16

Mrs. Robert G. Morrell

TRICKY TORTE

1 Sara Lee pound cake,
  cooled, not frozen
1 6-oz. pkg. chocolate bits
½ pt. sour cream
1 cup slivered almonds,
  sautéed

Slice pound cake into 7 layers while cake is cool from the refrigerator. Melt chocolate bits and stir in sour cream. Evenly frost all layers includ- ing top layer. Top with sautéed almonds, pressing lightly so they will not fall off when cake is sliced. Refrigerate. Let stand at room temperature awhile before serving.

Preparation: 15 min.   Easy
                              Must do ahead

Serves: 6 - 8

Mrs. G. Dwight Moore

TORTE

"A heavenly dessert."

6 egg whites
2 tsp. vanilla
½ tsp. cream of tartar
dash of salt
2 cups sugar
6 or more ozs. English
  toffee bars (Heath), crushed
2 cups heavy cream,
  whipped

Have egg whites at room temperature. Add vanilla, cream of tartar and salt. Beat to soft peaks, gradually add sugar and beat to stiff peaks. Cut 2 9" circles of brown paper, place on cookie sheets and cover each with half the meringue mixture. Bake at 275° for 1 hour, then let cool in oven.

Combine whipped cream and crushed toffee bars. Spread half between meringue layers, and half on top. Let chill in refrigerator at least 8 hours. Hint: Freeze Heath bars and they will be easier to crush.

Preparation:	30 min.	Easy	Serves: 10
Cooking:	1 hour	Must do ahead	

Mrs. William I. Jack

LEMON CREAM TORTE

"A very special dessert . . . melts in your mouth."

4 egg whites
dash salt
1 cup granulated sugar
1½ tsp. vinegar
½ tsp. vanilla
4 egg yolks, slightly beaten
dash salt
2 lemons, juice & grated
  rind
¾ cup sugar
½ cup heavy cream

Beat whites with salt until very stiff, adding sugar gradually. Mix vinegar and vanilla together and add to whites at any point. Place well-greased brown paper on a cookie sheet. Draw 2 8" circles and pile meringue within the circles, spreading evenly. Bake at 250° for 1 hour. Mix next 4 ingredients together and cook in top of a double boiler until

thick, about 10 minutes. Cool thoroughly. Whip ½ cup medium or heavy cream and mix with lemon filling. Pile between meringue layers and refrigerate. May use limes: ⅓ cup juice and grated rind of 1 lime. Add a drop of green coloring. Very attractive garnished with whole strawberries.

Preparation:	1 hour	Can do ahead	Serves: 6

Mrs. Richard Webster

PARCEL TORTE

"Unusual dessert, a chocolate lover's delight."

7 oz. Baker's semisweet
  chocolate
1 stick butter
7 oz. sugar
7 egg yolks
7 egg whites
chocolate shavings
sweet whipped cream

Melt the chocolate and butter in a saucepan. Add sugar and egg yolks, and beat for 3 minutes at high speed. In a separate bowl, beat egg whites until stiff (add a little sugar to help hold peaks). Fold egg whites *slowly* into the chocolate batter with a spatula. Pour only ¾ of the batter into an ungreased spring pan. Bake at 325° for 35 minutes. Let torte cool and fall. Then run knife around edge and remove frame. Pour the remaining uncooked batter over the top and chill. Garnish with chocolate shavings and serve with sweet whipped cream.

Preparation:	15 min.	Easy	Serves: 8-10
Baking:	35 min.	Must do ahead	

Mrs. F. Gordon Kraft

COFFEE MOUSSE

"Even folks who don't like coffee will love this one."

1 cup strong coffee
24 regular size marshmallows
½ pt. whipping cream, whipped

Dissolve cut up marshmallows in hot coffee. Fold in whipped cream. Pour into serving dishes. Chill until firm.

Preparation:	25 min.	Easy	Serves: 6 - 8
		Must do ahead	

Mrs. James P. Edson

RASPBERRY CLOUD SOUFFLE

"A marvelous light summer dessert."

2 10-oz. pkg. frozen berries
2 env. unflavored gelatine
¾ cup cold water
2 tbsp. sugar
1 tbsp. lemon juice
¼ tsp. almond extract
4 egg whites
dash salt
¼ cup sugar
1 cup whipping cream,
  whipped

Thaw berries (reserve some for garnish, wrap in foil, return to freezer). Soften gelatine in cold water. Combine raspberries, gelatine, 2 tbsp. sugar and lemon juice. Heat to dissolve gelatine. Add almond extract and cool this until consistency of egg whites. Beat egg whites and salt until soft peaks form, gradually add ¼ cup sugar until stiff. Whip cream, reserving ¼ cup for garnish. Fold egg whites and whipped cream into raspberries. Pour into 1-quart souffle dish which may be extended with a wax paper collar. Refrigerate until serving time.

Preparation:	25 min.	Must do ahead	Serves: 6 - 8

Mrs. James O. Borden

LOUISIANE ICE BOX CAKE
"Rich and delicious!"

½ cup sweet butter
1½ cup confectioner's sugar
4 egg yolks
3 oz. rum, cognac or sherry
2 heaping tsp. instant coffee
1 tsp. vanilla
½ cup slivered, blanched almonds
1 cup heavy cream, whipped
2 doz. ladyfingers
2 doz. large almond macaroons,
  crumbled
1 cup heavy cream, whipped
fresh berries

Cream butter and sugar until fluffy. Beat in egg yolks, rum, coffee, vanilla and nuts. Fold in 1 cup whipped cream. Place ladyfingers in a flat, oblong pan or 9" spring form and cover with half the cream mixture; then put in a layer of macaroons and pour over them the remaining cream mixture. Let stand at room temperature for about 30 minutes, then refrigerate for at least 24 hours before serving. Cover with second cup whipped cream and fresh berries.

Preparation: 30 min.   Must do ahead   Serves: 8
Refrigeration: 24 hours

Mrs. Ralph W. Massey

CREME BRULÉ
"Always a treat."

1 pt. heavy cream
5 egg yolks, beaten
3 tbsp. granulated sugar
fresh sliced strawberries or
  peaches
brown sugar

Boil cream for 1 minute; stirring constantly. Gradually beat hot cream into egg yolks and sugar. Return to saucepan and cook until thickened. Be careful not to overcook and scramble egg yolks.

Place fruit on bottom of individual ovenproof dishes; pour mixture over fruit and place in refrigerator until set. Sprinkle thickly with brown sugar. Melt brown sugar under broiler and refrigerate again. Serve cold. Will hold well only about 6 hours.

Preparation: 15 min.   Must do ahead   Serves: 4
Setting: 1 hour

Mrs. George B. Moore

DESSERT SAUCES

CHRISTMAS ICE CREAM SAUCE
"Delicious any time of year."

1 cup granulated sugar
1 cup brown sugar, packed
½ cup water
1 cup strawberry jam
1 cup orange marmalade
1 cup pecans, chopped
1 lemon, juice and grated
  rind
1 orange, juice and grated
  rind
2 tbsp. brandy
8 - 10 meringue shells
2 quarts vanilla ice cream

Two weeks before: Cook granulated and brown sugars with ½ cup water for 5 minutes. Mix in thoroughly jam, marmalade, pecans, citrus juices and rinds and brandy. Heat through. Let ripen in glass jar in refrigerator for two weeks (at least) before using. Heat in chafing dish and serve over ice cream in meringue shells.

Preparation: 15 min.   Easy   Serves: 8 - 10
                               Must do ahead

Mrs. Charles H. Weaver

RUM AND LIME SAUCE FOR MELON BALLS
"A refreshing summer dessert — cool & pretty, too."

⅔ cup sugar
⅓ cup water
1 tsp. grated lime rind
6 tbsp. lime juice
½ cup light rum
melon balls, 3 kinds
mint

Mix sugar and water in a saucepan and bring to a boil. Turn back to simmer for 5 minutes. Add rind and let cool at room temperature. Stir in lime juice and rum. Pour over melon balls — preferably 3 different kinds for color — and chill, covered, for 3 to 5 hours. Garnish with mint before serving.

Preparation: 30 min.   Easy   Serves: 6 - 8
Cooking: 5 min.   Must do ahead

Mrs. Edward A. Montgomery, Jr.

HOT FUDGE SAUCE

3 squares unsweetened
  chocolate
¼ cup butter or margarine
2 cups confectioner's sugar
dash salt
¾ cup evaporated milk
½ tsp. vanilla

Combine all ingredients except vanilla in saucepan. Cook and stir over medium heat until mixture boils and chocolate melts. Reduce heat to low and cook 5 minutes only, stirring often. Add vanilla. Store in refrigerator. To serve — heat over hot water, stirring often until smooth and hot. Especially good over ice cream pecan balls.

Preparation
& cooking: 20 min.

Easy
Can do ahead

Yield: 1¾ cups

Mrs. Robert G. Morrell

PEANUT BUTTER FUDGE SAUCE

"I spoon it over ice cream and it's too much!"

1 cup Quik (or other
  instant sweetened cocoa)
1 tbsp. milk or more
1 tbsp. peanut butter

Pour the Quik and the milk in the top of a double boiler. Cook, stirring constantly. When the sauce is smooth, add the peanut butter and keep stirring. If the sauce is too thick, add more milk.

Preparation: 10 min.   Easy   Yield: 1 cup

Don Brockett

ICE CREAM SAUCE

1 egg, beaten
¾ cup sugar
pinch salt
⅓ cup butter, melted
1 tsp. vanilla
1 cup heavy cream, whipped

Combine egg, sugar and salt; beat well. Add melted butter gradually, continuing to beat; add vanilla. Fold egg mixture into whipped cream. Chill thoroughly. Keeps only a few hours. Do not make ahead.

Topping for fresh berries, chocolate sponge or dessert calling for vanilla sauce.

Preparation: 10 min.   Easy   Yield: 2 cups

Mrs. Thomas M. Garrett

COOKIES

BALKAN DELIGHTS

"A marvelous cookie worthy of a special occasion."

1 cup butter
½ cup margarine
2 cups sugar
4 egg yolks
1 tsp. vanilla
6 cups flour
2 heaping tsp. baking powder
½ pint sweet cream (only use as much as needed)
1 jar of jelly
1 beaten egg (optional)
ground nuts & sugar (optional)

Cream butter and margarine until creamy. Add sugar gradually, then egg yolks and vanilla and continue until blended. Sift flour with baking powder. Add alternately with cream. Use as much cream as is necessary for soft dough.

Place ball of dough on floured board and roll until desired thinness. Cut out with doughnut cutter (other cookie cutters may be used). One half of dough to have hole in center and other half without. Continue rolling until all dough is used. Place on greased cookie sheet. The top cookie (one with hole) may be brushed with beaten egg and spread with ground nuts and sugar mixture before baking, if desired.

Bake in 350° oven until desired brownness. Cool and place 2 cookies together with your favorite jelly.

Preparation: 2 hours
Baking: 12 - 15 min.

Can do ahead

Yield: 3 - 4 doz.
Can freeze

Mrs. Helen Trumbetas

ALMOND ROLLED COOKIES

"This has been handed down in one family for two generations."

2 cups sugar
1 stick butter
3 eggs, well beaten
pinch salt
3 cups flour
1 tsp. almond extract

Cream butter and sugar. Add eggs and then remaining ingredients. Mix well. Chill dough for easier handling. Roll very thin on floured surface. Cut with cookie cutter and decorate with sprinkles.

Bake on greased cookie sheets for 6 - 8 minutes at 450° until edges are very light brown.

Preparation:	10 min.	Easy	Yield: 6 - 8 doz.
Baking:	6 - 8 min.	Must do ahead	Can freeze

Mrs. Richard Webster

BROWNIE DROPS

"Rich and yet light."

2 4-oz. bars German Chocolate
1 tbsp. butter or margarine
2 eggs
¾ cup sugar
¼ cup flour
¼ tsp. baking powder
¼ tsp. cinnamon
⅛ tsp. salt
½ tsp. vanilla
¾ cup finely chopped
  nuts (optional)

Melt chocolate and butter over hot water. Cool. Beat eggs until foamy, add sugar, 2 tablespoons at a time, beat until thickened, 5 minutes on medium speed. Blend in chocolate, add flour, baking powder, salt, cinnamon, and blend. Add vanilla and nuts. Drop by teaspoons onto greased baking sheet. Bake at 350° for 8 to 10 minutes.

Preparation:	25 min.	Can do ahead	Yield: 4 doz.
Baking:	8 - 10 min.		Can freeze

Mrs. John L. Baldwin

MAPLE PECAN WAFERS

2 egg yolks
½ cup granulated sugar
¾ cup brown sugar
1 cup chopped pecans
2 egg whites, beaten stiff
½ cup plus 2 tbsp. all-
  purpose flour
pinch salt
1 tsp. Mapleine

Beat egg yolks until thick and lemon colored. Add both sugars gradually, beating well. Add pecans, stiffly beaten egg whites, flour mixed with salt, and Mapleine. Drop from teaspoon on greased baking sheet and bake in moderate oven 350° for 10 minutes. Remove *at once* with spatula.

Preparation:	15 min.	Can do ahead	Yield: 4 doz.
Baking:	10 min.		Can freeze

Mrs. R. E. Albrecht

DATE PIN WHEELS

"A family recipe used for holidays and special affairs."

½ lb. chopped dates
⅓ cup water
½ cup white sugar
¼-½ cup chopped
  walnuts (optional)

Cookie Dough:

½ cup butter or margarine
½ cup brown sugar
½ cup white sugar
1 egg
2 cups sifted flour
½ tsp. baking soda
¼ tsp. salt

Mix in a saucepan dates, water, sugar and walnuts. Cook 5 minutes over medium heat, stirring to prevent sticking. Cool.

Cookie Dough — Cream together butter and sugars; add egg and mix well. Sift the flour with the soda and salt. Mix with the creamed butter, etc. and roll out to thin consistency, like pastry. Spread with the date mix and roll up like a jelly roll. Refrigerate for several hours, overnight, or longer. Slice thin; bake 10-12 minutes on a greased cookie sheet at 400°. It is easier to make two shorter rolls of cookies, rather than one long one.

Preparation:	20 min.	Easy	Yield: 3 doz.
Baking:	10-12 min.	Must do ahead	

Mrs. William Howard Colbert

FROSTED BANANA COOKIES

"Great for using those last two bananas nobody will eat."

¾ cup shortening or margarine
¾ cup sugar
1 egg
½ tsp. vanilla
2 mashed bananas
¼ tsp. salt
1 tsp. soda
2 cups sifted flour

Frosting:

6 tbsp. brown sugar
4 tbsp. butter or margarine
4 tbsp. cream or evaporated
  milk
confectioner's sugar
½ tsp. vanilla extract

Cream shortening. Add sugar and blend. Add egg, vanilla and bananas. Sift together flour, salt and soda. Place by teaspoons on greased sheet. Bake at 350° for 8 minutes. These brown only on the edges.

Frosting: Place in pan and bring to boil brown sugar, butter and milk. Remove from heat and add enough powdered sugar to make runny but spreadable. Add ½ teaspoon vanilla. Keep pan over warm water to keep frosting soft. If it gets thick, add a little hot water. Frost cookies while they are warm.

Preparation:	20 min.	Easy	Yield: 6 doz.
Baking:	8 min.	Can do ahead	

Mrs. J. Robert Van Kirk

MARSHMALLOW FUDGE-KINS
"A Chocoholic's delight."

3 sqs. unsweetened chocolate
2 sticks butter or margarine
4 eggs
2 cups sugar
½ cup all-purpose flour
1 tsp. baking powder
1 cup broken nuts
2 tsp. vanilla

Topping:

1 stick margarine
2 sqs. unsweetened
  chocolate
1 5⅓-oz. can evaporated
  milk
1 cup sugar
1 lb. box confectioner's
  sugar
1 tsp. vanilla
6 oz. mini marshmallows

Melt chocolate and butter in double boiler. Beat eggs until foamy. Add sugar. Beat well. Add other ingredients and chocolate mixture. Spread in greased 9 x 13" pan. Bake at 325° about 35 minutes.

Topping: In double boiler, melt margarine and 2 squares chocolate. Add evaporated milk and 1 cup sugar. Cook until well blended. Beat in confectioner's sugar and add vanilla.

As soon as cake is removed from oven, cover with mini marshmallows. Pour on hot icing. Wait until next day to cut into squares. Cut into 1" squares or larger if desired.

Preparation:	30 min.	Easy	Yield: 24 squares or
Baking:	35 min.	Must do ahead	40 bars

Mrs. Lloyd Booth, Jr.

RAISIN BARS
"Super"

1 cup + 2 tbsp. flour
1¼ cups sugar
⅓ cup butter
2 eggs, lightly beaten
½ tsp. baking powder
¼ tsp. salt
1 tbsp. orange peel,
  grated
2 tbsp. orange juice
¾ cup chopped seedless
  raisins
½ cup flaked coconut

Glaze:

1½ tsp. orange juice
1½ tsp. lemon juice
1½ tsp. butter
¾ - 1 cup confectioner's
  sugar

Preheat oven to 350°. Place 1 cup flour and ¼ cup sugar in bowl. Work in butter until crumbly. Press into bottom of greased 9" square pan. Bake 15 minutes. Meanwhile, combine eggs with remaining flour and sugar, baking powder and salt. Stir until smooth. Stir in orange rind, juice, raisins and coconut. Pour over hot baked layer and bake 20 - 25 minutes.

Glaze: Combine orange and lemon juices, butter and enough sugar to make a thin frosting. Spread over cooled mixture. Cut into bars.

Preparation:	25 min.	Can do ahead	Yield: 1 doz.
Baking:	40 min.		Can freeze

Mrs. Joseph J. Weibel

CHOCOLATE CHIP MERINGUES

"Great for a person with a 'sweet tooth'."

4 egg whites
1 tsp. vanilla
dash of salt
1 cup sugar
1 cup chocolate bits
1 cup chopped pecans
  or walnuts

Add vanilla and salt to egg whites (that are at room temperature), beat until frothy. Gradually add sugar. Beat until stiff peaks form. Carefully fold in chocolate bits and nuts. Drop by teaspoon on a greased cookie sheet. Put in preheated oven at 350°. Close door and *turn off* oven. Do not open for 4 - 5 hours. May be left in oven overnight. Cannot be made successfully on a humid or rainy day.

Preparation: 25 min.   **Must do ahead**   Yield: 2½ doz.
Baking: Overnight   Can freeze

Mrs. W. Duff McCrady

GINGERSNAPS

"Soft and chewy."

¾ cup shortening
1 cup sugar
¼ cup light molasses
1 beaten egg
2 cups flour
¼ tsp. salt
2 tsp. soda
1 tsp. cinnamon
1 tsp. clove
½ tsp. ginger
sugar

Cream shortening and sugar. Add molasses and egg. Stir in sifted flour, salt and soda, cinnamon, clove and ginger. Dough will be soft and a little sticky. Roll into walnut-sized balls and roll in sugar. Place on cookie sheet and bake at 350° for 7 - 8 minutes. They will flatten out while baking.

Preparation: 15 min.   Easy   Yield: 5 doz.
Baking: 8 min.   Can do ahead

Mrs. James E. Cavalier

LEMON SQUARES

"Superb taste."

1 cup flour
½ cup butter or margarine
¼ cup powdered sugar
2 eggs
2 tbsp. lemon juice
1 cup granulated sugar
2 tbsp. flour
½ tsp. baking powder
grated rind of 1 lemon
sifted powdered sugar

Blend flour, butter and sugar. Pat into 8" square pan. Bake at 350° for 15 minutes. Blend other ingredients and spread on top of first mixture. Bake at 350° for 25 minutes more. As soon as out of oven sprinkle with powdered sugar. Cut into squares.

Preparation: 20 min.   Easy   Yield: 1 doz.
Baking: 40 min.   Can do ahead   Can freeze

Mrs. Henry A. Sargent

THUMBPRINT COOKIES
"Unusually good — most will want to double recipe."

½ cup brown sugar
1 cup butter
2 - 3 egg yolks
2 cups flour
egg whites
1 - 1½ cups chopped
 nuts
raspberry preserves

Cream together sugar, butter and egg yolks. Beat flour into this mixture. Form balls and dip into slightly beaten egg whites. Roll balls in chopped nuts. Put on lightly greased cookie sheet and make a thumbprint on each ball. Bake at 350° for 8 minutes. Remove from oven and reset thumbprint. Bake 8 to 10 minutes longer. Fill print with raspberry preserves.

Preparation:	25 min.	Easy	Yield: 30
Baking:	18 min.		Can freeze

Mrs. James P. Edson

CINNAMON DANDIES
"Nice for afternoon callers."

1 cup butter or margarine
1 cup sifted powdered sugar
½ tsp. salt
¼ cup applesauce
1 tsp. vanilla
2½ cups sifted flour
½ cup sugar
1½ tsp. cinnamon

Cream butter. Gradually add powdered sugar and salt. Cream well. Add applesauce and vanilla. Gradually add flour. Shape scant teaspoonsful into balls. Place on ungreased cookie sheets. Flatten to ¼" with bottom of glass dipped in sugar. Bake at 325° for 15 to 18 minutes. Dust warm cookies in mixture of sugar and cinnamon.

Preparation:	15 min.	Easy	Yield: 3 - 4 doz.
Baking:	15 - 18 min.	Can do ahead	Can freeze

Miss Flossie E. Branch

SAND TARTS
"Everybody's favorite."

1 cup butter
3 tbsp. confectioner's sugar
1 cup ground almonds or
 walnuts
2½ cups sifted cake flour
1 tsp. vanilla
confectioner's sugar

Mix all ingredients well using wooden spoon. Pinch off small pieces of dough and roll to thickness of pencil. Form into crescents. Bake at 350° for 15 - 18 minutes, or until delicately brown. Roll immediately in confectioner's sugar.

Preparation:	30 min.	Easy	Yield: 40 cookies
Baking:	20 min.	Can do ahead	Can freeze

Mrs. M. E. McElman

ORANGE COOKIES

1½ cups dark brown sugar
1 cup margarine
¼ tsp. salt
2 eggs, beaten together
½ cup sour milk (½ tsp.
  vinegar to ½ cup milk)
rind & juice of 1 orange
1½ tsp. vanilla
1 tsp. baking soda
2 tsp. baking powder
4 cups flour

Frosting:

1 box powdered sugar
1 lump butter, size of
  an egg
rind & juice of 1 orange

Cream together sugar and margarine. Add all ingredients but flour, and mix well. Add flour gradually, mixing well. Grease cookie sheets and drop 1½" apart. Bake at 350° about 12 minutes. Check in 10 minutes. Remove to wire rack to cool. When cool, frost.

Preparation:	20 - 25 min.	Easy	Yield: 6 doz.
Baking:	12 min.	Can do ahead	Can freeze

Mrs. Lawrence W. Hitchins

MOLASSES COOKIES
"Very good."

¾ cup shortening (if using
  margarine, cut salt)
1 cup brown sugar —
  packed
1 egg
4 tbsp. light molasses
2¼ cups sifted flour
1 tsp. salt (½ tsp. if
  margarine is used)
1 tsp. soda
½ tsp. cloves
1 tsp. cinnamon
1 tsp. ginger
sugar (optional)

Cream shortening, add sugar, egg, molasses, then dry ingredients and spices. Spoon batter in size of walnuts and dip tops in sugar (optional). Press on buttered cookie sheet until rather thin. Bake at 375° for 9 - 12 minutes (or less).

Preparation:	20 min.	Can do ahead	Yield: 5 doz.
Baking:	9-12 min.		Can freeze

Mrs. William H. Guernsey

RICE KRISPIES COOKIES
"Cookies with snap, crackle and pop!"

1 cup sugar
1 cup brown sugar
1 cup softened butter
 (½ may be shortening)
1 tsp. vanilla
1 pinch salt
2 eggs
1 cup quick oatmeal
2 cups flour
1 tsp. soda
2 cups Rice Krispies

Mix all ingredients well, spooning in Rice Krispies last. Shape into long, thin rolls and freeze (double wrapped, if to be kept for a long period of time). Slice very thin when frozen, place on ungreased cookie sheet. Bake at 375° for 8 to 10 minutes until lightly browned. Keep the dough frozen and slice off what you need. Means having fresh, hot cookies on the table in 10 minutes.

Preparation:	5 min.	Easy	Yield: 5 - 6½ doz.
Baking:	10 min.	Must do ahead	Must freeze

Mrs. Edward I. Sproull, Jr.

TOFFEE COCONUT BARS

½ cup soft shortening or
 butter
½ cup brown sugar
1 cup sifted flour
2 eggs
1 cup brown sugar
1 tsp. vanilla
2 tbsp. flour
1 tsp. baking powder
½ tsp. salt
1 cup moist shredded
 coconut
1 cup chopped almonds
 (or use other nuts)

Mix butter and sugar thoroughly, and stir in flour. Press or flatten with hand to cover bottom of ungreased 13 x 9" pan. Bake 10 minutes at 350°.
Almond-coconut topping: Beat well 2 eggs and stir in sugar and vanilla. Mix together flour, baking powder and salt; add to egg mixture, and stir in coconut and almonds. Spread in pan. Return to oven and bake at 350° for 25 minutes or more until topping is golden brown. Cool slightly and cut into bars.

Preparation:	20 min.	Can do ahead	Yield: 2 doz.
Baking:	30 - 35 min.		

Mrs. Scott Sawhill

CHEWY NOELS
"Very easy and yummy."

2 tbsp. butter*
2 eggs
1 cup brown sugar
5 tbsp. flour
⅛ tsp. baking soda
½ tsp. salt
1 cup chopped walnuts
1 tsp. vanilla
*If 9" pan is used, increase
  butter to 3 tbsp.

Preheat oven to 350°. Melt butter in oven in 8" square pan. Beat eggs. Combine dry ingredients and add to eggs. Add nuts and vanilla. Pour mixture over melted butter in 8" pan. *Do Not Stir. Carefully,* slide pan into oven. Bake 20 minutes.
Remove from oven. Turn out of pan immediately onto a rack or foil. Allow to cool 5 - 8 minutes. Then sprinkle with confectioner's sugar. Cut into squares.

Preparation:	15 - 20 min.	Easy	Yield: 16 - 20
Baking:	20 min.	Can do ahead	Can freeze

Mrs. Kenneth Johns, Jr.

VITALITY SPICE BARS
"Good for lunch boxes."

1¼ cups firmly packed brown
  sugar
⅓ cup shortening
2 eggs, beaten
1 cup unbleached flour
½ cup wheat germ
1 tsp. baking powder
salt
mixture of cinnamon, nutmeg,
  cloves, allspice (abt. 2 tsp.
  total)
chopped walnuts, raisins, dates
  (whatever is on hand)
2 - 3 tbsp. well-seasoned
  applesauce

Cream sugar and shortening together, and add beaten eggs. Stir dry ingredients, including spices, together and add to creamed mixture. Mix well. Add walnuts, etc. Add applesauce. Spread mixture in well-greased 8" square pan and bake in 350° oven for about 45 minutes, or until mixture begins to pull away from sides of pan. These are very solid and chewy.

Preparation:	15 min.	Easy	Yield: 18 - 24 bars
Baking:	45 min.	Can do ahead	Can freeze

Mrs. Mary Cooper Robb

APRICOT DELIGHT COOKIES

"Worth every minute of preparation time."

1½ cups sugar
¾ cup margarine
2 eggs
3 cups all-purpose flour
½ tsp. soda
2 tsp. baking powder
1 tsp. salt
½ cup finely snipped dried
  apricots
⅓ cup sour milk (add 1 tbsp.
  lemon juice to ⅓ cup milk
  & let sit while making the
  cookies)
½ tsp. vanilla
apricot jam

Mix sugar, margarine and eggs until creamy. Sift together flour, soda, baking powder and salt. Add apricots, the dry ingredients and the sour milk and vanilla to the creamed mixture. Drop by teaspoonsful on ungreased cookie sheet and drop scant teaspoon of apricot jam on top, making hollow in middle of cookie with spoon. Bake at 375° for 12 - 15 minutes.

Preparation: 20 min.
Baking: 15 min.

Yield: 4 - 5 doz.

Mrs. W. Ralph Green

VIENNESE BROWNIES

"A delicious layered brownie."

1 8-oz. pkg. cream cheese,
  softened
⅓ cup sugar
1 egg
2 1-oz. squares unsweetened
  chocolate
½ cup butter
2 eggs
1 cup sugar
¾ cup flour
½ tsp. baking powder
½ tsp. salt

Grease 8 x 8 x 2" pan. Combine cream cheese, sugar and 1 egg; set aside. Melt chocolate and butter. Beat 2 eggs until fluffy; add 1 cup sugar and chocolate mixture. Add sifted dry ingredients; stir to blend.

Pour half chocolate mixture into greased pan. Spread with cream cheese mixture. Top with remaining batter.

Bake 40 - 50 minutes at 350°.

Preparation: 20 min.   Easy   Yield: 12
Cooking: 50 min.   Can do ahead   Can freeze

Mrs. Kenneth N. Myers

CANDIES

FUDGE

2 cups sugar
²/₃ cup evaporated skim
  milk
12 regular marshmallows
½ cup butter
¹/₈ tsp. salt
1½ tsp. vanilla
6 oz. semi-sweet chocolate
  bits
1 cup nuts (optional)

Mix sugar, milk, marshmallows and butter in a heavy saucepan. Cook, stirring constantly over medium heat until mixture comes to a boil. Boil and stir 5 minutes more. Remove from heat. Stir in chocolate bits until melted completely. Stir in vanilla and nuts. Spread in a buttered 8" square pan. Cool and cut.

Preparation: 20 min.   Easy   Yield: About 30
                                Can do ahead   Can freeze

Mrs. W. Lukens Ward

WHITE FUDGE

2 cups granulated white
  sugar
2 tbsp. white Karo syrup
½ cup whole milk
2 tbsp. butter
¼ cup each of ground
  pecans, walnuts, almonds
¹/₈ cup grated coconut (fresh
  or packaged)
1 tsp. each of vanilla and
  almond extracts

Over medium heat bring to a gentle boil the sugar, syrup, and milk. Boil until a few drops in cool water form a soft ball. Remove from heat and add butter and extracts. Set pot of candy in a pan of cool water and beat until creamy and thick. Pour into well-buttered 8 x 8" pan. When thoroughly cool, cut into squares. At Christmas

time add ½ cup each of red and green finely cut candied cherries.

Preparation: 15 min.   Easy   Yield: 24
Cooking: 10 min.   Can do ahead   Can freeze

Mrs. John A. Shoener

SOUR CREAM FUDGE

"Melts in your mouth."

2 cups sugar
2 tbsp. white Karo
2 tbsp. (heaping) cocoa*
½ cup sour cream
½ cup butter
1 tsp. vanilla
½ cup chopped nuts, if
  desired

Combine all ingredients except vanilla and nuts in saucepan. Cook over medium high heat and allow to cook about 3 or 4 minutes. Test in cold water until a soft ball forms. Remove pan from heat and place in cold water to cool slightly. Add vanilla. Do not leave in water more than 2 minutes. Remove from water, add nuts, and beat until it begins to look thick. It doesn't take as much beating as most other fudge. Put in an 8" greased pan. *You can use more or less depending on your preference for light or dark chocolate.

Preparation: 5 min.	Easy	Yield: 36-40 pieces
Cooking: 3-4 min.	Can do ahead	Can freeze

Mrs. Robert G. Morrell

BON BONS

2 sticks margarine, melted
2 cups crushed graham
  crackers
1 cup packed coconut
1 cup crunchy peanut
  butter (12 oz.)
1 box powdered sugar
1 12-oz. pkg. chocolate chips
½ inch wax (cut from block)
  melted in double boiler

Mix well margarine, graham crackers, coconut, peanut butter and sugar. Melt chips and wax in double boiler. Roll cookies into balls and dip in chocolate and wax. Put on wax paper. Refrigerate for 15 minutes.

Preparation: 1 hour   Yield: 5 doz.

Mrs. Charles Lewis

DIVINITY

"For the sweet tooth."

2 cups sugar
½ cup Karo Corn Syrup
½ cup boiling water
2 egg whites, beaten
1 cup chopped nuts
½ tsp. vanilla

Dissolve sugar and Karo in boiling water. Boil until brittle when dropped into cold water. Remove from heat and stir slowly into the beaten egg whites, stirring constantly. Add nuts and vanilla. When thick, turn onto a buttered platter.

Preparation: 30 min.	Easy	Yield: About 24 pieces
Cooking: 10-15 min.		

Mrs. Leonard Burnett

GRANDMA'S FUDGE (1912)

"This is the old-fashioned kind of fudge."

1 cup granulated sugar
1 cup light brown sugar, packed
¾ cup milk
2 squares unsweetened chocolate
1 tbsp. maple syrup (optional)
¼ tsp. salt
1 tbsp. butter or margarine
1 tsp. vanilla

Blend sugar and milk and stir over low fire until a rolling boil is reached. Then add chocolate and salt and increase heat. Stir frequently and scrape down sides. Cook until drop in cold water forms soft ball that can be picked up.* Then stir in butter, remove from fire, and beat with electric beater few minutes before adding vanilla. Continue beating until it begins to thicken. Finish beating by hand and when beginning to stiffen, pour quickly into buttered pan. Score into squares. Let cool few minutes before cutting. Half pieces of walnuts or pecans may be pressed into each square quickly before fudge hardens.

*If adding 1 tablespoon maple syrup, add before butter while still boiling - it seems to add flavor and smoothness.

Preparation: 10 min.   Easy   Can freeze
Cooking: 5 min.

Mrs. Sidney J. Ratcliffe

ALMOND TOFFEE

"Tricky to make, but heavenly to eat."

1 cup butter
2½ cups sugar
1½ cups unblanched sliced almonds
1 tsp. vanilla
9 oz. semisweet chocolate
1 cup finely chopped walnuts

In a heavy saucepan combine butter and sugar. Cook over low heat, stirring until the sugar is dissolved. Slowly raise the heat while continuing to stir, and wash down any undissolved sugar crystals clinging to the sides of the pan with a brush dipped in cold water until the mixture comes to a boil. Remove the pan from the heat and stir in almonds. Cook the mixture over moderately high heat, without stirring, until a candy thermometer registers 290°F. Add vanilla, pour the mixture into a buttered 12 x 18" jelly roll pan and let it cool completely. In the top of a double boiler set over simmering water, melt the semisweet chocolate over very low heat. Spread half the chocolate over the toffee with a metal spatula and sprinkle the surface with ½ cup of the walnuts. Let the chocolate set, invert the candy onto a piece of wax paper, and wipe any excess butter off the toffee with a paper towel. Spread the toffee with the remaining chocolate and sprinkle it with the rest of the walnuts, and let the chocolate set. Break the toffee into pieces and store in an airtight container.

Preparation: 1 hour   Must do ahead   Yield: 2½ lbs.

Mrs. James E. Cavalier

CHEFS'
SPECIALITIES

Duquesne Club
Pittsburgh

193

THE DUQUESNE CLUB

Behind the five-story brown stone facade on Sixth Avenue is the Duquesne Club, one of the best-known clubs in America. The fourteen story addition completed in 1931 expanded the number of private dining rooms to 65 and increased overnight accommodations for its approximately 2,500 members. Incorporated in 1881, it has counted among its members the nation's leaders in coal, iron, steel, aluminum, aerospace, oil, banking, glass, railroads and electric power.

Additional illustrations in this section:

The Courtyard entrance of the Harvard-Yale-Princeton Club.

Further examples of Bakewell Glass: "Ribbed Ivy," "Roman Key," "Mirror," "Rib," "Horn of Plenty."

Decanter — Example of Riverboat Glass and Bakewell Candlesticks.

Doors leading into 13th century French Gothic style Heinz Memorial Chapel, University of Pittsburgh, Oakland.

Duquesne Club — The Patio.

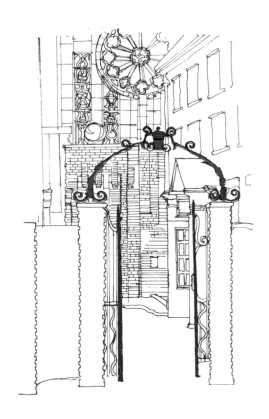

J. D. A.
"One of Pittsburgh's most popular drinks."

1 qt. clam juice
1 cup tomato juice
1 whiskey glass tomato ketchup
1 level tsp. celery salt
½ whiskey glass cocktail sauce
6 drops Tabasco sauce
salt if necessary

Mix well.

Yield: 1½ qts.

Nick Coletti, Chef
Duquesne Club

CRABMEAT a la HOELZEL

1 can fresh crabmeat (1 lb.)
2/3 cup olive oil
1/3 cup tarragon vinegar
salt & freshly ground pepper

Place the crabmeat on a terrapine plate. Combine the rest of the ingredients and pour over the crabmeat.

Serves: 4

Nick Coletti, Chef
Duquesne Club

MAD ANTHONY BOHMENSUPPE (Bean Soup)

"A thick, hearty soup."

1 lb. marrow beans
ham bone
10 cups water
½ cup chopped onions
¼ cup vinegar
¼ cup tarragon
salt & pepper

Soak the beans several hours
— then cook until tender with
a ham bone and 10 cups of
water. Add vinegar and spices.

Preparation: 3 hours   Easy   Serves: 10
Cooking: 3 hours

Mad Anthony's Bierstube

CANADIAN CHEESE SOUP

¼ cup chopped onion
¼ cup chopped celery
1 tbsp. butter
1 tsp. paprika
1 tbsp. flour
1½ cups chicken stock
1½ cups milk
½ lb. Cheddar cheese
½ lb. Old English cheese
$1/8$ tsp. Tabasco
1 tsp. salt
$1/8$ tsp. white pepper
1 tsp. dry mustard

Sauté onion and celery with
butter until onion is transparent. Add paprika and
flour and cook 5 minutes,
stirring constantly. Add
chicken stock and milk. Cook
on low flame. Add cheese,
Tabasco, salt, white pepper and
dry mustard. Stir and strain.

Serves: 5

John Eichmuller
Joseph Horne Co.

CHIPPEWA SOUP

"Rolling Rock's famous soup. For curry lovers."

½ gal. tomato soup
½ gal. pea soup
celery
onions
carrots
bay leaf
curry
ham bone
1 qt. heavy cream
sour cream (optional)

Mix soups. Sauté celery,
onions, carrots, bay leaf and
sharp curry to taste. Blend
with soups and add ham bone.
Bring to boiling point. Simmer
for 30 minutes. Strain. Add
about 1 quart heavy cream.
Can be served hot or chilled
with dollop of sour cream if
desired.

Preparation: 30 min.   Can do ahead   Yield: 1½ gal.
Cooking: 30 min.   Can freeze

Willy Daffinger, Chef
Rolling Rock Club

FRENCH ONION SOUP

1 lb. sliced onions
butter
salt & white pepper
1 bay leaf
1 oz. dry sherry wine
3 cups beef consomme
3 cups chicken stock broth
6 large croutons
6 tsp. grated Parmesan cheese
6 slices Provolone cheese

Sauté onion in the butter until light brown. Add salt, pepper and bay leaf. Add the sherry wine and simmer for a few minutes. Add beef consomme and chicken broth. Cook for approximately 20 minutes. Let boil for 10 minutes. Ladle into 6 French onion soup bowls. To each bowl add 1 crouton and ½ teaspoon Parmesan cheese. Lay 1 slice of Provolone cheese over each bowl and cover with a thin layer of Parmesan cheese. Bake in broiler until cheese is bubbly and brown. If broiler is not used, place in 425° oven until brown. Serve hot.

Serves: 6

Yong Su Yi, Chef
Le Bastille

POTAGE PARMENTIER (LEEK OR ONION & POTATO SOUP)

3 to 4 cups peeled potatoes,
  sliced or diced
3 cups thinly sliced leeks
  or yellow onions
2 qts. water
1 tbsp. salt
⅓ cup heavy cream or
  2 to 3 tbsp. soft butter
2 to 3 tbsp. minced parsley
  or chives

Simmer vegetables, water and salt together, partially covered, in 3-4 quart sauce pan 40 to 50 minutes until tender. You can use a pressure cooker and cook 15 lbs. pressure for 5 minutes. Release pressure and simmer uncovered for 15 minutes. Mash vegetables in soup with fork or pass soup through food mill. Season. Set aside uncovered. Reheat to simmer just before serving. Remove from heat and stir in cream or butter by spoonsful. Pour into tureen or cups and decorate with herbs.

Preparation: 30 min.   Can do ahead   Yield: 2 qts.
Cooking: 1 hour

Frederick Martin, Chef
Sewickley Heights Golf Club

TOMATO COB SOUP

8 large ripe tomatoes, peeled
  & chopped fine
1 cup celery, chopped fine
1 small red onion, chopped
  fine
salt & pepper
½ tsp. curry powder
2 cups Hellmann's mayonnaise

Put tomatoes through a grinder or blender. Combine pulp with celery and onion. Salt and pepper to taste. Mix well and chill several hours. When serving, combine curry and mayonnaise in a dish and put a tablespoon or more on top of each serving.

Preparation: 10 min.   Easy   Serves: 8
Must do ahead

Charles Bowman, Chef
Allegheny Country Club

COLD STRAWBERRY SOUP

2 qts. strawberries
2 cups water
1 cup sugar
lemon juice
Rhine or Moselle wine
grated rind of 1 orange &
  1 lemon
whipped cream

Wash and drain the strawberries thoroughly. Strain the berries through a very fine sieve. Meanwhile make a syrup by boiling the water and sugar for 10 minutes. Cool. Put both items in the refrigerator and when both are the same temperature, combine them and

add lemon juice and Rhine or Moselle wine to taste. Finish by adding grated rind of 1 orange and 1 lemon. Serve in cold cups with a little topping of whipped cream.

Must do ahead

Willi Daffinger, Chef
Rolling Rock Club

QUICHE LORRAINE
"Continental Classic"

Dough:
½ lb. butter
3½ cups flour
1 egg
¼ tsp. salt
½ cup warm water
⅓ lb. ham, chopped fine
⅓ lb. Swiss cheese,
 chopped fine
⅓ lb. bacon, chopped,
 sautéed brown
6 eggs
1 pt. whipping cream
dash nutmeg
dash salt
2 tsp. butter

Mix butter, flour, egg and salt together. Add warm water to form pie dough. Put in refrigerator. Cover and let sit for 24 hours. Using a 10" pie pan, make pie crust. Combine ham and Swiss cheese and sprinkle in pastry-lined pie pan. Add bacon. Beat eggs slightly; beat in whipping cream, nutmeg and salt. Pour cream mixture into pie pan. Dot with butter. Bake at 325° for 40 minutes. Good for appetizers, lunch, or late supper.

Preparation: 30 min.	**Must do ahead**	**Serves: 6-8 main dish**
Baking: 40 min.		**10-12 appetizer**

Yong Su Yi, Chef
Le Bastille

MELANZANE FILANTI
(Eggplant and Cheese Sandwich)

3 eggplants, med. size
salt
flour
olive oil
Mozzarella or Swiss cheese
thin Italian bread

Wash the eggplants and cut them lengthwise into slices about ½" thick. Sprinkle with salt and leave to drain on a sloping plate or in a colander for about 1 hour to rid them of their bitter juices. Pat dry, dust with flour and fry in hot oil until golden. Drain well. Place a layer of cheese between two slices of eggplant and press lightly, making a firm sandwich. Roll the sandwiches in flour and deep fry in hot oil until golden. Drain on absorbent paper and serve hot between thin Italian bread.

Serves: 6

Frank Sgro
Sgro's Restaurant

BEEF WITH TOMATOES
(FAN CHIEH NIU RUH)

"An authentic Chinese recipe."

(May be partially prepared
  ahead)
1 lb. sirloin steak
1 green pepper, cleaned
1 large onion
1 lb. tomatoes, peeled
2 tbsp. peanut oil or
  salad oil
1 tbsp. soy sauce
1 tbsp. dry sherry
½ tsp. salt
½ cup water
1 tsp. cornstarch
2 tbsp. cold water

Marinade:

1 tbsp. soy sauce
1 tbsp. dry sherry
½ tsp. salt
½ tsp. sugar

Slice meat against the grain
½" thick and cut into 1 x 2"
strips.

Combine marinade and mix
well. Add beef; toss to coat.
Marinate beef for 20 minutes.

Cut green pepper and onion
into chunks. Cut tomatoes into
wedges and remove seeds.

Heat 1 tbsp. oil in skillet over
high heat until very hot. Add
meat; stir-fry for 1 minute.
Remove and set aside.

Heat the remaining 1 tablespoon
oil in skillet over high heat. Add green pepper and onion; stir-fry for
1 minute. Blend in soy sauce, sherry, salt and water; cook for 2 minutes. Add tomato wedges, and meat, and mix well. Dissolve cornstarch
in 2 tablespoons water and stir in. Cook, stirring constantly until
thickened. Serve at once.

Preparation: 25 min.

Serves: 2 - 4

Anna Kao
Chinese Gourmet
Restaurant

MEDALLION OF BEEF

½ cup oil
8 green peppers, cleaned &
  chopped into 2" pieces
1 Spanish onion, cleaned &
  chopped into large chunks
10 mushroom caps, sliced
filet, cleaned & removed of
  all fat
salt & flour
glass of red wine
glass of beef gravy
chopped parsley

Put oil into skillet and heat
until hot. Add pepper, onion
and mushrooms. Sauté for 20
minutes. Cut filet into 12
slices. Add salt and flour to
both sides. Cook in very hot
skillet for 15 minutes. Remove
meat from skillet. Throw
away grease. Place wine, gravy
and cooked pepper, onion and
mushrooms in same skillet
and sauté for 3 minutes.
Pour over filet and arrange on a
platter. Sprinkle parsley on meat.

Preparation: 45 min.
Cooking: 50 min.

Serves: 6

Dominic More, Chef
Le Mont

BUL-KO-KI

"Charcoal beef Korean style."

2 lbs. top butt roast beef
5 pieces green spring onion,
  shredded
1 small carrot, shredded
1 small onion, thinly sliced
1 tsp. garlic, chopped very fine
3 tbsp. soy sauce
1 tbsp. sugar
3 tbsp. olive oil
1 tsp. sesame seed
1 tsp. Tabasco sauce
2 tbsp. dry red wine
dash of black pepper
½ tsp. salt

Slice beef in 2" long by 1" wide pieces. Combine all other ingredients and mix thoroughly. Pour over beef. Refrigerate for 12 hours. Broil to your choice. Serve with rice and a green vegetable.

Preparation: 15 min.	Easy	Serves: 6-8
Cooking: 6-10 min.	Must do ahead	

Yong Su Yi, Chef
Le Bastille

SIRLOIN OF BEEF WELLINGTON

Duxelle:

2 small onions, chopped
4 oz. chicken livers, blanched
½ lb. fresh mushrooms
½ cup butter
⅛ tsp. thyme
⅛ tsp. basil
1 clove garlic, minced
1½ lbs. finely ground
  veal & pork
1 tsp. chopped parsley
2 eggs
salt & pepper to taste
4 lbs. sirloin strip
salt & pepper
puff pastry
egg yolks

Duxelle:
Sauté onions, chicken livers and mushrooms in butter. Add thyme, basil and garlic. Cool mixture; chop finely. Add ground pork and veal, parsley, eggs, salt and pepper; mix thoroughly.

Meat:
Preheat oven to 400°. Trim excess fat from meat; season with salt and pepper. Brown in hot fat on both sides. Cook in oven 15 minutes. Remove from oven; chill.

Puff Pastry:
Roll out finished pastry to about 3 times the size of beef.

Spread some Duxelle in center of pastry. Place beef on Duxelle; cover completely with 1" layer of Duxelle. Fold dough around meat; brush with beaten egg yolks to seal seams. Turn upside down; decorate with dough ornaments cut from excess pastry. Let Wellington "rest" in refrigerator for at least 1 hour. Brush completely with beaten egg yolk; pierce with a fork. Bake 40 minutes in 375° oven for medium beef. Let stand 5 minutes before carving.

Serves: 4-6

Ferdinand Metz, Chef
H. J. Heinz Company

ITALIAN BRACIOLE WITH TOMATO SAUCE
"A nice change from Italian meatballs."

2 lbs. prime filet steak
  (cleaned of all fat)
salt
pepper
crushed garlic
hard boiled egg, chopped

Tomato Sauce:

olive oil
1 garlic clove,
  chopped very fine
plum tomatoes
chopped capers
salt
pepper
oregano

Braciole:
Slice steak into 4 steaks or pieces. Pound very thin. Season with salt, pepper, crushed garlic and chopped hard boiled egg. Roll and tie with string or a toothpick.

Sauce:
Heat olive oil. Brown garlic until golden brown. Add tomatoes, capers, salt, pepper and oregano. Let simmer 20 minutes. Add Braciole to sauce. Cook slowly until meat is done to your preference.

Preparation: 30 min. Can do ahead Serves: 4
Cooking: 30 min.

Chef Africo Lorenzini
Tambellini's

CHEF DECANINI BEEF STROGANOFF

Gravy:

¼ cup butter or margarine
4 tbsp. flour
3 10½-oz. cans condensed
  beef stock

¼ cup butter or margarine
1½ lbs. sirloin, cut in ¼" strips
2 cups sliced mushrooms
¼ cup finely chopped onion
pinch garlic powder
pinch parsley
¼ cup sherry wine
¼ cup tomato purée
1 cup sour cream

Gravy — Brown butter and flour in a 3-quart saucepan. Then add condensed beef stock and cook on slow heat about 5 minutes.

Heat butter in a large skillet and quickly brown sirloin strips. Add sliced mushrooms, chopped onion, garlic powder and parsley, and cook about 15 minutes until brown. Then add gravy, sherry and tomato purée. Cook until meat is tender, then add the sour cream and bring to a boil. Serve Stroganoff on buttered noodles.

Serves: 6-8

Dante Decanini, Chef
Edgeworth Club

MARINATED LIVER PORTUGUESE

¾ cup red wine
2 tbsp. dark vinegar
1 tsp. minced garlic
½ bay leaf, crushed
½ tsp. salt
½ tsp. black pepper
1 lb. calf's liver (or beef),
 ⅛ " slices
3 tbsp. olive oil
4 slices bacon
parsley

Combine wine, vinegar, garlic, bay leaf, salt and pepper in a bowl or dish. Add the liver and leave at room temperature for 2 hours, turning the liver 2 or 3 times. In a heavy skillet, heat the oil and cook the bacon until crisp. Remove and drain. Remove liver from marinade and pat dry with paper towels. Then add the liver to the skillet and cook 2-3 minutes each side.

Brown quickly and remove to heated platter. Add marinade to skillet and boil until reduced to half. Taste for seasoning. Crumble bacon over liver and pour sauce over all. Garnish with parsley. Serve at once.

Serve immediately   Serves: 4

Joseph D. Parrotta, Jr.
Executive Chef
University Club

STIR-FRY PORK WITH SNOW PEAS (SUEH TOU CHU RUH)

1 lb. lean pork, tenderloin
 or boneless pork
1 tbsp. peanut or other
 salad oil
1   8-oz. box frozen snow
 peas, defrosted & drained
½ cup sliced bamboo shoots
1 chopped scallion
1 tsp. soy sauce
1 tbsp. dry sherry
¼ tsp. salt

Marinade for Pork:

1 tsp. cornstarch
1 tbsp. soy sauce
2 tbsp. dry sherry
½ tsp. salt
1 tsp. sesame oil
 (optional)

Preparation: 40 min.
Cooking: 5 min.

Slice pork ⅛ " thick, or have butcher slice pork on #4, then cut into 1 x 2" pieces. Combine marinade and mix well. Marinate pork for 30 minutes.

Heat 1 tablespoon of oil in wok or skillet over high heat. Add pork; stir-fry 3 minutes. Add snow peas, bamboo shoots, scallion, soy sauce, sherry and salt. Stir-fry for 2 minutes longer. Serve hot. (Veal may be used instead of pork).

Serves: 2 - 4

Anna Kao
Chinese Gourmet
Restaurant

THE GREAT WALL SWEET AND SOUR PORK

8 ozs. pork, cut into 1" cubes
1 tsp. sherry
½ tsp. salt
¼ tsp. pepper
1 egg, beaten
1 tbsp. flour
2 tbsp. cornstarch
4 cups vegetable oil for frying
1 cup diced carrots, parboiled
1 cup diced cucumbers
½ cup diced onion
½ cup water
1 tbsp. soy sauce
1 tbsp. cornstarch
3 tbsp. sugar
3 tbsp. vinegar
3 tbsp. tomato ketchup
1 clove garlic, minced

Mix pork cubes with sherry, salt and pepper.
Mix egg, flour, and 2 tablespoons cornstarch.
Coat pork with the mixture.
Heat oil and drop in pork cubes, one by one. Deep fry until well done, over medium heat. Drain.
Fry carrots, cucumbers, and onion for 1 minute and drain.
Mix water, soy sauce, cornstarch, sugar, vinegar and ketchup. Heat 4 tablespoons oil, fry garlic, stir in the mixture and simmer until thickened. Add pork and vegetables and mix well. Serve hot.

Preparation: 25 min.
Cooking: 10 min.

Serves: 2

The Great Wall

BREAST OF VEAL WITH MUSHROOMS
"A tender tasty dish."

2½ lbs. breast of veal
1½ oz. lard
1 tbsp. flour
1¼ cups white wine
1 shallot, chopped
5 - 6 parsley sprigs
a sprig of thyme
half of a bay leaf
bouillon or water
12 small onions, browned
12 oz. mushrooms

Cut the breast in slices at right angles to the bone and brown well in the lard. Dust with flour, brown slightly, season, and add the white wine, the chopped shallot, and the herbs. Cover and braise slowly in the oven, adding a little bouillon or water from time to time. After 1½ hours, remove the herbs, add the browned

onions, done separately, and raw mushroom caps and finish cooking together. Skim fat off stock and pour over meat.

Preparation: 30 min.   Easy   Serves: 5
Cooking: 2 hours   Can do ahead   Can freeze

Anthony Talerico, Chef
Chartiers Country Club

VEAL CORDON BLEU

4 2½-oz. thin slices of
   veal cutlet
4 2-oz. slices Swiss or
   Mozzarella cheese
2 1-oz. pieces prosciutto
   ham or good smoked ham
flour
egg-milk mixture
bread crumbs
2 tbsp. butter

Layer as follows:
1 slice veal cutlet
1 slice cheese
1 slice ham
1 slice cheese
1 slice veal
Press together or hold with
tooth picks. Dip in flour
and egg-milk mixture, and
bread crumbs. Sauté in 2
tablespoons butter until brown
on one side only. Turn over and bake in 300° oven for 15 minutes or
until golden brown. Serving suggestions: Serve plain or with
Champignon Sauce.*

*There is a good Mushroom
 Wine Sauce on page 82.

Serves: 2

*Vincent Salpietro
Executive Chef and
Food Service Director
Interstate United Corp.*

VEAL SCALLOPS SEVILLANA

½ cup olive oil
½ cup chopped onion
3 cloves garlic
2 med. green peppers,
   chopped
¼ lb. washed &
   sliced mushrooms
3 med. tomatoes, peeled,
   seeded & chopped
2 tbsp. crushed almonds or
   walnuts (optional)
½ cup water
salt & black pepper
6 veal scallops (4-6 oz. each)
flour
½ cup oil
12 stuffed green olives,
   cut in half
¼ cup sherry

Heat olive oil in skillet, add
onions, garlic and green peppers.
Cook until vegetables are soft.
Add mushrooms, tomatoes,
almonds, water, salt and pepper.
Bring to a boil, stirring constantly.
Cook until half of the water
has evaporated, set aside.
Sprinkle veal with salt and
pepper and dust with flour. Heat
oil in skillet, sauté veal. Pour
off excess oil, add the above
mixture and the olives. Cover
and simmer 45 minutes. Add
sherry before removing from
skillet. To serve, arrange veal on
platter and pour sauce over.

Serves: 6

*Joseph D. Parrotto, Jr.
Executive Chef
University Club*

VEAL SCALLOPPINI MARSALA

1 lb. sliced mushrooms
5 oz. butter
juice of 2 lemons
2½ cups brown sauce
2 lbs. veal, 2 x 3" pieces
salt & white pepper
3 tbsp. grated Parmesan cheese
3 tbsp. flour
5 tbsp. shallots
½ cup butter
1½ cups Marsala wine

Sauté mushrooms in butter. Add juice of 2 lemons and brown sauce, set aside. Sprinkle veal on both sides with salt, pepper, Parmesan cheese and flour. In a skillet put butter and shallots. When hot, sauté veal until brown on both sides. Put veal in a casserole, discard butter and shallots from skillet. Add Marsala wine and Mushroom Sauce. Simmer for 5 minutes. Cover veal with sauce and bake at 400° until sizzling.

Serves: 5

Nick Fusco, Executive Chef
The Pittsburgh Hilton

SOUFFLE OF CHICKEN HASH WITH PLAIN SPINACH FLORENTINE

2 cups cooked chicken meat
  cut in small pieces (diced but
  not finely chopped)
1 cup sweet cream
1½ cups cream sauce
salt & pepper
1 oz. sherry wine (optional)
spinach
butter

Cheese Souffle:

½ cup melted butter
1 cup flour
2 cups boiling milk
½ tsp. salt
pinch pepper
a little nutmeg
5 beaten egg yolks
1 cup grated fine Parmesan cheese
6 egg whites

Heat the hash in sweet cream. When cream is reduced to half the original quantity, thicken with the cream sauce. Season with salt and pepper, and sherry if desired. Around a platter place a ring of cooked, buttered spinach. In center place the chicken hash and cover with a cheese souffle and smooth with a spatula. Sprinkle with finely grated Parmesan cheese. (The cheese souffle can be piped around the edges for a decorative effect.) Bake in 450-500° oven for 15 minutes, or until brown. *Cheese Souffle* — Mix the melted butter and flour, and let become light brown. Add the boiling milk carefully, mix with a whip and let boil slowly for at least 30 minutes. Season with salt, pepper and nutmeg. Stirring constantly, combine with egg yolks. When the boiling point is reached, remove from the heat and add the grated cheese. Beat the egg whites stiff and fold into the mixture carefully. Spread this over the chicken hash mixture so as to cover everything and make a mound in the center. Sprinkle a little cheese over and bake in a hot oven as described above.

Serves: 6

Nick Coletti, Chef
Duquesne Club

CHICKEN BREAST NEPTUNE WITH BRANDY SAUCE

4 oz. Alaska King Crabmeat
4 oz. raw lobster tail
2 tsp. chopped parsley
6 slices white bread
2 whole eggs
2 oz. milk or cream
salt, pepper, dry mustard
4 boneless breasts of chicken
butter

Brandy Sauce:

4 pieces green onions
½ lb. fresh mushrooms, diced
4 tbsp. butter
2 tbsp. flour
2 oz. brandy or cognac
2 oz. sauterne wine
3 cups chicken broth,
  chicken bouillon or water
salt, pepper, garlic

Chop crabmeat, lobster and parsley. Dice white bread and add to mixture. Add eggs, milk and seasonings to taste. Cut pocket and fill chicken breasts with above mixture. Place stuffed chicken breasts in pan with butter and bake at 350° for 20 minutes.

Sauté onions, mushrooms and butter until tender. Add flour and brown. Add brandy or cognac, wine and chicken broth. Season with salt, pepper and garlic to taste. Cook the above sauce for 5 minutes and pour over chicken breasts. Bake in 300° oven for 30-40 minutes.

Serves: 4

Vincent Salpietro
Executive Chef and
Food Service Director
Interstate United Corp.

ESCALLOPED CHICKEN AND SWEETBREADS

¼ cup chicken fat or butter
1 cup mushrooms
½ cup flour
2 cups chicken stock
1 cup milk
1 cup light cream
2 cups chicken, cooked
  & cubed
1 cup sweetbreads,
  cooked
¾ cup almonds, blanched
½ tsp. salt
½ cup crumbs
1 tbsp. butter
pie crust pattie shells

Preparation: 30 min.
Baking: 45 min.

Melt butter or chicken fat, add mushrooms, and sauté until tender. Stir in flour and when blended, add chicken stock, milk and cream. Stir until thickened. Add chicken, sweet-breads, almonds and salt. Cover with buttered bread crumbs (use 1 tablespoon butter) and brown in 350° oven for 45 minutes. Serve in pie crust pattie shells.

Serves: 8 - 10

Mrs. Gilbert McCune
College Club

STIR-FRIED SCALLOPS WITH ALMONDS
(Ch'ao Kao Pei)

Marinade for Scallops:
1 clove garlic, chopped
½ tsp. salt
1 tbsp. dry sherry
1 tsp. minced ginger
½ tsp. sugar
1 lb. scallops, cut in half
3 tbsp. peanut or other
   salad oil
½ cup sliced bamboo shoots
½ cup sliced water chestnuts
½ cup Chinese cabbage (celery
   cabbage), sliced diagonally
1 small onion, cut in chunks
3 Chinese dried mushrooms,
   soaked in hot water 20 min.,
   stems removed & quartered
1 tsp. salt
1 tsp. soy sauce
1½ cups water
1 tbsp. cornstarch
3 tbsp. cold water
½ cup blanched almonds, fried
   to light brown

Combine marinade and mix well. Add scallops and toss to coat well. Marinate for 15 minutes.

Heat 2 tablespoons oil in wok or skillet over high heat until very hot. Add scallops; stir-fry 1 minute. Remove and set aside.

Heat remaining 1 tablespoon oil in wok or skillet over high heat; add bamboo shoots, water chestnuts, cabbage, onion and Chinese mushrooms. Stir-fry 2 minutes; add salt, soy sauce and water. Bring to a boil. Stir in cornstarch dissolved in 3 tablespoons cold water. Cook, stirring constantly, until sauce is thickened. Add scallops and mix well. Sprinkle almonds on top. Serve hot.

Preparation: 45 min.   Can do ahead   Serves: 2 - 4

Anna Kao
Chinese Gourmet
Restaurant

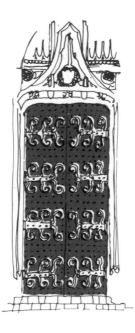

CRABMEAT IMPERIAL

"Crabmeat fit for a king."

½ cup chopped green pepper
1 tbsp. butter
½ tsp. salt
¼ tsp. black pepper
¼ tsp. dry mustard
1 tsp. Worcestershire sauce
¼ cup mayonnaise
1 lb. cooked fresh crabmeat
  (or if desired, an equal amount
  of mixed seafood such as
  shrimp, scallops, halibut, etc.
  may be used and called
  "Seafood Imperial")
⅓ cup chopped pimientos,
  well drained
⅔ cup soft bread crumbs
2 tbsp. melted butter
½ tsp. paprika

Sauté peppers in butter.
Add salt, pepper, mustard,
mayonnaise and Worcester-
shire sauce.
Add crab or seafood and
place mixture in casserole.
Combine pimientos, crumbs,
butter and paprika. Sprinkle
on top of casserole.
Bake in 350° oven for 30
minutes until crumbs are
brown.

Preparation:	10 min.	Easy	Serves: 4
Baking:	30 min.	Can do ahead	

L. J. Tokarz, Chef
Butler Country Club

SEAFOOD NEWBURG

"A grand dish for special company."

1 lb. or 3 cups clean,
  cooked crabmeat
1 lb. or 3 cups lobster
  tail (South African)
1 cup clean, cooked shrimp
⅓ cup butter
3 tsp. flour
½ tsp. salt
½ tsp. paprika
dash cayenne
1½ cups coffee cream
  (flavored with chicken
  bouillon)
3 large egg yolks, beaten
2 tbsp. sherry
toast points

Remove any shell or cartilage
from the shellfish, being careful
not to break the meat into small
pieces. Melt the butter and
blend in the flour and seasonings.
Add cream and cook until
thick and smooth, stirring constantly. Beat hot mixture into
egg yolks, a little at a time. Remove from heat and slowly
stir in sherry. Serve immediately
on toast points.

Preparation:	30 min.	Easy	Serves: 10
Cooking:	20 min.		

Romeo Victor Lupinacci, Chef
Cumberland Inn

FILLET OF SOLE WITH SHRIMP STUFFING

10 slices white bread
1 small onion
1 stalk celery
¼ lb. butter
1 lb. raw shrimp
2 whole eggs
dried parsley flakes
seafood seasoning to taste
  (if not available, use dash
  of poultry seasoning)
12 4-oz. pieces of sole
paprika
butter
½ cup water
salt

Soak bread in water, then squeeze out water until bread is moist. Dice small onion and celery, then sauté in butter for 4 or 5 minutes. Shell and devein shrimp, cut in ¼" chunks, add these to onions and celery until cooked, about 6 or 7 minutes. Add shrimp and vegetable mixture to bread. Add eggs and season to taste.

Place 6 pieces of sole on a greased baking pan. Portion stuffing evenly on sole, mounding slightly. Cut a slit in each of the remaining sole and place on top. Sprinkle with paprika. Place a small amount of butter on each and add ½ cup of water with a dash of salt to keep from drying. Place in a preheated oven at 375° for 15-20 minutes.

Serves: 6

Jack Rittleman, Assistant Chef
Edgeworth Club

STUFFED TROUT a la CITRONNIER

Stuffing:

1 lb. crabmeat, chopped
  coarse (any variety)
3 cups small-diced white bread,
  crust removed
½ cup minced celery
3 eggs
2 tbsp. lemon juice
2 tsp. minced parsley
½ tsp. dry mustard
salt & pepper to taste
water

Trout:

4 8-oz. trout, with or
  without head and tail
  removed
1 tsp. salt
cooking oil

Combine all ingredients for stuffing and mix thoroughly. If stuffing tends to appear dry, add a few drops of water.
Trout:
Rinse cavity of the trout and pat dry. Rub lightly with salt. Fill cavity with stuffing and sew together. Place in a baking sheet lined with aluminum foil and brush with oil. Bake at 350° 30 minutes.

Serves: 4

Jack Braun, Executive Chef
The Lemon Tree Restaurant

POMMES BOULANGÉRE

6 med. potatoes
3 sliced onions
½ cup butter
salt & pepper
½ cup chicken or beef broth
2 tbsp. butter

Wash and peel potatoes and cut into round ¹⁄₁₆" thick slices. Sauté onions in butter. Coat the inside of an oven-proof baking dish or skillet with sufficient butter. Arrange the sliced potatoes in the form of a flower on the bottom of the dish; season with salt and pepper. Cover with 1 layer of onions. Use the rest of the potatoes and onions and apply additional layers. Bring broth and 2 tablespoons butter to a boil. Pour over potatoes and bake in 450° oven for 25 to 30 minutes to a crisp golden brown color. Serve the potatoes upside down to get the effect of the flower arrangement. Serve with beef, lamb or pork.

Preparation: 10 min.
Baking: 25-30 min.

Serves: 6-7

Ferdinand Metz, Chef
H. J. Heinz Company

SPAGHETTI CON LE MELANZANE
(Spaghetti with Eggplants)

6 eggplants, med. size
salt & pepper
½ cup olive oil
2 cloves garlic, crushed
2 lbs. ripe tomatoes
2-3 sprigs basil,
  finely chopped
1½ lbs. spaghetti
¾ cup grated Pecorino or
  Parmesan cheese

Wipe the eggplants, peel them and cut them into thin slices. Sprinkle with salt and leave in a colander or on a tilted plate for 1 hour to drain off their bitter juices. Wipe the slices dry and fry in hot oil, a few at a time, until brown on both sides. Drain on paper towels. Pour about ½ cup oil into a small pan, sauté the garlic cloves until brown and discard them. Peel and chop the tomatoes, discarding seeds. Stir the tomatoes into the oil and cook for 20 minutes. Add salt, plenty of pepper and basil to taste. Bring a large pan of salted water to a bubbling boil. Add the spaghetti and cook until tender but still firm. Drain and dress immediately with the fried eggplants, the tomato sauce and the cheese. Serve at once with plenty of additional grated cheese.

Serves: 6

Frank Sgro
Sgro's Restaurant

MAURICE SALAD BOWL AND DRESSING

½ cup salad oil
½ cup mayonnaise or salad
  dressing
2 tbsp. pickle juice
¼ cup salad or apple
  cider vinegar
1 tbsp. Worcestershire sauce
3 hard-cooked eggs, minced
1 tbsp. minced onion
¼ cup minced candied
  dill strips
1 large head lettuce, broken
  into bite-sized pieces
1 cup julienne cooked chicken
1 cup julienne cooked ham
1 med. tomato, julienned

Using rotary or electric
beater, gradually beat salad
oil into the mayonnaise. Continuing to beat, add pickle
juice, vinegar and Worcestershire sauce. Stir in eggs, onion
and pickle. Allow to stand in
refrigerator at least 1 hour.
Mix lettuce with dressing,
place on individual salad
plates. Top with chicken,
ham and tomato.

Serves: 6

Harvard-Yale-Princeton Club

HOT CHICKEN SALAD

1 cup mayonnaise
  (not salad dressing)
1 tsp. grated lemon peel
2 tsp. fresh lemon juice
2 tsp. grated or finely
  minced onion
½ tsp. salt
2½ cups cooked diced chicken
1 cup chopped celery
1 cup sliced or chopped
  almonds, toasted
½ cup grated sharp Cheddar
  cheese
1 cup crushed potato chips
watercress

Blend mayonnaise with
lemon peel, juice, onion and
salt. Mix lightly with chicken,
celery and almonds. Spoon
into individual serving dishes or
a 1½ quart casserole. Top with
a sprinkling of cheese and
potato chips. Bake at 400°
for 15 minutes or until piping
hot. Serve on bed of watercress. You may also make this
using either cooked shrimp,
turkey, or crabmeat in place
of chicken.

Serves: 7-8

| Preparation: | 45 min. | Easy |
| Baking: | 15 min. | Can do ahead |

Chef George Weise
Longue Vue Club

FROZEN FRUIT SALAD

"Your bridge club will love this."

2 3-oz. pkg. cream cheese
1 cup mayonnaise
1 cup heavy cream, whipped
1 No. 2½ can fruit cocktail
½ cup maraschino cherries,
  quartered
2½ cups miniature marshmallows
few drops of cherry juice or
  red food coloring
cherries & mint leaves

Soften cream cheese and blend with mayonnaise. Fold in remaining ingredients. Pour salad mixture into 1 quart round ice cream container or ice cube trays. Freeze firm. To serve, let stand out for a few minutes, remove from container, slice, and place on crisp lettuce. Garnish with cherries and mint leaves.

Preparation: 20 min.   Easy   Serves: 10-12
Freezing: 1 hour   Must do ahead   Must Freeze

Frank Ambrose, Chef
Youghiogheny Country Club

WILLIAM PENN CHEESE CAKE

6 eggs
1½ cups granulated sugar
½ tsp. salt
½ tsp. vanilla
juice of 1 lemon
3 lbs. Philadelphia cream
  cheese, softened

Crust:

½ cup Zweiback crumbs
3 tbsp. granulated sugar
¼ tsp. cinnamon
white of 1 egg
½ cup graham cracker crumbs

Combine and mix eggs, sugar, salt, vanilla and lemon juice until thick and lemon colored, using mixer on low speed or hand whip. Further soften cream cheese with mixer and add gradually to egg mixture until soft and smooth.

Crust:
Combine all ingredients, mixing by hand, thoroughly. Grease a 10" spring-form pan. Sprinkle bottom and sides with crumbs mixture, pressing in

place with your hand. Pour in the cheese batter. Bake at 350° for 1 hour. When you take it out, if it seems pale, put it under the broiler for a few seconds to brown. Chill thoroughly. Invert on plate, browned side up.

Paul Wayman, Chef
William Penn Hotel

ALMOND MACAROONS

1 lb. almond paste
¼ cup cake flour, minus 1 tsp.
  (flour should not be packed)
2¼ cups granulated sugar
⅔ cup egg whites
granulated sugar

Break almond paste into small pieces and place in mixing bowl. In separate bowl mix together the cake flour and sugar. Start mixer while adding small amount of egg whites to almond paste. Then alternately add dry ingredients and egg whites until creamy and smooth. If mixture is too stiff, add a little extra egg whites. Using a pastry bag, squeeze out macaroons to the size of a half dollar on a greased and floured pan. Press tops with a damp cloth and sprinkle with granulated sugar. Bake in a slow oven (about 330°) for about 19 minutes.

Preparation: 25 min.
Baking: 19 min.

Yield: 56 cookies

Albert Brunn, Jr., Pastry Chef
Kaufmann's

PECAN CHEWIES

1 lb. small pecan pieces
¾ tsp. salt
2 cups packed golden brown
  sugar
1 tsp. vanilla
⅜ -½ cup egg whites

Blend the first 3 ingredients together by hand. Do not use electric mixer as pecans may be crushed. Add vanilla. Add the egg whites until the mixture holds firm when squeezed into a ball. Drop cookies from a teaspoon into small mounds on a greased and floured pan. Bake in slow oven (about 330°) until golden brown (about 16 minutes), or until slightly firm in the center. Remove from pan while slightly warm. Top surface of cookies should not blacken on edges. If this happens, your oven is too hot.

Preparation: 25 min.
Baking: 16 min.

Yield: 71 cookies

Albert Brunn, Jr. Pastry Chef
Kaufmann's

ZABAGLIONE

8 egg yolks
6 oz. Bristol Cream
  Sherry wine
2 oz. powdered sugar
fresh strawberries or
  fresh raspberries

Combine egg yolks, sherry and sugar in the top of a double boiler and cook until thick like a custard. Serve with fresh strawberries or raspberries.

Chef Carl Ristoff
Pittsburgh Press Club

SOUFFLÉ au GRAND MARNIER

1¾ cups milk
3 tbsp. butter
5 beaten egg yolks
4 tbsp. granulated sugar
3 tbsp. flour
¼ tsp. vanilla extract
5 egg whites + pinch of salt
3 tbsp. sugar
3-4 ladyfingers
¼ cup Grand Marnier
powdered sugar

Grand Marnier Sauce:
2 cups milk
½ vanilla bean or ½ tsp.
  vanilla extract
5 egg yolks
½ cup sugar
2 oz. Grand Marnier

Place in a double boiler the milk and butter. When milk is hot, add the egg yolks that have been beaten with the 4 tablespoons sugar, flour and vanilla, and stir vigorously until mixture comes to the boiling point. Remove to cool a little. In the meantime, butter a 6-cup souffle dish and sprinkle with granulated sugar. Beat the egg whites until stiff and add the 3 tablespoons sugar with the salt and beat a few seconds more. Fold this into the egg yolk mixture carefully and thoroughly. Put half this mixture into the buttered mold. Cover with the ladyfingers soaked in Grand Marnier. Fill dish with remainder of souffle and smooth the top with a spatula. Bake at 450° for 18 to 20 minutes. A minute or two before removing from oven, sprinkle with powdered sugar on top to glaze. Serve with Grand Marnier sauce.

Grand Marnier Sauce: Scald milk in a double boiler with the vanilla bean. Beat the yolks lightly and add sugar. Beat a little of the hot milk slowly into the egg yolk mixture. Return the egg yolk-milk mixture to the double boiler and cook, stirring continuously with a whip, until it thickens to a custard. Strain through a sieve and cool. Just before serving add 1 ounce Grand Marnier to the sauce and drizzle the remaining ounce over the Souffle.

Nick Coletti, Chef
Duquesne Club

BAKED FRESH FRUIT COMPOTE

"To serve with a goose or turkey. European style."

8 small apples, peaches
 or pears
2/3 cup red wine or water
2/3 cup sugar
½ stick cinnamon
4 whole cloves
1/8 tsp. salt
½ thinly sliced, seeded
 lemon (lime also will
 do)

Preheat oven to 350°. Pare
and core fruit. Place whole
or in thick slices in baking
dish. In another pan com-
bine the wine (or water),
sugar, cinnamon, cloves,
salt and lemon slices (or
lime) and heat, but do not
boil. Pour over fruit and
bake (may be covered or
uncovered) until fruit is

tender when tested with fork. If you are cooking fruit uncovered,
be sure to baste it every 10 minutes. Some people turn fruit over
after first two bastings.

Serves: 8

Chef Sint-Nicolaas
Carlton House

ORANGE WINE SAUCE

"Super served over baked chicken, turkey or duck."

1 fifth of sherry
2 lbs. butter
1 orange rind, grated
2 lbs. brown sugar
2 oranges sliced thin

Melt butter in sherry. Add grated
orange rind and brown sugar.
Cook and thicken to the consistency of a thin marmalade. Add
orange slices just before serving
(5 minutes).

Preparation: 15 min.   Easy   Yield: 1½ qts.
Cooking: 15 min.   Can do ahead

William Campbell
Carnegie Institute Cafeteria

FUNG MAI HAR (SAUCE)

2 med. sized onions,
 sliced thin
10 tbsp. bacon fat
1 oz. paprika
1 49-oz. can of jellied
 consomme madrilene
12 oz. honey
10 oz. wine vinegar
2 oz. arrowroot

Sauté onion in bacon fat. Add
paprika, madrilene, honey and
wine vinegar. Bring to a rolling
boil. Mix arrowroot with cold
water. Add to boiling mixture.
Wonderful over deep-fat
fried shrimp.

Chef Marcel Martin
Oakmont Country Club

NATIONALITY
FAVORITES

TAMBURITZANS

The Tamburitzans, a group of full-time college students at Duquesne University, present programs of music, singing and ethnic dancing of the southern Slavic peoples. This famous group has performed all over the world. The ethnic variety of Pittsburgh's populace contributes to its cultural richness. The foods, the art, the handcrafts, the music and the dancing provide a reflection of ethnic gifts to the city. Pittsburgh, "the melting pot," may be grateful that nationality groups have preferred not to melt in some ways, while adapting in others.

Additional illustrations in this section:

Ukrainian Catholic Church on Pittsburgh's South Side.

Further examples of Bakewell Glass: "Bell Flower," "Pear," "Ribbed Ivy," "Argus," "Tulip" and "Loop."

An 1897 switch engine and old caboose which were used in the steel industry now grace the front lawn of a Sewickley resident.

The Old Economy Fire Engine was built by the Harmony Society at Economy in 1826 to protect the village they had founded.

Old Economy.

Architectural details of some Pittsburgh churches.

LINSEN SUPPE (LENTIL SOUP)
"Delicious on a cold winter night."

1   1-lb. pkg. lentils
¼ lb. bacon, diced
2 med. onions, sliced
2 med. carrots, diced
2 qts. water
1 cup celery, sliced
2½-3 tsp. salt
½ tsp. pepper
½ tsp. dried thyme
2 bay leaves
1 large potato, pared
1 ham bone
2 tbsp. lemon juice

Night before: Wash lentils. Soak overnight covered in cold water. Early next day: Drain lentils. In Dutch oven, saute diced bacon until golden. Add sliced onions and diced carrots and saute until onions are golden. Add lentils, water, sliced celery, salt, pepper, thyme and bay leaves. With medium grater, grate peeled potato into lentil mixture; add ham bone. Simmer, covered, 3 hours. Lentils should be nice and tender. Remove bay leaves and ham bone. Cut all bits of meat from bone and return meat to soup. To serve at once, add lemon juice. For next day, refrigerate soup; then add lemon juice and reheat. This is a German recipe.

Preparation: 45 min.   Can do ahead   Yield: 9½ cups
Cooking: 3 hours

Mrs. Dominic Rondinelli

WINE SOUP

"Will make you tipsy."

5 egg yolks
2 tbsp. sugar
2 tbsp. cornstarch
1 cup water
2 cups dry white wine
1 tsp. grated lemon peel
2 cloves

In a large mixing bowl, beat together egg yolks, sugar and the cornstarch diluted in a cup of water. Pour into the top of a double boiler. Add wine, grated lemon peel and cloves. Place over boiling water and, with a wire whip, beat it continuously until the soup comes to a boil. This will take approximately 3 minutes. Remove immediately from the heat and serve. If you have a copper bowl and a wire whip, use the copper bowl instead of the top of a double boiler. This is a Hungarian recipe.

Preparation:	5 min.	Easy	Serves: 6
Cooking:	3 min.		Serve immediately

Maria Stacho

PYROHY

2 cups flour
1 tsp. salt
1 egg, or 2 yolks
½ cup water
onions
melted butter

Cottage Cheese Filling:

2 cups dry cottage cheese
1 beaten egg
salt to taste
sugar (optional)

Mashed Potato Filling:

mashed Idaho potatoes
salt & pepper
cubed Longhorn cheese

Lekvar:

Cooked pitted prunes
  may be used as a filling.
Sauerkraut may be used
  as a filling.

Mix flour with salt in deep bowl. Add 1 egg or the 2 yolks and enough water to make a medium soft dough. Knead on a floured board. Cut into 2" squares or rounds. Place filling in and press edges together with fingers, sealing well. Drop into rapidly boiling salted water, and boil for 3 or 4 minutes. Stir carefully. Pour melted butter with browned onions over the pyrohy.
Cottage Cheese Filling:
Combine cottage cheese with 1 beaten egg and salt to taste. If cheese is too dry, an extra egg may be added. Sugar may also be added.
Mashed Potato Filling:
Use only Idaho potatoes. To mashed potatoes, add salt, pepper, and cubed Longhorn cheese. This is a Ukrainian recipe.

Preparation:	30 min.	Can do ahead	Yield: 2½ dozen
Cooking:	3-4 min.		Can freeze

Mrs. Sam Finch

OLIE KOEKEN (OIL CAKES)

"A delicious Dutch variation on apple fritters."

1 cup sugar
3 cups flour
4 tsp. baking powder
¾ tsp. nutmeg
dash of salt
2 beaten eggs
1 cup milk
1½ tsp. lemon extract
1 cup raisins dredged in
  ½ cup flour
2 peeled, finely chopped
  apples
cinnamon & sugar

Preparation: 20 min.

Mix dry ingredients. Add eggs, milk, and lemon. Fold in raisins. Add apples. Drop by teaspoonsful in hot fat. Cook one side until it turns itself over. Fry until crispy. Drain. While hot, shake in cinnamon and sugar. Freezes beautifully before sugaring. Reheat in brown paper bag in 350° oven, and add sugar while hot. This is a Dutch recipe.

Yield: 4 doz.

Mrs. Neill Barker

NEW YEAR'S PRETZEL

"A traditional good luck bread of German families at New Year's."

⅔ cup dry milk
½ cup sugar
2 tsp. salt
2 cups lukewarm water
2 cakes yeast (or
  equivalent in dry yeast)
2 eggs
½ cup shortening
7-7½ cups flour
margarine
powdered sugar
nuts, cherries, etc.

Mix dry milk, sugar, salt and water. Stir in mixing bowl. Stir in yeast until it dissolves. Add eggs and shortening and stir in. Add flour, cup by cup, beating in with mixer on high speed, until about half the flour is used. Mix in remaining flour. Knead until smooth. Let rise until double. Punch down and let rise again. (If in haste, skip second rising.) Take half of dough and roll it to form a long strip and shape into a pretzel, twisting once at the center. Repeat with remaining half. Bake about 20 minutes at 350°. Remove from oven and brush with margarine. Frost while still warm with a thin powdered sugar and water frosting. Sprinkle with chopped nuts or decorate with candied cherries, etc., if desired. This is a German recipe.

Preparation: 20 min.   Must do ahead   Serves: 16
Baking: 20 min.   Can freeze

Mrs. John D. Rhodes

AKARA
"Soul Food"

2 cups black-eyed peas
1 med. red onion
½ tsp. red pepper,
  to taste
½ tsp. salt
peanut oil (preferred)
  or other vegetable oil
  for frying — In Africa,
  palm oil is used.

Soak the peas overnight. Drain and pound with masher to loosen the skins, floating them off in running water or spread on a board and use rolling pin to rub the skins loose. Soak further, if necessary, until the peas can be crushed. Grind purée in an electric blender, adding water as needed to a smooth consistency (similar to pancake batter). Grind very finely the onion and peppers if fresh, and add to the beans in the blender. Heat oil to 350 - 375° in deep fryer. Drop the mixture by spoonsful into the hot oil and fry until deep brown. Drain on paper towel. Many Africans would sprinkle the balls with additional red pepper. Eat them warm. Use as warm snacks or as bread substitute. This is a Nigerian recipe.

Preparation: 45 min.   Yield: 3 doz,
Cooking: 5 min.

Bernice Anderson

DEVONSHIRE SCONES

1 lb. self rising flour
1 tsp. salt
4 oz. butter
2 oz. sugar
1 cup milk

Sift flour and salt into a bowl. Rub in butter until mixture resembles fine bread crumbs. Add sugar and mix to a soft dough with the milk. Turn onto a lightly floured surface, knead quickly, then roll out to ½" thickness. Cut into 20 rounds with a 2½" cutter. Place scones on greased baking trays and brush tops with beaten egg or milk. Bake in a very hot oven, 450°, for 8 to 10 minutes. Cool on a wire rack. When cold, split and serve with strawberry preserves and whipped cream. This is an English recipe.

Preparation: 20 min.   Can do ahead   Yield: 20 scones
Baking: 9 min.   Can freeze

Mrs. Geoffrey J. Bicknell

OAT CAKES

"A different kind of scone."

4 oz. oatmeal
pinch of salt
pinch of baking soda
1 tsp. fat
hot water

Put oatmeal in bowl and add salt and soda. Make a well in the center and pour in melted fat. Add enough hot water to make a stiff paste. Knead and roll out as thinly as possible, cut in fours and cook on griddle. Brown on both sides. This is a Scottish recipe.

| Preparation: | 15 min. | Easy | Yield: 8 pieces |
| Cooking: | 10 min. | Must do ahead | |

Mrs. Gerald Robinson
"White Heather Pipes and Drums"

SAUERBRATEN

½ cup vinegar
½ cup water
1 sliced onion
salt & pepper
1 bay leaf
1 clove
1½ lbs. beef, shoulder
1 marrow bone
2 tbsp. fat
1 chopped onion
1 chopped tomato

Sauce:

1 tbsp. flour
vinegar or lemon juice
pinch of sugar
salt
butter
1 tbsp. cream or wine

Cook vinegar, water, sliced onion and seasonings together for 10 minutes. Steep beef in the marinade 2 to 3 days. Drain, save liquid. Brown meat and marrow bone in hot fat. Add the onion, tomato and ½ cup of the marinade, cover and simmer on top of range for 1 hour. Turn the meat so it is cooked on all sides. Carve and put on a warm platter. *Sauce:* Mix flour with pan liquid until smooth. Add the rest of the marinade and stir until smooth and thickened. Sauerbraten sauce calls for more ample ingredients than other sauces. Add, to taste, a little vinegar or lemon juice, a pinch of salt, sugar, a little fresh butter and a tablespoon of cream or wine. Strain and pour over meat or serve as a separate sauce. This is a German recipe.

| Preparation: | 15 min. | Must do ahead | Serves: 3-4 |
| Cooking: | 1 hr. 10 min. | | |

Mrs. Peter Freymark

SPANAKOPITA

3 lbs. fresh spinach
3 bunches chopped green
 onions
1 tbsp. dill weed
¼ cup chopped parsley
5 eggs, slightly beaten
1 tbsp. farina
½ lb. crumbled Feta
 cheese
¼ cup shredded Roman
 cheese
¼ cup olive oil
16 sheets filo
salt to taste
melted butter

Preparation: 20 min.
Baking: 45 min.

Wash spinach. Set aside to drain, sprinkle with salt and cut. Squeeze spinach well to remove excess moisture. Combine with onions, dill, parsley, eggs, farina, cheeses and oil. Arrange 8 filo, brushing each with butter, in a large pan. Pour in spinach mixture. Cover with 8 filo, brushing each with melted butter. Seal edges to retain filling. Brush top with melted butter. Bake in 350° oven for 45 minutes or until golden brown. This is a Greek recipe.

The Committee

MACARONOPITA

8 oz. elbow macaroni
5 or 6 eggs, beaten
2½ cups lukewarm milk
1½ sticks butter
salt
1 cup Feta cheese,
  crumbled
½ cup cottage cheese
½ cup grated Roman or
  Parmesan cheese
½ lb. filo (phyllo) leaves

Cook macaroni in boiling salted water until almost done. Drain well. In separate bowl beat eggs, add milk, ½ stick melted butter. Pour into macaroni, add cheeses and stir lightly to mix. Melt remaining butter. Carefully line 9 x 13" greased pan with 6 sheets filo, brushing each filo with melted butter. Pour mixture into pan, topping with additional 6 sheets filo and brushing each sheet with butter. Bake at 350° for 40 minutes. Lower temperature after 15 minutes if top is getting too brown. This is a Greek recipe.

Preparation: 20 min.
Baking: 40 min.

The Committee

PASTITSO (MACARONI AND MEAT)

"Well worth the time it takes to prepare."

1 large grated onion
¼ lb. butter
2 lbs. ground meat
1 tbsp. salt
¼ tsp. black pepper
½ tsp. cinnamon
4 tbsp. tomato paste
½ cup water
1 egg

Macaroni:

1 lb. elbow macaroni
3 eggs, beaten
1¾ cups grated Romano
  cheese

White Sauce:

¼ lb. butter
½ cup flour
3 cups milk
5 egg yolks
¼ cup grated Romano
  cheese

Brown onion in butter. Add meat. Keep stirring until meat is browned. Add salt, pepper, cinnamon, tomato paste and water. Cook, uncovered, over medium heat about 20 minutes, stirring occasionally (until water is absorbed). Remove from heat and allow to cool. Beat 1 egg very well and add to meat mixture.

Macaroni — Cook macaroni according to directions on package. Rinse under hot water, drain, and in large bowl toss macaroni with beaten eggs and cheese.

White Sauce — Melt butter, add flour, mix well. Gradually add cold milk, stir well. Cook until thick, stirring often. Remove from heat. After 5 minutes, while sauce is cooling, beat egg yolks very well and blend into sauce. Add cheese.

Butter a 10 x 14" pan. Put ½ of macaroni mix in pan. Put meat mixture over macaroni, spreading evenly. Put rest of macaroni on top, also spreading evenly. Put white sauce all over. Bake at 375° for 45 minutes or until golden brown. This is a Greek recipe.

Preparation: 45 min.   Serves: 8
Baking: 45 min.   Can do ahead

Mrs. James A. Boumbouras

TURKOPITA

1 lb. Feta cheese,
  crumbled
5 egg yolks
½ stick melted butter,
  cooled
2 lbs. diced cooked
  turkey
5 beaten egg whites
16 filo (phyllo) sheets
melted butter

Mix Feta cheese, egg yolks and melted cooled butter with turkey. Fold in beaten egg whites. Place 8 buttered filo in buttered pan. Pour in mixture and cover with remaining filo, brushing each with butter. Bake at 350° for 1 hour.
This is a Greek recipe.

Preparation: 20 min.
Baking: 1 hour

The Committee

RICE PILAFF
"Delicious with chicken."

3 tbsps. minced onion
3 tbsps. butter
1½ cups chicken broth
⅛ tsp. cracked pepper
¾ cup raw rice
⅓ cup slivered almonds,
   blanched & lightly toasted

Sauté onion in butter (use medium size pot) until tender. Add chicken broth, pepper, and rice. Bring to a boil and simmer for 5 minutes. Stir in almonds. Place cover on pot, reduce heat, and simmer until done; usually 20 minutes.
This is a Greek recipe.

Preparation: 5 min.   Easy   Serves: 4-6
Cooking: 30 min.

Mrs. James A. Boumbouras

FISH — PAPRIKASH CHRISTMAS CASSEROLE
"A traditional first course for Christmas Eve dinner."

8 med. baking potatoes
1 tbsp. salt
salt & pepper to taste
2 large onions, finely
   chopped
4 tbsp. cooking oil
2 tbsp. sweet paprika
1 cup water
1 cup clam juice
1 cup sour cream
6 pieces carp or
   haddock, ½ lb each
½ tsp. salt
6 strips bacon, thick
   slices
2 tomatoes, peeled &
   sliced
1 green pepper, seeded
   & sliced crosswise
½ cup butter to baste

Potato layer — Place the raw potatoes in a large pot; cover with cold water and add 1 tablespoon salt. Bring to a boil, cover and cook for 20 minutes. Drain the potatoes and peel them. Cut into ⅛" thick slices. Arrange sliced potatoes in layers over the bottom of a buttered baking dish. Season with salt and pepper.
Sauce — In a saucepan, sauté onions in oil until golden brown. This takes approximately 5 minutes. Add paprika and mix well. Add water and clam juice and bring to a boil. Cover and simmer for 15 minutes. If you have a blender, put sauce through the blender. Mix with sour cream and pour over potatoes in baking dish. Sprinkle the fish with salt. Make a small incision in each slice and place a strip of bacon in it. Arrange fish side by side in a row on top of potatoes and sauce. Decorate with green pepper and tomato slices. Baste with butter. Cover with foil. Bake in preheated 350° oven for 30 minutes, and finish under the broiler for 3 minutes, 6" away from the heat. Serve with French bread and a full bodied white wine.
This is a Hungarian recipe.

Maria Stacho

Preparation: 1½ hours   Easy   Serves: 6
Baking: 30 min.   Can do ahead

CHEESE AND PASTA IN A POT

2 lbs. lean beef, ground
vegetable oil
2 med. onions, chopped
1 garlic clove, crushed
1   14-oz. jar spaghetti sauce
1   16-oz. can stewed tomatoes
1   3-oz. can sliced
   mushrooms
8 oz. shell macaroni
1½ pt. sour cream
½ lb. sliced Provolone
   cheese
½ lb. sliced Mozzarella cheese

Cook beef in a little vegetable oil in large deep frying pan until brown, stirring often with fork. Drain off excess fat. Add onion, garlic, spaghetti sauce, stewed tomatoes and undrained mushrooms. Mix well. Simmer 20 minutes or until onions are soft. Meanwhile, cook macaroni shells according to package directions. Drain and rinse with cold water. Pour half of the shells into a deep casserole, cover with half of the tomato sauce. Spread half of the sour cream over the sauce. Top with the Provolone cheese. Repeat the layers, ending with the Mozzarella cheese. Cover casserole and bake at 350° for 35 to 40 minutes. Remove cover and bake until cheese melts and browns. This is an Italian recipe.

Preparation:	30 min.	Easy	Serves: 10-12
Baking:	1 hour	Can do ahead	Can freeze

Mrs. Frank G. Vucetich

MANICOTTI

4 eggs
1 tsp. salt
2 tbsp. Mazola oil
2 cups warm milk
2¼ cups flour

Filling:

2 lbs. Ricotta cheese
3 egg yolks
¼ cup Romano cheese,
   grated
½ cup Mozzarella cheese
⅛ tsp. black pepper,
   freshly ground
¼ cup finely chopped
   flat leaf parsley
tomato sauce

Beat eggs well in mixer bowl. Add salt, oil, milk, and flour and beat until smooth. Fry batter in well oiled 6 or 7" skillet, 2 tablespoons at a time. Rotate pan with batter so that pancake cooks evenly. When thick, but not brown, flip and cook on other side. Remove and set on paper towels to cool. Yields 28 to 30.

Filling — Mix all filling ingredients together except tomato sauce. Put 1 tablespoon filling on each pancake and roll. Pour tomato sauce on bottom of baking dish and lay rolled manicotti in single layer. Fill baking dish. Pour more tomato sauce over top along with Romano cheese. Bake at 350° for 30 to 45 minutes. Serve hot. This is an Italian recipe.

Preparation:	1 hour	Easy	Serves: 15
Baking:	30 - 45 min.	Can do ahead	Can freeze

Mrs. Joseph Matzzie

EASTER PIE

"Favorite choice for springtime picnics on the Italian Riviera."

Pastry:

3 cups flour
½ tsp. salt
1 cup butter, cut
  into pieces
1 egg yolk
3 tbsp. cold water

Filling:

3 tbsp. olive oil
2 large onions, finely
  chopped
1½-2 lbs. fresh spinach
  leaves or 2 10-oz.
  pkgs. frozen, chopped
  spinach
3 1" thick smoked
  pork chops (1 lb.),
  boned & diced
1½ cups freshly grated
  Parmesan cheese
1 cup Ricotta
salt & freshly ground
  pepper
4 eggs, lightly beaten
1 egg white

Place flour, salt and butter in bowl. Work flour into the butter until it looks like coarse oatmeal. Mix egg yolk with water and sprinkle over mixture. Stir with a fork, adding only enough extra water so that dough clings together. Wrap dough in wax paper and chill briefly.

Filling — Heat oil and sauté onion until tender, not brown. Place washed spinach, stems removed, in large saucepan. Cover tightly and cook until leaves wilt. Drain well and chop. (If frozen spinach is used, cook according to package directions; drain well.) Combine drained spinach and onion; cool. Add diced smoked pork, Parmesan cheese, Ricotta, salt and pepper to taste, and eggs to cooked spinach mixture. Preheat oven to 425°. Roll half of pastry out and put into 10" pie plate. Brush the bottom and sides of pie shell with lightly beaten egg white. Pour in filling. Roll out remaining dough and cover filling. Seal and decorate edges, make a steam hole, and place leaves made from extra pastry around hole. Bake 40 minutes until golden brown. Let stand 10 to 15 minutes before cutting. Delicious hot or cold. The pie may be made early in the day and reheated in a 375° oven for 40 minutes. Cover loosely with foil to prevent over-browning. It may be frozen after cooling, wrapped in foil, for up to 2 months. Thaw for 3 hours. Bake for 1 hour in 375° oven. This is an Italian recipe.

Preparation: 1 hour	Can do ahead	Serves: 8
		Can freeze

Marie Torre

ITALIAN MEATBALLS

"Meatballs for special spaghetti suppers."

½ lb. ground beef
½ lb. ground pork
1 cup coarse bread crumbs
1 cup evaporated milk
1 egg
¼ cup parsley
½ tsp. black pepper
½ clove garlic, minced
¾ tsp. salt
¼ cup imported Romano
  cheese, grated
1 tsp. olive oil

Mix all ingredients together and form into meatballs. These can then be put into spaghetti sauce or frozen.

Preparation:	15 min.	Easy	Serves: 6
Cooking:	30 min.	Can do ahead	Freezes well

Mrs. Henrietta Yacovoni

EGGPLANT SAUSAGE CASSEROLE

"A hearty dinner of eggplant and wine sauce."

1 lb. pork sausage (mild bulk)
3 tbsp. chopped fresh parsley
2 tbsp. chopped green onions
½ cup red wine
¼ cup ketchup
1 tsp. curry powder
½ lb. fresh mushrooms
1 can Cheddar cheese soup
1 large eggplant
cooking oil
1 large tomato
¼ cup soft bread crumbs

Sauté sausage until the redness disappears. Pour off any excess fat and, while cooking, separate with a fork. Add parsley, onions, wine, ketchup and curry powder. Cook for 5 minutes stirring often.

Wash mushrooms, slice and add to the mixture. Cook for another 5 minutes. Spoon in the soup, mix well and remove from stove.

Remove the stem from the eggplant, and slice thinly lengthwise. Sauté in oil on both sides until tender. Drain on absorbent paper. Arrange one layer in bottom of a shallow 1½-quart casserole. Cover with a layer of the sausage mixture and top with a layer of eggplant. Peel and slice tomato and arrange over top. Sprinkle with bread crumbs. Bake at 350° for 30 minutes. This is an Italian recipe.

Preparation:	45 min.	Can do ahead	Serves: 8
Baking:	30 min.		Can freeze

Mrs. Annette Hrimika

PAT GMITER'S STUFFED CABBAGE (GOLUMKI)

1½ cups rice
1 large head cabbage
2 med. onions, chopped
8 strips bacon
pinch paprika
½ lb. ground pork
½ lb. ground beef
1 tsp. each salt & pepper
1 small can sauerkraut
1 8-oz. can tomato sauce
1 can tomato soup
1 tbsp. sugar

Cook rice and let cool. Parboil cabbage and separate leaves using the largest. Cut ribs off and let cool. Sauté onions with 5 strips of minced bacon and a pinch of paprika. Mix onions and bacon with ground meats. Thoroughly mix in cooked rice, salt and pepper. Roll cabbage with 1 heaping tablespoon of mixture in center. Thoroughly drain sauerkraut and spread on bottom of small roaster. Take remains of cabbage head and dice and lay on top of sauerkraut. Place cabbage rolls tightly together on top of diced cabbage, with seam side down. Pour cans of tomato sauce and soup over, and enough water to cover. Lay remaining 3 strips of bacon on top. Sprinkle 1 tablespoon sugar over rolls and simmer covered in 300° oven for 1½ hours. Uncover and simmer 30 minutes more. Cooking time should not exceed 2 hours. Add more water if needed. This is a Polish recipe.

Preparation: 45 min.   Yield: 3 - 4 doz.
Baking: 2 hours   Can do ahead

Pat Gmiter

231

LAMB AND CABBAGE CASSEROLE (FÅR I KÅL)

"Economical and delicious too."

3½ lbs. breast of lamb,
cut into chunks
2½ cups beef or chicken
stock, or water
1½-2 lbs. white cabbage,
washed, cored, & sliced
into 1" wedges
¼ cup diced celery
¼ cup chopped onions
2 tbsp. whole peppercorns,
tied in cheesecloth &
lightly bruised with a
rolling pin
2 tbsp. salt
¼ cup flour

Boil the meat in the stock for about 1 hour. In a casserole, arrange cabbage, meat, celery, onions and peppercorns in layers and sprinkle with salt and flour. Add the stock and boil slowly for 2 hours. This is a Scandinavian recipe.

Mrs. Karl A. Olson

Preparation:	20 min.	Easy	Serves: 6
Cooking:	3 hours	Can do ahead	

BILL CARDILLE'S KOLBASI AND SAUERKRAUT

"Try this one next New Year's."

2 lbs. fresh or smoked kolbasi
2 large cans sauerkraut
2 large onions
small piece salt pork or
smoked bacon
salt & pepper
2 tbsp. flour
2 tbsp. bacon fat

Bake kolbasi in 325° oven for 1 hour in pan with water to cover. Thoroughly rinse and drain sauerkraut. Place in pan with 2 whole onions and salt pork, add salt and pepper to taste. Add water to cover; simmer 45 minutes. When kolbasi is cooked, drain, cut into 4" pieces, add to sauerkraut, and continue cooking for 30 minutes. Brown flour in bacon fat. When golden brown, add to kolbasi and sauerkraut and mix thoroughly. This is a Polish recipe.

Preparation:	10 min.	Can do ahead	Serves: 8
Cooking:	2 hours 15 min.		

Bill Cardille

PIROGY WITH FREESTONE PLUMS

5 cups flour
3 eggs
4 tbsp. sugar
½ tsp. salt
12 tbsp. cold water
  or more
45-50 Freestone plums
sugar
butter

Cheese Filling:

  (Can be used instead of
  Freestone Plums)
1 cup dry
  cottage cheese
2 egg yolks
1 tbsp. butter
¼ tsp. salt

Mix first 5 ingredients with enough water to make a medium soft dough. Knead by hand until dough holds together. Let dough rest ½ hour before rolling. Roll (¼ of the dough at a time) thin, cut in squares, and place ½ of a freestone plum (add ¼ teaspoon sugar to each plum) on each square. Fold in half to make triangles. Press with salad fork to seal. Drop in boiling salted water and cook until all pirogys rise to the top of the water, and become transparent. This will take between 5 and 10 minutes, depending on the quantity.

Cook for 5 more minutes. Remove gently, drain in colander, then place in fry pan in melted butter and swish butter generously to prevent from sticking together. Can be frozen — then heated slowly before serving. Combine ingredients for filling and mix thoroughly. This is a Polish recipe.

Preparation: 1 hour, 15 min.
Cooking: 10-15 min.

Yield: 95
Can Freeze

Mrs. Leo Gaca

233

CHEESE
"A traditional Ukrainian Easter Cheese."

1½ lbs. dry cottage cheese
¼ lb. butter
4 tbsp. sugar
pinch of salt
6 eggs

Work cottage cheese through a strainer with a wooden spoon into a large bowl. Beat in butter until fluffy. Add sugar and salt. Add eggs, one at a time, beating well after each.

Pour into a shallow pan (pie, cake, etc.). Set into larger pan with water in it (as for custard). Bake at 350° for 45 minutes. Test with butter knife in center for doneness (as for custard).

Preparation: 20 min.   Easy   Yield: 2 lbs.
Baking: 45 min.   Can do ahead

St. Mary's Sisterhood
St. Vladimir Ukrainian
Orthodox Church

EGG NOODLES
"How easy! Try them."

½ lb. flour
2 eggs

Put flour into bowl and make a well. Add the eggs. Mix with a fork taking in flour gradually.

Knead the dough until smooth. Roll out until paper thin, and let dry. When dry, cut with a knife as thin as you wish. Let noodles dry. This is a Croatian recipe.

Preparation: 15 min.   Easy
                           Must do ahead

Confraternity of Christian Mothers
Holy Trinity Roman Catholic Church

POLISH KLUSKI
"Serve these as an accompaniment to beef stew."

2 cups grated
 raw potatoes
1 egg
½ tsp. salt
¾ cup flour
chopped onion
butter

Drain and squeeze the grated potatoes. Add egg, salt and flour. Form into small balls or drop by teaspoonsful into a large kettle of boiling, salted water. Cover, bring to a boil, and cook until they float. Transfer the dumplings with

a slotted spoon onto a hot platter. Sauté onions with butter and pour over the dumplings.

Preparation: 25 min.   Serves: 6
Cooking: 5-10 min.

Mrs. Jean Surowiec

HERRING SALAD (SILLSALAD)

"This received rave comments at Folk Festival."

2 large salt herrings
(1 lb. each)
3 cups diced cooked
potatoes
3 cups diced pickled
beets
⅔ cup diced pickled
gherkins
1 cup diced peeled
apple
1 med. onion, peeled
& chopped
¾ cup vinegar
¼ cup water
¼ cup sugar
1 tsp. white pepper
2 cucumbers
2 tsp. salt
½ cup mayonnaise
1 hard cooked egg
pressed through a
ricer or sieve

Clean fish, removing heads and tails, and soak 12 hours in cold water; changing the water once during this time. Drain, skin and fillet. Be sure to get all bones out. Dice the fillets and mix with the potatoes, beets, gherkins, apple and onion. Mix ¼ cup of vinegar, water, sugar and pepper. Add to the herring mixture and stir gently until well mixed. Pack into a 2-quart bowl and chill well. Slice cucumbers paper thin and sprinkle with salt; mix well, cover and let stand for an hour. Drain and rinse very well with cold water. Pour ½ cup vinegar over cucumbers and let stand 15 minutes. Drain. Turn out salad and garnish with the wilted cucumbers, mayonnaise and egg. Can also be served with sour cream tinted with a little beet juice. (Better if left to marinate in refrigerator 2 days.) This is a Scandinavian recipe.

Mrs. A. A. Lindberg

Preparation: 1½ hours   **Must do ahead**   **Serves: 12**

SWEDISH CRAB SALAD (KRABBSALLAD)

"A different and most enjoyable salad."

1 7½-oz. can crabmeat
1 10-oz. pkg. frozen peas
4 oz. fresh mushrooms
sliced lengthwise
1 5-oz. can asparagus tips,
drained & cut in pieces
lettuce leaves

Dressing:

½ cup whipping cream
⅓ cup mayonnaise
3 tbsp. chili sauce
fresh dill sprigs

Quickly rinse the crabmeat in cold water. Let the peas thaw. Combine crabmeat, peas, mushrooms and asparagus in a salad bowl lined with lettuce leaves. Whip the cream and mix with mayonnaise and chili sauce. Pour the dressing over and carefully toss the salad with 2 forks. Garnish with fresh dill sprigs. This is a Scandinavian recipe.

Preparation: 15 min.   **Easy**   **Serves: 4-5**

Mrs. Edward H. Peterson

WARMER KARTOFFELSALAT (HOT POTATO SALAD)

2 lbs. small white
  potatoes, unpeeled
1 tsp. salt
½ cup diced bacon
½ cup minced onion
1½ tsp. flour
4 tsp. sugar
1 tsp. salt
¼ tsp. pepper
¼ to ⅓ cup vinegar
½ cup water
¼ cup minced onion
2 tbsp. snipped parsley
1 tsp. celery seeds
½ cup sliced radishes
  (optional)
celery leaves

About 1 hour before serving, cook potatoes in their jackets in 1" boiling water with 1 teaspoon salt in covered saucepan until fork tender, about 35 minutes. Peel and cut into ¼" slices. In small skillet, fry bacon until crisp. Add minced onion and sauté until tender, not brown. In bowl, mix flour, sugar, 1 teaspoon salt and pepper. Stir in vinegar (amount depends on tartness desired) and water until smooth. Add to bacon; simmer, stirring until slightly thickened. Pour hot dressing over potatoes. Add ¼ cup minced onion, parsley, celery seeds and radishes. Serve lightly tossed and garnished with celery leaves. This is a German recipe.

Preparation: 1 hour
Cooking: 35 min.

Serves: 4-6

Mrs. Dominic Rondinelli

CHEESE CAKE

"Try this with sliced strawberries on top."

Crust:
16 double graham
  crackers, crushed
1½ tbsp. sugar
4 tbsp. butter
½ cup chopped nuts
Filling:
3 8-oz. pkgs. cream
  cheese, softened
5 eggs
1 cup sugar
1½ tsp. vanilla
Topping:
1½ pts. sour cream
½ cup sugar
1½ tsp. vanilla
sliced strawberries
  (optional)

Crust: Mix all ingredients together until well blended. Place on bottom of 13 x 9 x 2" glass baking dish. Set aside. *Filling:* Beat softened cheese with electric beaters until smooth. Add eggs one at a time and beat well. Add sugar and vanilla. Cream well. Pour into crust. Bake at 300° for 1 hour. *Topping:* Allow cake to cool 5 minutes after baking before icing. Mix ingredients well and put on top of cake. Return to oven for 5 minutes longer to bake at 300°. Allow to cool, then refrigerate. May be served with fresh strawberries on top. A Carpatho-Russian recipe.

Preparation: 30 min.
Baking: 1 hr. 5 min.

Easy
Can do ahead

Serves: 12-16

Mrs. G. F. Semenko

FLANCATS

2½ cups flour
12 egg yolks
½ pt. sour cream
1 tbsp. milk
¼ tsp. salt
1 tbsp. sugar
½ tsp. vanilla
salad oil
powdered sugar

Sift flour, add egg yolks, sour cream, milk, salt, sugar and vanilla. Mix all together. Work flour dough until it makes bubbles. Cut into 7 pieces and make each into a ball. Sprinkle each with flour. Separate in wax paper and cover with a clean dry cloth. Let stand 4 to 5 hours. Roll 1 ball at a time like noodle dough because they dry quickly. Cut into squares and stretch. Fold 2 corners together. Be quick when frying, and use hot salad oil. Brown lightly on each side, let cool. Sprinkle with powdered sugar. This is a Croatian recipe.

| Preparation: | 5 hours | Must do ahead | Yield: 3½ doz. |
| Cooking: | 30 min. | | |

Confraternity of Christian Mothers
Holy Trinity Roman Catholic Church

OBST TORTE

¾ cup flour
¾ tsp. baking powder
⅛ tsp. salt
2 eggs, separated
¼ cup plus 2 tbsp.
  cold water
½ cup plus 3 tbsp.
  sugar
½ tsp. vanilla

Filling:

3-4 cups fresh, canned
  or frozen fruit
1 tbsp. cornstarch
1 cup whipping cream

Preheat oven to 350°. Sift the flour, baking powder, and salt together. In a large bowl, beat the egg yolks with water, using a rotary type or electric beater, until foamy. Gradually beat in sugar. Add the sifted flour to the egg mixture, beating well. In a separate bowl, using clean beaters, beat the egg whites until foamy; add vanilla and continue to beat until whites stand in stiff peaks. Fold egg whites into the batter, do not beat. Pour batter into a well-greased flan pan. Bake at 350° for 20 minutes.

Filling: Drain canned or frozen fruit, reserving juice, or crush 1 cup fresh fruit to make juice. Sweeten to taste. Boil juice. Mix cornstarch with a little sugar; stir into juice and cook until thick. Fill baked shell with fruit. Pour cooled juice over fruit, and chill. Decorate with whipped cream. Torte is excellent with peaches, strawberries, cherries, or pineapple. May be made the morning of the day it is to be served. This is a German recipe.

| Preparation: | 45 min. | Can do ahead | Serves: 12 |
| Baking: | 20 min. | | |

Theresia Timcheck

PALACHINKA OR CREPE SUZETTES

"Translated from an original Croatian cook book."

3 eggs
1 qt. milk
¾ tsp. salt
½ cup sugar
3¾ cups unsifted flour
6 tbsp. melted butter

Cheese Filling for
 Palachinka:

2 lbs. cottage cheese
½ cup sugar
dash salt
2 tbsp. butter
1 tsp. vanilla

Thoroughly mix all dry ingredients with milk and eggs. Add melted butter and blend well. Spread ¼ cup batter on hot greased pan. Tip pan to get very thin pancake. Whip cheese, sugar, salt and butter with wooden spoon. After blending well, add vanilla. Spread on hot pancake, and roll up.
This is a Croatian recipe.

Preparation: 10 min. Easy Serves: 24
Cooking: 30 min.

*Confraternity of Christian Mothers
Holy Trinity Roman Catholic Church*

BAKLAVÁ

2 lbs. pecans or almonds,
 coarsely ground
1 cup sugar
grated rind of 1 orange
1½ tsp. cinnamon
dash allspice
¼ tsp. ground cloves
½ cup farina (optional)
1½ to 2 lbs. melted
 sweet butter
1½ lbs. filo
whole cloves

Syrup:

4 cups water
4 cups sugar
1 cinnamon stick
rind of whole orange
2 lb. jar of honey

Combine nuts, sugar, orange rind, cinnamon, allspice, cloves, and farina. Mix well. Grease 11 x 16" pan with melted butter. Line pan with 4 filo, brushing butter on each as it is placed in pan. Sprinkle with a thin layer of nut mixture. Cover with another filo and alternate filo and nut mixture, making sure each filo is brushed with butter. Finish with 6 filo on top. Cut diagonal lines through top 6 filo to form diamond shapes. Then stick a whole clove into center of each diamond. Heat remaining butter until sizzling, taking care not to burn, and pour over entire pan. Bake at

300° for 1 hour. Pour warm syrup over the Baklava which has been slightly cooled.
Syrup: Boil water, sugar, cinnamon stick and rind of a whole orange and cook into medium syrup. Remove from heat and add honey.
This is a Greek recipe.

Preparation: 30 min.
Baking: 1 hour *The Committee*

CITRONFROMAGE

"A light Danish dessert."

3 eggs, separated
1 cup sugar
1 env. Knox gelatin
½ cup cold water
juice of 2 lemons or
  ¼ cup
rind of 1 lemon
½ pt. whipping cream

Beat egg yolks and sugar until lemon colored. Soak gelatin in ½ cup cold water, then melt over hot water (not boiling) in top of double boiler. Combine gelatin with egg yolks and add lemon juice. Place in refrigerator until it begins to thicken. Fold in rind and whipped cream. Fold in beaten egg whites. Place in a pretty bowl. Refrigerate. This is a Danish recipe.

Preparation: 30 min.   Easy   Serves: 6
Cooking: 10 min.   Must do ahead

Mrs. Kristian Kristensen

HUNGARIAN KICHLI

"Cookies or sweet rolls."

3 cups all-purpose enriched
  flour
½ lb. butter
⅛ tsp. vanilla
3 well-beaten egg yolks
1 small cake Fleischman's
  yeast (or ⅓ of the house-
  hold size)
8 tbsp. cream or top milk
1 tbsp. granulated sugar
1 cup apricot preserves
1 beaten egg (for glaze)

Sift flour and cut in butter (as for pie) with pastry blender or fork. Blend in vanilla, well-beaten egg yolks and yeast which has been crumbled and dissolved in the cream and sugar. The less you handle the dough the better. At this point you should have a sort of elastic dough. Separate dough into 3 sections. Take each section in turn. Roll out in circle on lightly floured board or cloth to about ¼" thickness. Spread apricot jam lightly over surface of dough. More jam may be used if you like. Cut circle into about 16 wedges. Roll each wedge into a crescent shape, starting from the broad base and rolling towards the point. Place on lightly greased cookie sheet. Glaze tops of horns with well-beaten egg. Bake in 350° oven about 20 to 25 minutes or until slightly browned. Makes about 4 dozen cookies depending on size of wedge. If you like a very rich cookie mix some finely ground nuts with the apricot jam for the filling. You can also make the horns in a larger size (larger wedges) and serve them as breakfast rolls. This is a Hungarian recipe.

Preparation: 30 min.   Yield: 4 doz.
Baking: 20 - 25 min.   Can do ahead

Mrs. Elizabeth Besser

CRÉMA KARAMELÁ

1¾ cups sugar
5 eggs
1 qt. milk, warmed
1 tsp. vanilla or
 lemon rind
few drops brandy
 (optional)

Melt 1 cup sugar over medium heat, stirring constantly until caramel consistency. Pour into bottom of 1½ quart mold or 12 5-oz. custard cups. Brandy or whiskey may be sprinkled over melted sugar, if desired. Beat eggs with ¾ cup sugar.

Add milk gradually, with flavoring. Pour into mold or cups, and place in a pan of hot water. Bake at 350° until firm. Cool thoroughly and place in refrigerator. When ready to serve, turn upside down on serving plate. This is a Greek recipe.

Preparation:	15 min.	Easy	Serves: 12
Baking:	45 min.	Must do ahead, same day	

The Committee

KOULARAKIA a la GREEK
"These are not too rich."

½ lb. sweet butter
1 cup sifted powdered sugar
4 egg yolks
2½ cups sifted all-purpose flour
½ tsp. baking soda
2 tsp. vanilla
1 cup chopped walnuts
half pieces of walnuts for
 decorations
powdered sugar

Cream butter and sugar together. Add egg yolks, one at a time, beating well. Sift soda with flour and add to egg and butter mixture. Add vanilla and then nuts. Form dough into crescent forms about 3 x 1'', and put nut meat half on top. Bake in 325°-350° oven for 20 to 30 minutes. Remove from cookie sheet to rack. Cool

slightly, then lightly sift powdered sugar over top of cookies. This is a Greek recipe.

Preparation:	20 min.	Easy	Yield: 20 - 24
Baking:	20-30 min.	Can do ahead	Can freeze

Mrs. James A. Boumbouras

POLISH KRUSCIKI

"A delicious fried cookie."

6 egg yolks
3 tbsp. grated orange rind
½ tsp. salt
½ pt. sour cream
3 cups flour
1 cup powdered sugar,
  sift after measuring
deep fat
powdered sugar

Beat egg yolks with fork, add grated orange rind, salt and sour cream. Put aside ½ cup flour. Add 2½ cups flour and powdered sugar to egg mixture. Mix well, then add last ½ cup flour and work in by hand to form a soft dough. On a floured board, roll out dough a quarter at a time. Roll thin. Cut dough in small rectangles and twist in center to make bows. Fry in deep fat. Drain and dust with powdered sugar.

Preparation: 30 min.   Can do ahead   Yield: 80

Mrs. Leo Gaca

MARIE'S KRINGLE

"Always a favorite with guests."

Filling:

4 tbsp. butter
⅓ cup sugar
1½ oz. raisins
¼ cup chopped almonds

Dough:

½ cup milk
1 extra large egg
¾ of 2 oz. yeast cake
½ tbsp. sugar
dash of salt
2 cups flour, scant
1 stick plus 5½ tbsp.
  butter

Topping:

1 beaten egg,
  brushed on
sliced almonds
coarse sugar or
glaze frosting after baking

Filling: Combine all ingredients for filling in a small bowl.
Dough: In a large bowl, mix milk, egg, yeast (crumbled), sugar and salt. Mix in 1 cup flour until no longer lumpy. Work in another ½ cup flour. Put other ½ cup flour on table top and rolling pin. (Use no other flour.) Turn dough onto table top and sprinkle with some of this remaining flour. Slice some butter and place on top of dough. Fold dough over butter and roll in. Add more butter in same way. Keep folding and rolling it in a little at a time until all butter is used. Roll until dough is elastic and desired size (about size of cookie sheet). Spread prepared filling on dough. Fold dough over, pinch ends.

Place on greased cookie sheet. Let rise until double in bulk. Either put topping on and bake, or glaze after baking. Bake 20 minutes at 325°. This is a Danish recipe.

Preparation: 30 min.   Can do ahead   Serves: 12
Baking: 20 min.

Mrs. Thomas Jensen

241

INDEX

ENTREES

CHEESE AND EGGS

BEEF

LAMB

PORK AND HAM

VEAL

POULTRY & GAME

FISH AND SEAFOOD

SANDWICHES

SAUCES, PICKLES, AND RELISH

SWEETS

CAKES

PIES

DESSERTS

DESSERT SAUCES

COOKIES

CANDIES

CHEF'S SPECIALTIES

NATIONALITY FAVORITES
(Listed by country of origin)

CARPATHO-RUSSIA

CROATIA

DENMARK

HOLLAND

GERMANY

GREECE

HUNGARY

ITALY

NIGERIA

POLAND

NOTES:

NOTES:

THREE RIVERS COOKBOOK
CHILD HEALTH ASSOCIATION OF SEWICKLEY, INC.
POST OFFICE BOX 48
SEWICKLEY, PENNSYLVANIA 15143

Please send me_____copies of THREE RIVERS COOKBOOK at $5.00* plus 50 cents handling per copy.

Enclosed is my check for $_____, payable to Child Health Association of Sewickley, Inc.

NAME_____

STREET_____

CITY_____ STATE_____ ZIP_____

All profits from the sale of this book will be returned to Allegheny County child-oriented agencies through the Child Health Association of Sewickley, Inc.

*PENNSYLVANIA RESIDENTS MUST ADD 30 CENTS TAX PER BOOK.

Please enclose ☐ *do not enclose* ☐ *gift card.*

THREE RIVERS COOKBOOK
CHILD HEALTH ASSOCIATION OF SEWICKLEY, INC.
POST OFFICE BOX 48
SEWICKLEY, PENNSYLVANIA 15143

Please send me_____copies of THREE RIVERS COOKBOOK at $5.00* plus 50 cents handling per copy.

Enclosed is my check for $_____, payable to Child Health Association of Sewickley, Inc.

NAME_____

STREET_____

CITY_____ STATE_____ ZIP_____

All profits from the sale of this book will be returned to Allegheny County child-oriented agencies through the Child Health Association of Sewickley, Inc.

*PENNSYLVANIA RESIDENTS MUST ADD 30 CENTS TAX PER BOOK.

Please enclose ☐ *do not enclose* ☐ *gift card.*

THREE RIVERS COOKBOOK
CHILD HEALTH ASSOCIATION OF SEWICKLEY, INC.
POST OFFICE BOX 48
SEWICKLEY, PENNSYLVANIA 15143

Please send me_____copies of THREE RIVERS COOKBOOK at $5.00* plus 50 cents handling per copy.

Enclosed is my check for $_____, payable to Child Health Association of Sewickley, Inc.

NAME_____

STREET_____

CITY_____ STATE_____ ZIP_____

All profits from the sale of this book will be returned to Allegheny County child-oriented agencies through the Child Health Association of Sewickley, Inc.

*PENNSYLVANIA RESIDENTS MUST ADD 30 CENTS TAX PER BOOK.

Please enclose ☐ *do not enclose* ☐ *gift card.*

THREE RIVERS COOKBOOK
CHILD HEALTH ASSOCIATION OF SEWICKLEY, INC.
POST OFFICE BOX 48
SEWICKLEY, PENNSYLVANIA 15143

Please send me_____copies of THREE RIVERS COOKBOOK at $5.00* plus 50 cents handling per copy.

Enclosed is my check for $_____, payable to Child Health Association of Sewickley, Inc.

NAME _____

STREET_____

CITY_____ STATE_____ZIP_____

All profits from the sale of this book will be returned to Allegheny County child-oriented agencies through the Child Health Association of Sewickley, Inc.

*PENNSYLVANIA RESIDENTS MUST ADD 30 CENTS TAX PER BOOK.

Please enclose ☐ do not enclose ☐ gift card.

THREE RIVERS COOKBOOK
CHILD HEALTH ASSOCIATION OF SEWICKLEY, INC.
POST OFFICE BOX 48
SEWICKLEY, PENNSYLVANIA 15143

Please send me_____copies of THREE RIVERS COOKBOOK at $5.00* plus 50 cents handling per copy.

Enclosed is my check for $_____, payable to Child Health Association of Sewickley, Inc.

NAME _____

STREET_____

CITY_____ STATE_____ZIP_____

All profits from the sale of this book will be returned to Allegheny County child-oriented agencies through the Child Health Association of Sewickley, Inc.

*PENNSYLVANIA RESIDENTS MUST ADD 30 CENTS TAX PER BOOK.

Please enclose ☐ do not enclose ☐ gift card.

THREE RIVERS COOKBOOK
CHILD HEALTH ASSOCIATION OF SEWICKLEY, INC.
POST OFFICE BOX 48
SEWICKLEY, PENNSYLVANIA 15143

Please send me_____copies of THREE RIVERS COOKBOOK at $5.00* plus 50 cents handling per copy.

Enclosed is my check for $_____, payable to Child Health Association of Sewickley, Inc.

NAME _____

STREET_____

CITY_____ STATE_____ZIP_____

All profits from the sale of this book will be returned to Allegheny County child-oriented agencies through the Child Health Association of Sewickley, Inc.

*PENNSYLVANIA RESIDENTS MUST ADD 30 CENTS TAX PER BOOK.

Please enclose ☐ do not enclose ☐ gift card.